The
Narcissistic Abuse
RECOVERY
Bible

SPIRITUAL RECOVERY
from NARCISSISTIC
and EMOTIONAL ABUSE

SHANNON L. ALDER

PLAIN SIGHT
PUBLISHING An imprint of Cedar Fort, Inc.
Springville, Utah

ISBN 13: 978-1-4621-2224-0

Published by Plain Sight Publishing, an imprint of Cedar Fort, Inc.
2373 W. 700 S., Springville, UT 84663
Distributed by Cedar Fort, Inc., www.cedarfort.com

LIBRARY OF CONGRESS CATALOGING-IN-PUBLICATION DATA

Names: Alder, Shannon L., author.
Title: The narcissistic abuse recovery bible : spiritual recovery from
    narcissistic and emotional abuse / Shannon L. Alder.
Description: Springville, Utah : Plain Sight Publishing, an imprint of Cedar Fort, Inc., [2018]
    | Includes bibliographical references.
Identifiers: LCCN 2018028109 | ISBN 9781462122240 (perfect bound : alk. paper)
Subjects: LCSH: Psychological abuse--Religious aspects--Christianity. |
    Narcissism--Religious aspects--Christianity.
Classification: LCC BV4596.P87 A43 2018 | DDC 261.8/3227--dc23
LC record available at https://lccn.loc.gov/2018028109

Cover design by Shawnda T. Craig
Cover design © 2018 Cedar Fort, Inc.
Edited by Allie Bowen and James Gallagher (Castle Walls Editing LLC)
Typeset by Kaitlin Barwick

Printed in the United States of America

10 9 8 7 6 5 4 3 2 1

Printed on acid-free paper

I dedicate this book to the women who stole my privacy.
God's greatest hope is that you will one day stop being enablers and
step into the role of women of integrity, dignity, and humility.

Also by

Shannon L. Alder

*350 Questions Parents Should Ask
during Family Night*

*350 Questions LDS Couples Should
Ask before Marriage*

*300 Questions LDS Couples Should
Ask for a More Vibrant Marriage*

*300 Questions to Ask Your Parents
before It's Too Late*

Contents

Acknowledgments

Dear Family and Friends,

First and foremost, I would like to thank my loving husband, Jim, who has supported me throughout this process. Thank you for being my best friend, but most of all thank you for being an example of what a Son of our Heavenly Father should look like. You have been my light in the darkest years of my life. I am grateful for your love, compassion, forgiveness, and kindness every day.

I also want to thank my therapist, Kay Marlow. You started me on this journey and knew my words were the only thing that would bring closure to a very long chapter in my life. You reminded me that I deserved something more than abuse. Thank you for your encouragement and wisdom!

I want to thank Dr. Sean Prystash for treating me during my narcissistic abuse. You restored what was taken from me and gave me balance during a traumatic time in my life. You gave me back my focus so I could write, the most important part of my recovery. Thank you for believing in me!

Finally, I wish to praise Jesus Christ and my Heavenly Father. Thank you for answering my prayers and comforting me during this storm. Thank you for using my story to help so many people who have suffered as I have. Thank you for giving me justice when I thought all hope was lost. Thank you for your mercy and forgiveness, but most of all, thank you for loving me.

With all my love,
Shannon L. Alder, a Strong Daughter of our Heavenly Father

PS: "There are no ordinary moments." (Dan Millman, *Way of the Peaceful Warrior*)

Introduction

If you are reading this, then rejoice and know that God has led you to the answers in this book. It is time to take back your peace and happiness! But first, God wants you to know that he loves you. He has heard your prayers. He knows what you have been through. He knows that you are a good person who has survived a bad situation for a very long time. He wants you to know that he has never left your side. However, he needs you to find the courage to move beyond being simply a victim or survivor of abuse. He wants you to step into a different role—a thriving son or daughter of our Heavenly Father.

From this day forward, you will wear God's armor, which is one of faith, dignity, courage, and action. Whether you are still in a relationship with a narcissistic partner or have left him or her, there is a message for you in this book and a key to unlock the door to peace, the very door you have been searching for. Even if you were never in a relationship with the narcissist, but you were targeted for narcissistic supply or attention and forced to endure an endless sea of mind games, there is a message of hope in these very pages.

I want you to know that you are not alone. I know that you have suffered greatly because I have been where you are, not once, but twice in my lifetime. I know what it is to love someone and have them abuse you. I know what it is to lose someone and not have closure. I know what it is like to spend endless days ruminating over old conversations and actions to discern what was sincere and what was a game or lie. I know what it feels like to have someone smear your name without one person believing your side of the story. I know what it is like to feel helpless.

Something didn't seem to add up. How could my narcissist appear so nice to strangers or friends outside the relationship, but behind closed doors be so manipulative and disrespectful to the person they professed to love? How could people who claimed to believe in God

1

have a total lack of empathy, devaluing and discarding me without an explanation? How could they wage a smear campaign against me after all the love and attention I gave them?

The first narcissist to target me was a boyfriend. In our two-year romance, he stole my heart and talked about us getting married. I was swept off my feet. In the beginning, it was like a fairy-tale romance. However, as our relationship progressed, he changed. He began to belittle my dreams and nitpick the way I looked. I soon learned that I was nothing more than an extension of his ego, and appearances were everything to him. His behavior escalated when I tried to stand up for myself. No matter how much I explained myself and tried to fix or justify things, I was blamed for everything. Fights were always followed by him giving me the silent treatment. Just when I thought I had enough, he would take me back through the honeymoon stage, only to repeat the cycle again when he wasn't getting complete adoration and compliance from me. Then one day, unexpectedly, he decided he wanted to move in with some friends and play the bachelor. Only two weeks before he had said he wanted to marry me. His actions and words left me confused and heartbroken. Without a legitimate reason, he discarded me. I was given no closure or explanation. Even worse, it was followed by a smear campaign. I found myself in a whirlwind of gossip at church. Everyone sided with his version of events, events that were made up to portray him as a saintly Christian and me as the weak individual he discarded.

The second narcissist to target me seemed like a nice person on the outside. I didn't know of anyone who didn't say he was soft-spoken, polite, and kind. He was quite the charmer and flattered me by telling me how beautiful he thought I was. I will admit I was attracted to him too, but we never entered into any type of relationship because we were involved with other people. He told me he was a man of traditional values and if he were to pursue me, then I would need to be single. However, his self-righteousness was nothing more than a lie. I didn't leave my relationship and in return, he punished me. He did this by waging a campaign to steal my privacy and smear my name. It took three months before I realized that my home computer was being hacked, as well as my cell phone. To keep his infatuation with me a secret, he lied to his wife by painting an unflattering and untrue picture of me that resembled Glenn Close in the movie *Fatal Attraction*.

My character was portrayed as an unstable woman with a crush that needed to be monitored because I was considered unpredictable and mentally ill. I imagine that is how he waged his twisted smear campaigns to convince the women in his life that his criminal activity was warranted and to prove he was faithful. However, unknowingly to his ex (whom he was in a relationship with at the time we met) and his wife, he told me that he was attracted to me and that timing was the only thing that stood between us. All I needed to do was get a divorce and then he would be free to pursue me. While he was denying to his wife that he had feelings for me, behind her back he was committing emotional infidelity, which was satiated by him invading the privacy of someone he admittedly was attracted to. Also, he had his sibling try to get my attention on social media sites. When that failed he had one of his hacker friends email me a letter to let me know he was still interested, if I would only leave my current relationship.

I felt helpless to defend myself against his smear campaign because I had no way to communicate my side of events to his wife or ex. The people in his life didn't run in the same social circles as I, so it was impossible to let them know that he was being deceitful. He was a liar who knew how to create drama and play the victim game to cover up his true motives for invading my privacy. He desired attention, so he created a lot of unneeded drama over me. I was used so other men could envy him and keep the women in his life fighting for his attention. I later found out this is called narcissistic triangulation.

When your computer and cell phone are hacked, the hacker has access to your email, text messages, Google history, passwords, financial information, and personal files. In my case, he also had remote access to my computer's desktop and could see me opening files on my computer and searching the internet. In addition, he used the speakerphone on my cell phone to listen into conversations going on in my room. That meant if I had sex with my husband and my cell phone was in the room, he overheard the event. The men who assisted him and his family member also listened in on my life. My intimate moments became public knowledge to a group of sick, perverted strangers. Sadly, he succeeded in punishing me in the worst way.

After months of speaking to countless computer forensic specialists and researching how to find the backdoor Trojan that allowed his hacker friends to gain remote access to my computer system, I was told it would be difficult to trace the hacking back to his computer's IP address. Thus, I wouldn't be able to convict him in a court of law. I was left victimized with no justice or trial. Sadly, he continued to hold his position at his church and play the part of the fake righteous husband, without a care in the world about what he did to his wife, ex, or me. It wasn't until his wife left one of her social media sites open to the public that I found a psychiatric reason for this man's abuse. She posted several narcissistic quotes about her husband that made it apparent that she had "accepted" that he had this disorder and was disloyal. Many of her quotes suggested he was emotionally and verbally abusing her, not to mention emotionally cheating. Of course, he denied everything. However, God witnessed all the evil he did and was just as appalled as we were.

When I look back at both of the situations that I have encountered with narcissism, I notice one consistent theme, not only in myself, but also in the people who enabled these men. All of us wasted our time on people who didn't deserve the pleasure of knowing us. Somehow and somewhere, in our abuse, dignity got lost. Either it was taken from us or we gave it away. Regardless, being around a narcissist has a way of taking you farther and farther away from the person you once were. You are left feeling as if you're one hundred years old—drained and lifeless. To say your happiness was the only thing taken from you would be too mild a description of narcissistic abuse. Narcissism steals your spirit. It has a way of unraveling your very faith.

What do you do when you're in a relationship with or know some-one who presents symptoms of narcissistic personality disorder? How do you stay strong in your faith when you are being abused? How do you forgive someone who shows no remorse? I also wanted to know the answers to those questions, and they weren't easy to come by because they weren't found in one source. One of the things I noticed in the many books about narcissistic recovery is that next to none of them talk about spiritual recovery in any biblical sense. They will give you a wealth of information about what narcissism is, but the chapters on recovery always left out spiritual recovery. Instead, they offer counsel-ing as the main solution. Having been in therapy for my narcissistic abuse, I can tell you that spiritual healing is not the focus of mental health practitioners. They deal mostly with building self-esteem and fixing unhealthy behaviors. During my healing process, I still felt something was lacking in my therapy sessions. I realized if I wanted to fully recover, it would be up to me to mend the shattered parts of my faith. On my own, I was able to piece together the missing components essential to true healing, which stitched my wounds shut with spiritual wisdom. I created rules to live by and boundaries that safeguarded my worth. Then I rebuilt my faith in God.

In my situation, both of my narcissists outwardly displayed devotion to their religion. Of course, behind closed doors their behavior made them poor examples of how Sons of our Heavenly Father should act. After the abuse each narcissist put me through, I found myself becoming angry with God. I wanted to know why they did this to me and why God allowed it. I could not see any lesson in these situations or feel any healing message from God because my heart was clouded in so much anger. I was impatient with my prayers, feeling that they weren't being answered in a timely manner. I could not forget or ignore how these abusers had smeared my good name to any believing soul to look like the saintly, upstanding people that they weren't.

Immediately after being abused by my last narcissist, I sought out people to validate what I had been through. I found friends on online narcissistic abuse recovery boards echoing the same sentiments. Survivors like me also felt their faith had dwindled. We all agreed that narcissistic abuse has the power to shake the foundations of our belief systems. Being rejected or abused does something to your faith. Don't we all want to believe in the dream that divine intervention caused us to meet our loved one? Who wouldn't? When you break up or are devalued by a narcissist, you start to question your own intuition. If you are not careful, you find yourself sliding down a slippery slope of questions that leave you with doubt that God is protecting you. You might be asking: Why didn't God warn me? Why did he let me waste my time and emotions on someone so abusive, someone who would change his feelings toward me so easily? Wasn't my marriage ordained? Am I supposed to stick it out because of my vows, for better or worse? Why can't God fix this person's illness if he values families staying together? Why would God allow this person to smear my name to other people, even church members?

It is not only these questions that can unravel your faith, but your own faulty conclusions. Many survivors I met online shared faith-shaking thoughts such as "If I can't trust my own intuition, which should have warned me about this person, maybe I can't trust my intuition about other important things such as my faith," or "If my narcissist can convince others at church of their holiness and lead people astray, maybe God doesn't care enough about me." Many of my online friends admitted to me that there were times when they thought, "Maybe I need to stick it out, because I don't deserve something better. Maybe this is the only plan God has for me and I am being too sensitive about what my partner is doing to me." They stuck it out without standing up for themselves and paid the price, losing much of their self-esteem.

These unanswered questions and conclusions can foster bitterness, which can lessen one's faith in God. Sadly, several of the victims I met online had fallen away from Christianity because they had been so abused that they didn't feel God could possibly have been in their relationship from the beginning. Therefore, they couldn't trust that he was guiding their footsteps in their life either. Even those who weren't in the relationship with the narcissist but were used for narcissistic supply began to question if God was looking out for them. Many expressed that they felt lost and confused. All of these victims admitted to sticking it out in hopes that somehow God would intervene and fix their narcissist. However, they felt let down when they didn't change.

Through my research and spiritual journey after these encounters with these narcissists, I was able to heal myself. Today, I can proudly say that I have reclaimed my dignity and I am a faithful daughter of our Heavenly Father. I have found my peace, and I am stronger than I ever was. And I am going to help you through this process. But first, I want you to know that God is leading your footsteps! Don't let what you have been through cause you to doubt his love for you. He has been with you the entire time! He has seen your tears. He has heard your prayers. He is trying to help you through this, but he needs you to change your perspective on a few things before peace can come. That is where I plan to help you.

Things might not make sense now, but they will, so hang on! You will face your greatest opposition when you are closest to your biggest miracle. In the chapters ahead, I will help you regain your inner peace and confidence so you can thrive, not just survive. However, before we do that, there is a message from your Heavenly Father. He wants you to read these words and believe in him. I want you to believe too, because you are a special son or daughter of our Heavenly Father, and you deserve more than what you have been through. You are so loved! It is time to heal and reclaim your dignity, respect, and power!

Your Friend,
Shannon L. Alder

My Beloved Child,

You may not know me, but I know everything about you. (Psalm 139:1)
I know when you sit down and when you rise up. (Psalm 139:2)
I am familiar with all your ways. (Psalm 139:3)
Even the very hairs on your head are numbered. (Matthew 10:29–30)
For you were made in my image. (Genesis 1:27)
In me you live and move and have your being. For you are my offspring. (Acts 17:28)
I knew you even before you were conceived. (Jeremiah 1:4–5)
I chose you when I planned creation. (Ephesians 1:11–12)
You were not a mistake, for all your days are written in my book. (Psalm 139:15–16)
I determined the exact time of your birth and where you would live. (Acts 17:26)
You are fearfully and wonderfully made. (Psalm 139:14)
Strength and *dignity* are to be your clothing. (Proverbs 31:25)
I knit you together in your mother's womb. (Psalm 139:13)
And brought you forth on the day you were born. (Psalm 71:6)
I have been misrepresented by those who don't know me. (John 8:41–44)
I am not distant and angry, but am the complete expression of love. (1 John 4:16)
And it is my desire to lavish my love on you. (1 John 3:1)
Simply because you are my child and I am your Father. (1 John 3:7)
I offer you more than your earthly father ever could. (Matthew 7:11)
For I am the perfect Father. (Matthew 5:48)
Every good gift you receive comes from my hand. (James 1:17)
For I am your provider and I meet your needs. (Matthew 6:31–33)
My plan for your future has always been filled with hope. (Jeremiah 29:11)
Because I love you with an everlasting love. (Jeremiah 31:3)

My thoughts toward you are countless as the sand on the seashore. (Psalm 139:17–18)

And I rejoice over you with singing. (Zephaniah 3:17)

I will never stop doing good to you. (Jeremiah 32:40)

For you are my treasured possession. (Exodus 19:5)

I desire to establish you with all my heart and all my soul. (Jeremiah 32:41)

And I want to show you great and marvelous things. (Jeremiah 33:3)

For if you seek me with all your heart, you will find me. (Deuteronomy 4:29)

So, delight in me and I will give you the desires of your heart. (Psalm 37:4)

For it is I who gave you those desires. (Philippians 2:13)

I am able to do more for you than you could possibly imagine. (Ephesians 3:20)

For I am your greatest encourager. (2 Thessalonians 2:16–17)

I am also the Father who comforts you in all your troubles. (2 Corinthians 1:3–4)

When you are brokenhearted, I am close to you. (Psalm 34:18)

As a shepherd carries a lamb, I have carried you close to my heart. (Isaiah 40:11)

One day I will wipe away every tear from your eyes. And I will take away all the pain you have suffered on this earth. (Revelation 21:3–4)

I am your Father, and I love you even as I love my son, Jesus. (John 17:23)

For in Jesus, my love for you is revealed. (John 17:26)

Know that I am not counting your sins. Jesus died so that you and I could be reconciled. (2 Corinthians 5; 18–19)

His death was the ultimate expression of my love for you. (1 John 4:10)

I have always been your Father, and will always be your Father. (Ephesians 3:14–15)

My question is . . . Will you be my child? (John 1:12–13)

I am waiting for you. (Luke 15:11–32)

Love,
God

The Devil Defined

"Hell is empty and all the devils are here."

—William Shakespeare, *The Tempest*

Theater and literature have been full of narcissistic characters throughout history. The word *narcissist* first appeared in Book III of the *Metamorphoses*. It tells the story of a "talkative nymph" who falls in love with a hunter named Narcissus, but he rejects her love. Then Narcissus, "tired from both his enthusiasm for hunting and from the heat," rests by a spring, and whilst he drinks, "a new thirst grows inside him" and he is "captivated by the image of the beauty he has seen." The image is his own reflection. He falls deeply in love with "all the things for which he himself is admired." He then wastes away with love for himself. Shakespeare was also familiar with Narcissus and refers to him in his poem "Venus and Adonis." No doubt, Shakespeare had a thing for narcissistic characters, who appear in many of his most famous plays. Therefore, it is fitting that we open this first chapter—or act, if you will—with the dance of the devil on stage, unmasked and defined.

Narcissists will tell you they hate drama. However, if you have ever been in a relationship with one, you know they thrive on drama and create it at every opportunity. Narcissists and other emotional abusers are not unlike actors on a stage. They construct a story of how their life should be, and anyone who shares their life is cast in a role, whether they want to be or not. You might be the trophy husband who proves his wife's worth to the world, or you might be the Stepford wife who waits on her husband hand and foot. Alternatively, you could be the other man or woman, whom they string along for narcissistic supply. Regardless of what role you play, you can always count on three phases of the relationship (or acts, if you will): idolization, devaluation, and discard. Discard doesn't always mean that the relationship is over. As *how do you stop having feelings?*

long as you have feelings for them, you can be sucked back into their drama to play your assigned role over and over again.

> All the world's a stage,
> And all the men and women merely players:
> They have their exits and their entrances;
> And one man in his time plays many parts.

> —William Shakespeare, *As You Like It*

When you enter into a relationship with a narcissist, you are choosing to dance with the devil on his or her stage. Author Tucker Max once said, "The devil doesn't come dressed in a red cape and pointed ears. He comes as everything you ever wished for." Narcissists know how to charm a person. They have spent a lifetime perfecting their image. However, beneath all the superficial charm and looks is something different—a hidden level of negativity and annoyance with other people. This darkness inside of them manifests in mind games, rages, and bullying. Years ago, they gave up on the notion that decency and kindness get them places in life. Instead, they adopted the attitude that manipulation is the fastest way to meet their needs. If you find yourself trying to explain decency to an adult narcissist, then you haven't accepted that they know what decency is already. They simply choose not to show it, preferring to act in their way for their gain. Out of all the mental disorders a person could be unlucky enough to acquire, narcissism is by far the worst, because the symptoms and manipulative games narcissists play go against the teachings of Christ.

Many of the objectives that Satan has in store for us are already in the character of someone with narcissistic personality disorder. Satan's objectives in our world are clear. He is here to do the following:

- Satan is here to draw us away from God.
- Satan seeks to thwart God's purpose and plan for our lives. He seeks to get us off track and not believe in God's words or those of his disciples.
- Satan seeks to deny God the glory, honor, and praise due him.
- Satan seeks to destroy us—literally and eternally.

For those still in a relationship with a narcissist, it might be hard to swallow the concept that narcissists have so much evil in them. After all, you have seen good qualities in them also. However, let me remind you that it takes a lot of Satan's influence to do the mean-spirited things they do. They have good and bad moments. Often, the amount of toxic behavior they have dulls the light of Christ inside them.

Let's look at that list of objectives again.

- **Satan is here to draw us away from God.** If you spend any time being abused by a narcissist, you will start to lose faith in yourself and in God. You might argue my opinion by saying, "But wait, I am holding on to God tightly. I am praying to him every day that he will change this person." Let me counter your perspective by asking, "How is it you think God would ever want you to remain in a relationship with someone abusive? How is it he would want your children to watch you be abused? How is it that God would want them to be abused?" Maybe you're hanging on to God, but you are not even hearing God's message for you to remember who you are—a person of dignity, who has a life purpose that goes far beyond simply settling for abuse because someone is kind once in a while. To live with dignity, you need to not ignore abuse or live with it. It is next to impossible to dwell with someone's evil behavior and not be affected by it.

- **Satan seeks to thwart God's purpose and plan for our lives.** How can you truly feel the spirit in your life if you are in a constant state of depression from your abuse? If you are constantly trying to mend your relationship by changing another person, where does that leave room for dignity and self-respect? How can you trust that God has a better plan for you if you are chasing after someone's affection or constantly proving your worth to him or her? God wants to use you in some way to better this world. He wants the best you have to offer. You can't tell me your life purpose has not been affected when you have been abused.

- **Satan seeks to deny God the glory, honor, and praise due him.** How can narcissists truly follow Christ if they believe kindness and decency are optional when trying to fulfill their needs? How can someone sincerely praise God without trusting his ways and applying them? If those things are optional, this denies God's way as the right way in order to live in favor of mind games and manipulation.

- **Satan seeks to destroy us—literally and eternally.** Time spent in a relationship with a narcissist takes its toll on a person's health. Living with someone who lies and disrespects a person does not

11

create an atmosphere of trust and happiness. It can cause depression, anxiety, post-traumatic stress disorder (PTSD), or physical ailments, as well as taking an emotional toll on a person's happiness or self-esteem. Over time, it can take a person further and further away from who they are spiritually. This is evident in the behavior of my narcissist's wife and ex. He convinced both of them to do criminal activity. If he were a righteous man, he wouldn't have asked his wife or ex to participate in such a thing as hacking. He would have said, "This is wrong," and given up the idea because he valued their souls. He went to church. He knew this wasn't the way a Christian should act. However, he didn't care, so he pulled both of them down to his level. He didn't think about their eternal salvation or their roles as daughters of their Heavenly Father. Can you say that your narcissist has your eternal salvation in mind?

As you can see, narcissistic personality disorder goes beyond mental illness. Your loved one has a spiritual illness as well. I am not saying that narcissists don't have good in them. Of course they do! However, much of what they do to feed their need for attention requires the cunning of the devil. You can't combat evil and cast it out of your life if you are not willing to acknowledge that it exists in a person. To stand for Christ, you must become just as cunning to understand them.

I will describe the games that narcissists play and how to navigate their dance steps. During your recovery, I ask that you remain in prayer with your Heavenly Father. Pray that he helps you remain honest with yourself about the fears that keep you connected to this person. Pray as you work through the to-do lists in the following sections. Also, ask God to help you develop courage to be nothing less than a person of dignity. You will need courage to maintain the boundaries you will be setting later.

Now let's begin the first step in your recovery. Unfortunately, this will be the hardest part of your healing. You need to accept that your partner is a narcissist and that you have been holding on to a false dream of who you think they are. This dream can be so strong and beautiful that we superimpose it on the narcissist. Every little spark of kindness from the narcissist enforces that dream. We see the good in them even if it is few and far between, because we love them. What little girl doesn't want the fairy-tale ending? What boy doesn't want to win the princess? That childhood desire doesn't change when we grow up. It is this romantic notion that keeps us at a seemingly safe distance from what is really happening. Your partner is playing evil games to manipulate you, and he is playing with your feelings in order to use you for narcissistic supply. At some point, it is necessary to see the dream for what it is, rather than the Disney ending we hoped for. You have to stop giving excuses for their behavior and you have to stop living the lie that this is what all relationships go through. Because they don't! You must accept that it is impossible to be loved by a narcissist in the way that normal people love. Let me repeat that. *Narcissists can't love you in the way you love them.* They have made themselves completely unavailable to unconditional love. It isn't your fault; it is their disorder.

This might seem like a cruel start to your healing process, especially if you still love this person. However, I plan to keep it real for you! I won't sugarcoat your experience. You must wake up from this dream-like state and deal with the reality of what you have allowed to occur in your life. Christ demands this of you: "Watch and pray always" (Luke 21:36). "Be sober, be vigilant; because your adversary the devil walks about like a roaring lion, seeking whom he may devour" (1 Peter 5:8). Christ is not just talking about all the criminals, rapists, and murderers in the world. He is also talking about the people you have allowed in your life whose bad behavior is taking you farther and farther away from the person God wants you to become.

Other narcissistic recovery books will tell you that narcissists have no redeeming qualities worth saving a relationship over. I can tell you that I wouldn't have been in a relationship with a narcissist if I hadn't see something wonderful in him from the beginning. However, those moments became few and far between as the relationship progressed. Likening your relationship to dancing with the devil is not meant to demonize the person you care for but to wake you up to the evil it takes to play the games they have. Their behavior is being judged, not the whole of them. Narcissists are sons and daughters of our Heavenly Father and he loves them as much as he loves you. However, they are ill! They developed narcissistic personality disorder in their youth, and unfortunately their coping mechanisms for control employ many of Satan's tools to live deceitfully. They can't sustain happiness unless it is derived from an outside source, and they will play cruel games to get their drug of choice, which is attention.

Can you imagine living an entire existence dependent on what people thought of you? Narcissists will deny they care about what people think. They prefer to come off as confident, but underneath their façade is someone who holds tight to fitting in and conformity rather than individuality. Don't let their stories about how rare and special they are fool you. Deep inside they want to be accepted. They have created a false image they live behind. I will help reveal the real them in the pages that follow.

But before we begin, if you are reading this book to figure out how to stay in a relationship with your narcissist, then heed my advice. You will not only play your part in his or her play, but you have elected to take on the role of caretaker as well. You are choosing to care for a mentally and spiritually ill person. They will require mental health therapy and spiritual therapy in order for real change to take place. Getting them to accept that they are narcissists will be next to impossible. You will come up against resistance—blaming, anger, and more games to shift the attention away from them. If you do get them into therapy, they might try their manipulation games on the therapist in an effort to downplay their behaviors and shift the focus to you as the problem in the relationship. You have to understand that they have safeguarded a broken child deep inside of them for years, and they will rebel against the very notion that they are flawed in some way. If you choose to stay, you must be willing to accept that there is no fairy-tale ending in mental illness. You can't cure narcissism. It is like any other disorder: *it can only be managed*. We will talk more about your decision to stay or leave in another section.

Before you begin learning more about your narcissist, I make one request of you during your recovery. I ask that you read this section as much as you want for a week and then no more after that. I have met survivors on narcissistic recovery forums who have been members for years. They still talk about their significant others. You don't want to be the person who is stuck. God has a plan for you that doesn't involve being a victim. Neither do you want to be the person who alienates your friends and family by rehashing the dynamics of your broken relationship for years.

Once I realized my second narcissist had this disorder, I couldn't believe bad luck had struck me twice. I found myself digging through Pinterest pins and websites for more information so I could avoid people like him in the future. I hate to admit it, but I set up camp emotionally by reading the countless stories of recovery on the internet. What I wanted was validation for what I went through. I wanted someone to believe me and tell me they went through it also. Unfortunately, I let my need for validation turn into months of self-imposed torture, which kept the situation alive in my mind by reliving it.

Constantly looking up narcissistic personality traits or frequenting online forums is simply a form of self-abuse. Victims do this as a way to feel in control of what is happening to them. However, it is a false sense of control. Repeatedly looking up information about a disorder doesn't fix the situation or heal a broken heart. So trust in your Heavenly Father and me! There is a season for all things and a season to let go. If you are reading this, then you are validated. What happened or is happening to you is real. You are not crazy! Someone very ill played a bunch of mind games and treated you poorly. Now is your time to take the knowledge in this book and make life changes. If you need support for what you went through, let me suggest a positive solution. I created a Facebook community called Staying Positive University, where abuse victims can receive positive quotes and affirmations instead of the constant quotes about narcissism that recovery boards are full of. You don't need to learn any more about narcissism after this section. You need to move past having your experiences validated and get on with your recovery. Choose to fill your mind with a positive outlook for the future instead of dwelling on the negative.

People who wonder whether the glass is half empty or half full are missing the point about their experiences and recovery. The glass is refillable! You can make your life full of positivity whether you stay in a relationship with a narcissist or leave. You are the only person in charge of how you feel. Don't give that power away! In addition, positivity is free and you can get it every day. My Facebook page is run like a classroom. You get daily quotes to uplift you and homework assignments to journal. Each semester, the theme of the quotes changes. We talk about self-esteem, empowerment, and healthy relationships. Plus, you get plenty of articles to inspire you. It is one step on your road to recovery.

Visit http://facebook.com/stayingpositiveuniversity.

Please consider joining my tribe and committing yourself to a positive life!

Let's continue your recovery by defining your dance partner. Narcissism comes in degrees like any other disorder. At one end of the spectrum are the verbally and physically abusive narcissists. At the other end of the spectrum are emotional abusers who passive-aggressively undermine everything. Symptoms make all narcissists equal in manipulativeness and mind games. However, they can vary in the way they present themselves to the world. The first narcissist I was in a relationship with had lots of friends and was outgoing and talkative. He made a big show of how cool he thought he was and had a large audience that bought the act. The second narcissist was quiet and had few friends, but he was just as manipulative as the first. I believe he earned his audience through acting like a victim. As different as their personalities were, the same games lay behind both of them. So if you are trying to determine if your loved one has this disorder, remember it is a spectrum.

As mentioned before, all narcissists put their targets through three phases: idolization, devaluation, and discard. In the idolization phase, they will love bomb you and move quickly to secure you in their life. This might mean over-the-top love letters, talks about you being soul mates early in the relationship, constant romantic dates, comparing you positively to other partners they have been with, and liking all the same things you do. Whatever it takes to woo you, they will do it on a fast and grand scale. They'll study you and pretend to give you what you need. Then, later, they will withhold it for control. If you are in another relationship with someone else, they might tempt you by talking about timing between you and them. They are letting you know they are interested, in order to string you along for narcissistic supply. This is their infatuation stage, and they rarely go beyond this type of love to something unconditional. Their love is superficial, and because of this they can't sustain the phase after the newness of the relationship wears off or they have grown tired of trying to get you to leave your current relationship in order for them to date you.

I know what you are thinking. "Is she trying to tell me that my partner was faking his love or attraction for me the whole time?" No, that is not what I am telling you. Narcissists have a different version of love. It revolves around their needs only. You were needed for something—their image, sex, a fix for loneliness or boredom, status, or financial help. Whatever the need was, it is why they were in a relationship with you or pursued you. You have become an extension of their ego and a supplier of admiration and attention. I am sure they enjoyed your company and were attracted to you. However, if you think that they chose you because you were going to make them into a spiritual person, you would be wrong. Any talk about you being their soul mate or the timing between you was simply a hook to keep you hanging on and putting up with their bad behavior. They don't go that deep to consider changing themselves for another. They might talk like they do. However, their actions speak otherwise. They live in the superficial. They might have told you they love you or were interested in dating you. However, their definition of love and their motives for attraction to you are shallow.

Once the newness is gone and they become bored, they move into the devaluation phase. This is where they belittle you, compare you, and sculpt you into what they need. All the little annoying things about you become big things to them and they don't have a problem telling you about them. This is when they whittle away at your self-confidence to have control over you. You start to see how one-sided your relationship truly is. They are a taker, and you the giver. After a while, you might feel like a roommate rather than a person in a committed relationship. You also might feel like you have to compete for loyalty and attention. In this stage, they have found other narcissistic supply, which is usually another person or thing (hobby, emotional or physical affair, adoring friends or fans) that gives them an ego boost. This supply demands their attention, so they keep you appeased while focusing their energy elsewhere. When you complain about lack of time spent with you, they either deny there is a problem or, if pushed, will blame you. Manipulatively, they want you to feel insecure about their disconnection from you. They want you to feel like you could be replaced and therefore should tread carefully, neither annoying them nor complaining when their behavior bothers you. This is their arrogance and entitlement. Also, during this phase, they blame you for the unhappiness in the relationship and take no responsibility for their behavior. There is little insight in them, so they are unlikely to see they are the problem or make even minute progress toward owning up to the fact that they are hurtful with their actions. Any acknowledgment that they hurt you is often an insincere and manipulative attempt to resolve the situation so you will get off their case.

If you were never in a relationship with them but were flirted with instead, they will turn around and devalue you in order to get sympathy from others. They might make things up about you, such as that you were the only one that had the crush. They might even lie and say they were never interested in you and that you won't leave them alone. You are suddenly being used for all sorts of purposes: making other people jealous, ego boosting, or getting attention from family and friends. They lie because you were either not available for them to date and this ticked them off, or they were never really interested. They just wanted to use you for the reasons mentioned above.

The final stage is when they discard you. This is when you stop meeting their needs. It could be as shallow as your looks not being as beautiful as those of another woman or man they fancy, or the idea that financially they are better off without you. The list of shallow reasons is as endless as their superficial love. However, the discard stage doesn't always mean they have to get rid of you. They might simply be talking about a divorce or a breakup because they are losing control over you. You have complained too much about their treatment of you or you haven't lived up to what they expect of you, so they are conditioning you to back off and change or they will leave. Threats are their way of regaining control and creating drama. When you rebel, they will either truly get rid of you in exchange for the other narcissistic supply in their life or they'll keep you strung along by taking you back through the idolization or "honeymoon" phase, only to repeat the devaluation phase after you have stopped complaining about their behavior.

It is hard to think of someone you love or are infatuated with being this calculating. These games seem well thought out, like a con artist's. I believe many narcissists enter relationships like con artists who plan the games they will use on you. However, I also believe there are narcissists who don't even realize they are playing games. They are in denial that they are doing anything wrong. They just do it out of habit because it works best for them. These individuals truly believe how they react and treat people is normal behavior. They minimize their bad behavior for various reasons—shame being one (more about this later).

This much is true about narcissism: *once you see the true character of the narcissist, you can't unsee it.* Everything they do is an act on their stage. If you don't take your script and act your part in their twisted drama, you will see the most appalling screenplay writer to ever walk the planet. After enough cycles through the three phases, you will begin to see yourself as a two-bit actor who was blessed to snag a role in their play. Whether you accept that they have a disorder or not, you will have to constantly audition for the spot to keep them in your life or you will be replaced, either by them actually leaving for someone else or by them focusing on other sources of supply.

The character I have just described is appalling! However, it is important to understand that this is how the disorder works. They might have moments of kindness and goodness, but, to maintain their self-esteem, they work on such a completely different level of manipulation that it overshadows their good qualities.

I believe love has a way of blinding people to what is truly going on in their life. I hope to wake you up from your dream and get you to the point of acceptance if you are not already there. Remember that the person you love is spiritually and mentally ill. The problem is their behavior and your reaction to it. If you're anything like me, a forgiving person, then you're going to go through denial that they have narcissism, because you have seen the good in them. Please don't make that mistake, like I did. Don't expect them to play every manipulative game listed in this book or have every symptom exactly as I have mentioned to meet your criteria for this disorder. Narcissism is a spectrum. Regardless of whether you accept that they are narcissistic, please at least acknowledge that they are an emotional abuser. Yes, there is good inside of them, but there is also a lot of evil manipulation and insincerity. Let me help you find a way to reclaim your dignity, rather than wasting more time ignoring bad behavior to keep the peace.

It took me a long time to figure out that the two men I knew had narcissism—probably because I bought the outward façade they had worked so hard to create and witnessed random acts of kindness by them. However, as things progressed, I kept seeing discrepancies in their characters. How could they profess to be Christian but so often be mean-spirited behind the scenes? Therefore, I began to research narcissism, but I was skeptical about them having this disorder. Narcissistic personality disorder would be obvious to everyone if they had it, right? That was the flaw in my thinking. Narcissism is not so obvious! Narcissists do such a great job of creating the appearance of a perfect person or life that sometimes only the people closest to them ever detect the disorder. Besides, society has created a stigma about narcissism. They are often portrayed as overachieving, loudmouthed, arrogant men who look in the mirror too often. Sadly, so many quiet and reserved types fly under the radar because of that stereotype. If you are still unsure whether your loved one truly has narcissistic personality disorder or just an inflated ego, then look closely at the *Diagnostic and Statistical Manual of Mental Disorders* (*DSM*) criteria for this disorder. The *DSM* lists the bolded items below as symptoms; below each one I have added my thoughts and what the Bible says about this characteristic.

- **They have an exaggerated sense of self-importance.**
  Narcissists feel special, so they latch on to things that support that idea. It can be as silly as saying they are related to a Cherokee ancestor and have 1 percent of that DNA running through their veins, or it can be something more tangible, such as knowing someone famous. Therefore, they believe they are important through association. They can take the most common talent, like playing an instrument, and turn it into a reason for being admired. In the dating phase, they might talk about themselves as if they were the rarest person in the world. You might even feel as if they are convincing you of their value.

  One clue of their exaggerated ego might be found on their social media. Their Facebook page might look like a boasting board and their YouTube video channel is going to star only them doing everything that makes them look cool. They might even be the king or queen of selfies. Oddly, they will even go so far as to idolize a mental illness, if they have one, to feel special. For example, they might state all people with ADHD are more creative and can focus more than most, leading to a state known as "hyperfocus." Thus, they may feel unique simply for having the disorder. They are either trying to sell you on their brokenness or trying to hide it.

  Even though narcissists often lack empathy (more on that later), they are skilled at reading people and they know what to say and do to appear extremely impressive, even at the expense of knocking people down to look good. Their intent is to let you know that they are superior. Imagine yourself working out. Instead of saying that they are happy for you because you're doing something about your health, they might say, "When I was your age, I was running marathons." This one-upmanship often comes across in subtle ways when they are annoyed with you. You might not see this in the idolization phase, but it comes out as subtle digs in the devaluation phase.

Narcissists like to categorize people into classes, not unlike what you experienced in high school. There are the geeks, nerds, in-crowd, and the outcasts—or whatever else they want to make up. Of course, they think they are part of the popular crowd, which is above all other people. Usually healthy individuals out-grow this adolescent classification. However, narcissists don't mature past this way of thinking. They believe other people label and classify people based on their looks, finances, career, and all things superficial. Therefore, they do too. Their goal is to remain at the top of this hierarchy, because it determines their worth. Realize that a narcissist will deny that they classify people, in order to look like the king or queen of equality, but the truth is they are not above snobbery.

What the Bible warns: *"And whoever exalts himself shall be abased; and he that shall humble himself shall be exalted" (Matthew 23:12).*

"And the devil said unto him, All this power will I give thee, and the glory of them: for that is delivered unto me; and to whomsoever I will I give it. If thou therefore wilt worship me, all shall be thine. And Jesus answered and said unto him, Get thee behind me, Satan: for it is written, Thou shalt worship the Lord thy God, and him only shalt thou serve" (Luke 4:6–8).

- **They expect to be recognized as superior even without the achievements that warrant it.**
  Narcissists thrive on being the best. They just don't act as if they are better; they actually believe it! In their minds, they are above you and are deserving of respect and special treatment. In public, they simply think they are cool, like an egotistical drummer thinking he is in a famous band when in reality he just plays with a couple of local musicians during Sunday services. There is no fan base or album, but in his mind, he is being worshiped by church members and is part of the popular crowd that is deserv-ing of respect and admiration. They have fantasies about who they are, when the reality is they are not all that.

In a relationship, a narcissist might act superior by being a know-it-all. For example, they might have entered your relationship with a lousy financial reputation (bad credit, bankruptcy), but they will tell you that they should be responsible for the finances in the house despite this track record. To family and friends, they might put on the persona of the expert at fixing things—cars, houses, you name it. However, nothing gets done around the house because they are fixated on their enjoyment and hobbies, not yours.

They might flaunt their job, talent, or whatever they have acquired in their life ferociously. They have adopted a "look at how cool I am" attitude. They expect attention even if they have no achievement that warrants it. For example, they could go to a party and not talk to anyone, but be upset after the party because no one was approaching them for a conversation. They think people should be falling over themselves to speak to them because, after all, they are cool and interesting. This lack of interest in speaking to others is followed by cutting down the people who blew them off so they can be elevated back to the status of being more important.

Narcissists are also very competitive. However, if they can't compete, they have a dozen excuses for why they are not superior. Narcissists suffer from what I call the "Wizard of Oz Complex." They want people to think of them as the great and powerful Oz, but the reality is that they are the circus performer behind the curtain.

What the Bible warns: *"The wicked, through the pride of his countenance, will not seek after God: God is not in all his thoughts" (Psalm 10:4).*

- **They exaggerate their achievements and talents.**
  Narcissists are great storytellers. They captivate you with stories of personal triumphs, heroism, and even spiritual self-righteousness. However, when you look further, you discover they have rewritten history. The fantasy becomes mythology. This can range from outright lies to embellishment of their talents, career, or finances. He might tell you he knows how to play an instrument and was on the way to stardom, but had to quit the band because his ex was insecure about him being on the road traveling all the time. However, when you start to investigate their past, you find things

grossly exaggerated. The truth is that he wasn't that talented. Or he might tell you how he used to be financially well off before his ex ran up the credit cards, leaving out the fact that she supported him when he didn't have a job and paid the start-up costs of his new company.

They are consumed with being admired and are not above lying about themselves to give the appearance that they are superior. Some will outright say they know people they don't know or have degrees they don't have. Others will tell white lies. For example, they might say they are friends with someone famous, but in reality they ran into that person one time and had a conversation. Or they might say they attended a prestigious college like Stanford, when in reality they took one online class there while all their other classes were at a local community college. Regardless, embellishment of the truth is lying, and they don't feel any shame in doing it.

What the Bible warns: *"Lying lips are abomination to the Lord: but they that deal truly are his delight" (Proverbs 12:22).*

- **They are preoccupied with fantasies about success, power, brilliance, beauty, or the perfect mate.**

    Narcissists can fixate on fantasies like nobody's business. These fantasies protect them from feelings of emptiness and shame, so facts and opinions that contradict them are ignored or rationalized away. The fantasy is about being better than what they are right now. It is normal to have dreams, but this goes a step further. They let these dreams ruin relationships. They might spend time away from you engrossed in a hobby or talent. They might be fixated on bodybuilding or competitive sports. A female narcissist could be involved in a social club or project that puts her in the spotlight. A narcissist could be the person who spends more time with their business than with you. Often their cell phone or computer gets more attention than anything in your relationship does.

    It is not uncommon for narcissists to spend a lot of time away from family because they are preoccupied with their narcissistic supply. You might feel you have to track them down. Anything that threatens to burst their fantasy is met with extreme denial, defensiveness, and rage. In my situation, when I was the narcissistic supply for my hacker, he was preoccupied with my reaction to him invading my privacy. He overheard my complaints to family and friends when he listened to my private cell-phone conversations. He would sift through my online files like a pervert looking through my underwear drawer. He had access to my Google search history and passwords to social media sites. My experience is an example of how obsessive narcissists can be and how their fantasies can destroy their own relationships.

What the Bible warns: *"Whoesover committeth sin transgresseth also the law: for sin is the transgression of the law. And you know that he was manifested to take away our sins; and in him is no sin. Whosoever abideth in him sinneth not: whosoever sinneth hath not seen him, neither known him. Little children, let no man deceive you: he that doeth righteousness is righteous, even as he is righteous. He that committeth sin is of the devil; for the devil sinneth from the beginning. For this purpose the Son of God was manifested, that he might destroy the works of the devil"* (1 John 3:4–8).

"Love not the world, neither the things that are in the world. If any man love the world, the love of the Father is not in him. For all that is in the world, the lust of the flesh, and the lust of the eyes, and the pride of life, is not of the Father, but is of the world. And the world passeth away, and the lust thereof: but he that doeth the will of God abideth forever" (1 John 2:15–17).

- **They believe they are superior and can only be understood by or associate with equally special people.**

  In their personal life, they will seek out attractive, empathetic, and intelligent partners, and popular friends who have something to offer them. It is a great cover-up for their narcissistic character. They expect people to believe they are kind, loving, and intelligent because they associate with someone who has these qualities. It is important to them to make their image rock solid so if things don't turn out with you, they have a support group that will believe their version of events. In their professional life, they will seek smart and highly motivated people to whom they can delegate most of the work, and then they will take the credit for themselves. They are not above using others for their gain. That gain always goes back to making themselves look good to other people, because they are consumed with what people think about them.

They are not the type of person to be friends with someone whom others speak poorly of or who has a bad reputation. They don't want someone tarnishing their status. However, if they can make a big deal about being the savior to the poor friend down on his luck, then of course they will use them to look good to others. However, the narcissist is still going to gossip and put them down behind their backs unless the righteous-rescuer façade is working for them.

What the Bible warns: *"These be they who separate themselves, sensual, have not the Spirit" (Jude 1:19).*

- **They require constant admiration.**
We all like to be admired. We all have egos. However, narcissists take this to extremes because they are reliant on other people's opinions to boost their self-confidence. The occasional compliment is not enough. Narcissists surround themselves with enablers who are willing to give them attention and admiration. Often these relationships are one-sided. The narcissist constantly takes and rarely gives. When you stop providing them with their "fix" of constant positive attention, they take this as betrayal. This is when they put you through the devaluation stage.

It is safe to say that narcissists don't want love; they want admiration and attention! They are willing to invent drama to get it. You can tell your narcissistic partner you love them all you want. Sure, they want those reassurances. However, to them they are simply words that show they have you hooked. However, that doesn't take top priority in the things they would prefer to hear from you. They would rather know you are impressed with them. And if they can't get positive attention, they will take negative attention. After all, a negative reaction is attention. For example, if you opened your Facebook page and cried about this person to your friends, you can bet the narcissist would be thrilled. They might even stalk your Facebook page to make sure you continue talking about them. It is an ego boost knowing you're pining away for them. Of course, if you don't give them admiration, they will punish you and accept your rage. Either way, they win because they get a reaction. To them, getting a reaction means they have control over you, which makes them feel powerful. And if your focus is on them, that must mean they are important.

25

What the Bible warns: *"But the Lord said unto Samuel, Look not on his countenance, or on the height of his stature; because I have refused him: for the Lord seeth not as man seeth; for man looketh on the outward appearance, but the Lord looketh on the heart"* (1 Samuel 16:7).

- **They have a sense of entitlement.**
  Narcissists live with a constant need for entitlement. Life is to revolve around them and their needs. They feel they deserve the royal treatment, but they rarely treat others the same way. This often shows up in relationships. They enjoy the sex, the financial security, and the other benefits of being together as a couple, but they don't want the responsibility. Their sense of entitlement might whisper to them that mundane tasks like doing the dishes, laundry, and cleaning are beneath them. With passive-aggressive behavior, they might create situations where other people do things for them. For example, they might complain when you get upset about them not helping out around the house by saying, "Well, you always complain when I do it, and besides, you're better at it." But they're simply roping you into situations where they get to blame you and at the same time butter you up so you will do the chores for them. If that tactic doesn't work, they might deliberately create time away from the house to avoid chores. They will hang out with their friends or spend time engrossed in a hobby, leaving you to tend to the responsibilities of the household while they spend their time in leisure.

  Another example of entitlement is displayed in their lack of loyalty. Many narcissists don't see a problem with flirtation or even with emotional or physical infidelity. They always deny this sense of entitlement, and they go to great lengths to avoid being caught. For example, they might not want you present when they pick up their kids from their ex's house because they want the opportunity to flirt with their ex. In addition, they might delete text messages or search histories from their computers and cell phones, especially if they involve people of the opposite sex. They might make stuff up about you, like you being insecure, to elicit sympathy from their other narcissistic supply. Simple requests for loyalty are met with accusations of you being paranoid. For example, you might ask them to unfriend the ex or their ex's family on Facebook. The narcissist might refuse to do this and then shift the blame on you by stating, "You don't trust me because you have trust issues." Narcissists expect to be free from relationship rules. However, they hold you to a higher standard.

My narcissist hacker was willing to risk being caught just to hack my cell phone and computer because he feels extremely entitled. He wasn't just risking himself, but risking his kids. If I were able to prove what he did, he would be spending five years in jail for violating my civil rights. His love of the game was more important than being separated from his own children. Not to mention, he risked his marriage by playing this game.

Narcissists want what they want. *They desire people, but they don't value them.* They don't give a lot of thought about other people's feelings. They don't understand that when a person tells you that you hurt them, you don't get to decide that you didn't. A narcissist's entitlement leads them to overlook your pain. It is not acknowledged as a valid emotion you are justified in having. Remember, you are not entitled; they are.

What the Bible warns: *"Ye adulterers and adulteresses, know ye not that the friendship of the world is enmity with God? Whosoever therefore will be a friend of the world is the enemy of God. Do you think that the scripture saith in vain, The spirit that dwelleth in us lusteth to envy? But he giveth more grace. Wherefore he saith, God resisteth the proud, but giveth grace unto the humble"* (James 4: 4–6).

"Treasures of wickedness profit nothing: but righteousness delivers from death" (Proverbs 10:2).

- **They expect special favors and unquestioning compliance with their expectations.**
  It's the narcissist's way or the highway. They are into themselves. Therefore, you might expect them to be annoyed if they're asked to do you a favor with no benefit to them. Yet they might ask you for a large favor when they have given very little in the relationship. For example, they might ask to go on a two-week trip with their friends, but when you ask to borrow their truck to visit family for the day in another town, they give a million excuses why you can't borrow it, because they don't want to be inconvenienced. Or they might expect you to act a certain way or look a certain way to meet their expectations. After all, you are now an extension of their image. When you gain a little weight, they

might treat you with subtle or outright criticism. However, if they gain weight, it is no big deal.

What the Bible warns: *"Love is patient, love is kind. It does not envy, it does not boast, it is not proud. It does not dishonor others, it is not self-seeking, it is not angered, it keeps no record of wrongs. Love does not delight in evil but rejoices with the truth. It always protects, always trusts, always hopes, always perseveres"* *(1 Corinthians 13:4–7).*

- **They take advantage of others to get what they want.**
  This character trait makes nurturing people especially vulnerable if they end up in a relationship with a narcissist. Most of us are willing to go above and beyond for loved ones, but narcissists don't return the favor. They take advantage of others to obtain everything from admiration to material possessions to professional connections. This person treats you horribly in the relationship but doesn't have a problem spending your hard-earned money while they are doing it. Or this person uses your social status to boost their own. Some take it as a conquest or make a sport of winning things over. It is not uncommon for them to enjoy pushing you to the brink of leaving just to win you back. They enjoy the game and the control they have over you. They don't have respect for the people they are in relationships with because over time they find it easy to manipulate people and win their approval over and over again.

  Narcissistic relationships are unbalanced regarding mutual giving and fairness. You will also notice how spoiled and selfish they become if they don't get their way. It is like a grown-up child throwing a tantrum full of passive-aggressive games. In many ways, they view the people in their lives as objects, there to serve their needs. If you try to point out their bad behavior, they can't see it. To them you deserved it. The only thing they understand is how to use manipulation to meet their needs.

  What the Bible warns: *"You shall not steal, neither deal falsely, neither lie one to another" (Leviticus 19:11).*

  "Recompense to no man evil for evil. Provide things honest in the sight of all men" (Romans 12:17).

- **They have an inability or unwillingness to recognize the needs and feelings of others.**

  They simply can't put themselves in the shoes of another person. They say they can, but the truth is shown in their actions. Often, you will find yourself desperately trying to convince them they have hurt you. However, they don't buy your version of events and think you're exaggerating the situation. They can't deal with shame, so they constantly blame you instead. Let's say you get into an argument with your partner and start crying in public. It would be reasonable for your partner to stop arguing and comfort you. However, a narcissist would be more concerned with getting you out of sight because you're embarrassing him or her. They are more concerned about how it looks rather than your feelings of pain and despair. They want you to stop crying because it makes them feel uncomfortable rather than because they are truly upset that you are hurting.

  It's important to remember that narcissists are not looking for partners; they're looking for obedient admirers. Your desires and feelings don't count, though they will tell you they do to appease you if you're thinking about leaving the relationship. Your sole value to them is being their primary narcissistic supply. You are to inflate their ego and keep up the act that they're living a wonderful life people should envy.

  There is debate among some psychologists about whether narcissists feel empathy or not. The consensus at this time is that narcissists don't feel empathy. That is not to say that the narcissist in your life won't donate to a charity at Christmastime or give a home to a dog that was to be put down. It simply means you can bet that they don't plan to keep that act of charity to themselves. It is something they are going to tell family and friends about. All acts of altruism go back to reinforcing their image to gain attention.

  What the Bible warns: *"Take heed that ye do not your aims before men, to be seen of them: otherwise ye have no reward of your Father which is in heaven. Therefore when thou doest thine aims, do not sound a trumpet before thee, as the hypocrites do in the synagogues and in the streets, that they may have glory of men. Verily I say unto you, They have their reward. But when thou doest aims, let not they left hand know what thy right hand doeth: That thine aims* *may be in secret: and they Father which seeth in secret himself shall reward thee openly" (Matthew 6:1–4).*

"We then that are strong ought to bear the infirmities of the weak, and not to please ourselves" (Romans 15:1).

- **They are envious of others and believe others envy them.**

Narcissists like to be the best guy or gal around. They will belittle another person's accomplishments if that person upstages them in any way, sometimes by taking credit for other people's success. Oddly, they believe they are widely envied, even by people who have had enough of them and their bad behavior. They are threatened by people who are confident and popular or who don't kowtow to them. Their defense mechanism to combat this feeling is contempt. This could be shown by outright name-calling, bullying and insults, or through something subtle like patronizing or passive-aggressive games.

They live in a fantasy world and are consumed with being admired. Therefore, it makes sense that they would feel that their enemies hate them because they are jealous of them in some way. Remember, they perceive themselves as significant, superior, and special. In their mind, people in their life fall into one of two categories: fans or enemies. There is no middle ground.

If they couldn't date you or you rejected their advances, you become the person that is beneath them and is jealous of whomever they are with now. This is part of their smear campaign against you. Strangely, they actually believe you are pining away for them, even though you have made it apparent you no longer want anything to do with them.

What the Bible warns: *"But God hath chosen the foolish things of the world to confound the wise; and God hath chosen the weak things of the world to confound the things which are mighty; And base things of the world, and things which are despised, hath God chosen, yea, and things which are not, to bring to nought things that are: That no flesh should glory in his presence" (1 Corinthians 1:27–29).*

"Let nothing be done through strife or vain glory, but in lowliness of mind let each esteem other better than themselves" (Philippians 2:3).

- **They behave in an arrogant or haughty manner.**

  This is supported by their inability to handle criticism. They might be extremely critical of others (especially when it elevates them), but any criticism or perceived criticism of them is enough to send them into a spiral of anger and defensiveness. Whether it is constructive or destructive criticism, they can't handle it because it threatens their sense of superiority. They are good at blocking out things that challenge their view of themselves as being unique and admired.

  Both of the narcissists I endured had an arrogant side. One day my narcissist hacker told me that he had a lot of women as fans because of his talent. He told me it gave him an ego boost. This offhanded statement seemed odd, and I wondered why he said it to me. However, looking back at that conversation, I see his arrogance as plain as day. He was trying to let me know he was desired by women. Therefore, I should know his value and leave my current relationship because he was all that.

  The other narcissist was a name-dropper. He would talk about all the important people he knew with stunning frequency. He truly thought he was important by association and wanted people to know it. Not to mention he was a snob. He classified people into categories—popular or rejects—rather than as individuals. He wouldn't be caught dead wearing an unpopular brand of clothing or driving something that didn't let other people know he had money.

  What the Bible warns: *"The fear of the Lord is to hate evil: pride, and arrogancy, and the evil way, and the forward mouth, do I hate"* (Proverbs 8:13).

  "And I will punish the world for their evil, and the wicked for their iniquity; and I will cause the arrogancy of the proud to cease, and will lay low the haughtiness of the terrible" (Isaiah 13:11).

Those are the *DSM* criteria. Remember, narcissistic personality disorder is a spectrum. Some of the symptoms might be prominent or mild. The point is that they have the symptoms, regardless of degree. Did any of these traits strike a chord?

You don't have to decide yet if your partner has the disorder or not. If you venture beyond the *DSM*, victims of narcissistic abuse would add more traits to the list. Indeed, I think it is safe to say that survivors would rewrite the section about narcissistic personality disorder in the *DSM* if they had the chance. Below are other characteristics I have heard many survivors of narcissistic abuse recount in recovery forums.

- **They hate to be alone.**
  To say narcissists don't like being alone would be an understatement. They hate it! Remember that they are actors on a stage and need an audience. They consider their partner their primary narcissistic supply. It isn't because you haven't given them enough attention that keeps them looking for it elsewhere. They are easily bored. They don't do well when the relationship settles in and there is nothing new to discover about their partner.

  When a relationship finally ends, they will often run to their other narcissistic supply. This could be someone new or a previous ex. They don't really care who it is, as long as that person will pick up where you left off. They are shallow individuals. You need to remember that! Just because they quickly get into another relationship doesn't mean they have more love for their new supply than they gave you. They are incapable of real love. They just want people to know they are desired and at the same time get their desires met. It doesn't get any deeper than that.

  What the Bible warns: *"But after they hardness and impenitent heart treasurest up unto thyself wrath against the day of wrath and revelation of the righteous judgement of God" (Romans 2:5).*

  "Remember therefore from whence thou art fallen, and repent, and do the first works; or else I will come unto thee quickly, and will remove thy candlestick out of his place, except thou repent" (Revelation 2:5).

- **They are excellent liars.**
  Narcissists are excellent actors, manipulators, embellishers, and liars. They don't think they are because, in their mind, anything they do to benefit themselves is part of surviving and is justifiable. Oddly, they prefer to lie even when telling the truth would be beneficial. Maybe that is because they can't keep the story straight. Lying requires a good memory!

  All narcissistic abuse victims agree that there is no such thing as a truthful narcissist. They lie to keep control. They lie to look good. They lie to win people over. They lie. They lie. They lie, and it never ends!

What the Bible warns: *"They speak vanity every one with his neighbor, with flattering lips and with a double heart do they speak"* *(Psalm 12:2).*

"Lying lips are an abomination to the Lord: but a just weight in his delight" *(Proverbs 12:22).*

- **They are hypocrites.**

Narcissists have extremely high expectations for fidelity, respect, and adoration. However, that applies to you, not them. This person might be in a respected position at church while cheating and lying on the side. Or they might boast about being an honest person in their business dealings, but they don't have a business license. They love to call other people fakes and hypocrites, but they don't see their actions in the same way. They see it as surviving or white lies that everyone tells. To them it is no big deal.

They also take away your basic right to be mad at them for hurting you. No matter how badly you're treated, they believe you shouldn't raise your voice higher than theirs in an argument. Anger is only reserved for them. Therefore, any anger on your part is disrespectful. In essence, they can dish it out, but they can't take it!

What the Bible warns: *"Then spake Jesus to the multitude, and to his disciples, Saying the scribes and the Pharisees sit in Moses' seat: All therefore whatsoever they bid you observe, that observe and do; but do not ye after their works: for they say, and do not. For they bind heavy burdens and grievous to be borne, and lay them on men's shoulders; but they themselves will not move them with one of their fingers. But all their works they do for to be seen of men"* *(Matthew 23:1–5).*

- **They have a victim attitude.**

To everyone outside their world, they project that life is wonderful, but behind closed doors, narcissists are negative. Somewhere in the beginning of a narcissist's life, they adopted the "glass is half empty" mentality. They will tell stories of past betrayals and abusive partners whom they always tried to make happy. People who believe this storytelling will offer words of comfort. They will assure the narcissist that they deserved better. This enables them to get away with pretending to be a victim, their reputation still intact while getting attention.

Over time, you might find yourself responsible for giving them a happy outlook on life. However, if you nurture their outlook too often, they will constantly remain in the victim role to garnish attention. Eventually, narcissistic abuse victims say they didn't sign up to be their partner's motivational coach, but they also didn't realize that they were cast into that role. Remember, you are playing a part in their play! You will have the role of therapist as well.

Narcissists are angry, negative people, but this isn't because they have never experienced love. They have been given it by many people and pushed it away. They are bitter because they are not as powerful and awe-inspiring or successful as they wish and, in their minds, deserve to be. They live with a constant, nagging need for adoration and attention. This can never be fulfilled. Happiness is fleeting. They live on a roller-coaster ride of emotions. Their daydreams stubbornly refuse to come true or stay true for any real length of time. They are their own worst enemy. Because of this, they have unmitigated paranoia, seeing adversaries plotting everywhere and feeling discriminated against, disrespected, contemptuously ignored, and slighted.

What the Bible warns: *"But mark this: There will be a terrible times in the last days. People will be lovers of themselves, lovers of money, boastful, proud, abusive, disobedient to their parents, ungrateful, unholy, without love, unforgiving, slanderous, without self- control, brutal, not lovers of good, treacherous, rash, conceited, lovers of pleasure rather than lovers of God, having a form of godliness but denying its power. Have nothing to do with such people"* (2 Timothy 3:1–5).

"Get rid of all bitterness, rage and anger, brawling and slander, along with every form of malice" (Ephesians 4:31).

- **They have trust issues.**
Most survivors report that narcissists tend to be more paranoid and untrusting than other people. This would make sense if they had a long history of broken relationships. When they are not willing to self-reflect and see problems in themselves, then they perceive that their partner is to blame for their unhappiness. Therefore, they create the limiting belief that not all people are worth trusting in a relationship. This lack of trust can cause them not to value the words "I love you" from a partner. They prefer

34

being in a place of control over their partner rather than taking their partner's word for it.

Often, the narcissist believes that people are "faking it." They are convinced that others' "feelings" are grounded in ulterior motives. In emotional situations, they become suspicious, feel embarrassed, are compelled to avoid them, or, worse, experience surges of almost uncontrollable aggression in the presence of genuinely expressed sentiments. These remind them how poorly equipped they are.

Many narcissists are paranoid. This means they are afraid of people and of what people might do to them. Wouldn't you be scared if your happiness depended on the attention of others? The narcissist depends on others providing narcissistic supply. To counter this overwhelming feeling of helplessness, the narcissist becomes a control freak. It is their way of managing the paranoia and a lack of trust.

What the Bible warns: *"A stone that causes people to stumble and a rock that makes them fall. They stumble because they disobey the message—which is also what they were destined for"* (1 Peter 2:8).

- **They care too much about how you make them look.**
The narcissist will frequently give comments about how you look, implying they dislike your looks or that you're no longer as attractive as you once were. These could be subtle remarks about what you are wearing or about other women or men who are more in shape. They also will go beyond your looks to scrutinize your hobbies or anything you do that might embarrass them. Appearances are everything, and you must remain the trophy partner, because you are an extension of their ego. This was apparent in the relationship I had with my narcissist. When we met, he told me I was the most beautiful thing he had ever seen. However, he treated me as if I could lose my looks after eating one Big Mac. I was a healthy weight for my height and age, yet he constantly criticized me for eating any fast food. I had to remain super skinny and play the part of the model girlfriend. I could never throw on a pair of sweats and walk around with messed-up hair or no makeup. I was to represent what he was capable of getting, which required me to be perfect 24/7. From that experience I have learned that one of the greatest

regrets in life is being what others want you to be rather than being yourself.

What the Bible warns: *"Charm is deceptive, and beauty is fleeting; but a woman who fears the Lord is to be praised" (Proverbs 31:30).*

- **They give to get.**
  If they want to cover something up, win you back, or need something, they might give you a gift. This gift might be a compliment, acknowledgment, or recognition that can seem like a glimmer of hope in your relationship. This can be done to take you back through the idolization phase again or to shift the attention off the narcissist's bad behavior. The point is that they don't give for the sake of giving. They expect credit for doing it. They believe that people give to get and the concept of simply giving without recognition is pointless.

  What the Bible warns: *"In everything I did, I showed you that by this kind of hard work we must help the weak, remembering the words the Lord Jesus himself said: 'It is more blessed to give than to receive'" (Acts 20:35).*

These characteristics are widely seen in people with narcissistic personality disorder. It can be overwhelming to see so many negative traits about your loved one. You might be asking, "How could anyone love someone like this?" However, you and I both know that it is easy to love when you have a good heart. People with good hearts want to see the best in people and overlook the rest. We want to give second chances. And again, they are sons or daughters of our Heavenly Father who are truly lost in this life, but they are still loved by God. They need our prayers and our pity for the shallow lives they live. But most of all, they need our love like Christ loves us. Our job as sons and daughters of our Heavenly Father is not to hate them. They are suffering enough through their own hate of their true selves. *However, God doesn't want us to love them at the expense of our dignity, life mission, health, faith, or joy.* When it comes to the point of losing any of those five things, then it is time to walk away from the drama.

I don't know your situation. You could still be with your narcissist, you might have been discarded by them, or maybe you are the one who left the relationship. Regardless of what place you find yourself in, God doesn't want you to lose track of who you are meant to be and what you are meant to do in this lifetime. These two things take precedence over your love for them.

Throughout this book, I will give you work to do to aid in your recovery. My first request is that you invest in a journal to complete the writing assignments in this book. It is important to write down your responses, because I will ask you to refer back to your answers.

If you have gotten this far, don't give up now! I know it is hard to accept that your loved one is ill. The dream of living happily ever after can be strong. At first, I wanted to dismiss that these two men in my life were narcissists. I wanted to believe I was being too hard on them. I wanted to believe that God was going to step in, do his magic, and get them to a point of remorse for what they had done. The truth I had to accept was that they were both ill, and I was becoming ill because of their toxic responses to anything I said or did. God was trying to rescue me. He wasn't going to do it by changing these two people into what I wanted. He was going to change me. Allow yourself to be the one who changes. Trust in God to see you through this! Don't dig through this book looking for the right words that will change your narcissist. You won't find it. This book is about changing you!

Now that you know the symptoms of narcissism, let's get started by doing something on this road to recovery!

To-Do List

1. Get a journal. Make sure this book is out of sight of your narcissist; need I say more?
2. In your journal, write down the characteristics your narcissist displays.
3. After each characteristic, write an example of how he or she disrespects you or others by having this trait. Again, you will be referring back to this when you get to Act II, the section on setting boundaries.
4. Write about how these characteristics make you feel. Also consider how they affect others, especially the children (if you have any).
5. Make two columns in your journal. Label one "Traits My Partner Should Have" and the second "Traits My Partner Has/Had." Write qualities for both lists (for example, "kindness" and "forgiveness" as traits they should have). Now compare the lists. Do you see a contrast?

6. Below the two columns, write why you are worth being with someone with the qualities you are looking for and why you are not. I think it is important to know your level of self-esteem. Seeing it on paper helps to determine what you will need to work on before you set boundaries in a relationship.

Who Do Narcissists Target?

As I mentioned before, narcissists usually search for attractive partners whom others would consider a real "prize" or "trophy." They have no interest in someone that *anyone* could get, unless they are with you for reasons other than love. So you might want to pause for a moment and ask, "Why are (or were) they with me?"

We already spoke about narcissists as users and takers. Is it possible this person is or was in the relationship because they were bored, needed help financially, or thought you had a social circle that would help their image? Maybe you were being used to make an ex jealous or to help them get back on their feet after their ex threw them out. The point is that narcissists' criteria for a mate consists of a shallow list of how you can serve their needs. They will say that they love you. Yet how can they love you and still engage in manipulative games? It's a shallow, toxic love. Whatever you might be to them, you are called "narcissistic supply" by psychiatric professionals. Narcissistic supply is adoration, interpersonal support, or sustenance a narcissist draws from the people around them, and it is essential to their self-esteem. This could be from a fan base, friends, coworkers, church members, or other men or women they are attracted to (or are attracted to them). That is all you are to them.

They usually target empathetic and caring souls—the type of person who will go the extra mile to please them. This giving soul is willing to forgive over and over again. They are usually a fixer and will bend over backward to make things work. Narcissists look for someone they can cross boundaries with. **They are not going to go for someone who is independent, opinionated, and difficult to control.** They don't want you to look or act inferior, but they do need you to be a forgiving individual, gullible and blinded with love, so they can get by with their behavior.

As you can imagine, narcissists see people as objects to satisfy their need for attention. They might have an internal dialogue with themselves about you. *Does this person make me look good? How easily can I get sex from them? How much better financially will I be with them? How much easier will they make my life?* There is nothing wrong with having a checklist of things we would like to have in a mate. However, a narcissist's reasons are superficial.

I wanted you to write down the checklist of traits you want in a partner to remind you that God already has a checklist for you. He wants you to be with someone who has spiritual characteristics! Go back and look at the list of traits you want in a partner. Are any of them spiritual? I can guarantee you that the list of qualities a narcissist looks for is a lot shallower. They don't have internal dialogues that ask, *How will this person make me grow spiritually? How can this person help me be better morally?* They might ask, "How will this person make me *look* spiritually?" but they never seek out qualities in a mate that they feel would improve their behavior. This is not to say that narcissists are not deep thinkers. They have a lot of views on life, but many of their actions don't line up with the teachings of Christ. Their symptoms won't allow it for very long.

What Causes Narcissism?

As with many personality disorders, the exact cause of narcissism is unknown. We do know that it isn't a chemical imbalance like bipolar or other disorders, and there is no evidence to believe it is brain-development based. Therefore, this leaves us with the conclusion that narcissism is created through habitual conditioning.

Narcissism first reveals itself with low self-esteem, or feeling inferior. A narcissist might put on a show that they are confident, but behind that act is a dysfunctional, wounded child. This is called the "true self" and is often suppressed for protection. Real or perceived threats to this suppression lead to anxiety, which in turn leads to the development of defense mechanisms to protect the narcissist's ego. Healthy individuals face shortcomings with humility. However, narcissists face shortcomings with shame, though this is well disguised. This surface disguise of cool confidence, or the "false self," hides the frail person the narcissist is inside. It becomes what they want people to see and what they need to be. It is their armor. In the "false self," they are superior to others and have a corresponding sense of entitlement.

They may have developed the false self to feel empowered when they were powerless as a child raised in a dysfunctional family. They might take the stance that their victimization entitles them to act cruel if need be because, after all, cruelty was shown to them.

The superior image of themselves that they formed for protection becomes a delusion. In a real sense, they overcompensate by thinking they are special. They are suffering from what I like to call "Harry Potter syndrome." They want to believe they are as special as the character in author J. K. Rowling's children's books. The narcissist sees themselves as a kid who grew up in a dysfunctional family and was an outcast for being different. Then finally they discover they are special—a wizard. No one understands that except the people allowed into their inner circle. Everyone is an ordinary Muggle except the narcissist. And of course they have been marked for greatness, so everyone should give them special treatment! The problem with this is that the narcissist doesn't realize they are as bad as Harry Potter's enemy Draco Malfoy. Obviously, that is just a popular children's book and narcissists don't think they are wizards, but they do take this "specialness" thing almost that far. The delusion is much easier to believe than the truth, which is that they were never good enough for a parent who damaged them earlier in life.

Now we come to their past. It is said that early childhood experiences and psychological factors contribute to the formation of narcissism. Instead of being provided with the unconditional love all children need, the narcissist was subjected to poor parenting. The dysfunctional parent possibly had unpredictable and inexplicable bouts of temper, rage, searing sentimentality, envy, prodding, infusions of guilt, and other unhealthy emotions and behavior patterns. They may have had a mental illness like Borderline Personality Disorder. They either smothered their child too much and made them believe they were better than other people or they did the opposite. In the latter case, the narcissist reacted by retreating to a made-up world, where they imagined they were omnipotent and omniscient and therefore immune to such vicious opinions. They stashed their vulnerable "true self" deep inside and chose to present to the world a "false self" that was safer.

Because the narcissist is divorced from their true self, they cannot hold on to good feelings. Instead, they can only operate within the range of painful feelings. All "good" feelings for a narcissist are delusional, obsessive, and ego driven, which can be seen through the actions of their false selves. That is why so many of them are so quick to anger. Narcissists can't and don't detach from people's assessments of them. Their identity is established by feedback. That is why it is important for them to ensure, create, and keep the type of narcissistic supply that will maintain the self-worth that they lack and sustain their false self. Even your anger with them gives them supply because it means you are affected by them. Therefore, they have control and exist. They live with constant low levels of frustration. Happiness is reliant on the positive or negative attention we give them.

Narcissists' natural reaction to your hurt feelings is always non-accountability. They react this way because they can't deal with the emotional pain and powerlessness that come from accepting blame. They can't be unacceptable. Somewhere in their early upbringing, they couldn't handle emotional pain, so they split from it and created a false self, which was a grandiose and accepted version of their self. Ego is always the first defense to protect ourselves from pain and fear. However, the narcissist develops a personality disorder because of discarding his true self, which he finds weak and unacceptable.

They are detached from their false self and the things they do. They actually have a hard time connecting to having done something wrong. They truly feel like a victim and believe it is outrageous to be held accountable. This might be because they are incredibly insecure and interpret the tiniest slight or criticism as a personal attack against them. The narcissist doesn't have the resources from their "true self" to shrug these opinions off. Therefore, they harbor resentment and inflate what people have done to huge proportions, which demands a cruel reaction. Healthy people can let things go, but a narcissist can't. Because narcissists believe in "me versus you" and the need to use pathological tactics to get by, they suspect everyone else is doing the same thing. Narcissists have trust issues and don't feel supported by anyone.

The narcissist is never in the moment but always stuck in the past, dealing with wounds that gnaw at them relentlessly. This pushes them to secure narcissistic supply for temporary relief from those wounds.

So now you know why they blame you and make you the bad guy. They can't tolerate adding to the vast sea of wounds that have remained unhealed in their life. Of course, their behavior seems insane to us. However, the narcissist's reality is that you did something wrong, not them, and they actually believe their own lies. To convince the narcissist of your version of events, you would have to rewire their mind. They might occasionally own up to something, but you will find out much later that all that honesty has disappeared. They are back to their stance that you are the problem—probably because they never believed they were the problem and were appeasing you so you would leave them alone.

Unfortunately, therapists usually can't diagnose narcissism in people until they are adults and the personality is fully developed. Therefore, narcissists don't get help early on, or if they do, it is for other disorders. Narcissism can look like other disorders if not diagnosed correctly.

Regardless of whether the narcissist was treated poorly as a child, it is safe to say that healthy self-esteem is not formed if a child is not valued for their own self-worth but instead is only used for the benefit of the parents' self-esteem and to further the parents' needs. A narcissistic personality may be formed to make up for this lack of support and encouragement from parents.

The following are early childhood risk factors for developing this disorder:

- Trauma
- High expectations that would be extreme for any child
- Insensitive parenting
- Spoiling by parents
- Poorly imposed discipline
- Idealization of the child—overpraising and excessive pampering—when parents focus intensely on a particular talent or the physical appearance of their child as a result of their own self-esteem issues
- Unpredictable or negligent care
- Excessive criticism
- Emotional or physical abuse

Other possible factors:

- Genetic abnormalities impacting psychobiology—the connection between brain and behavior
- An oversensitive temperament

Still another possibility could be our changing culture. Many people, including many psychologists, believe that narcissism is a product of our times and our system of values. In the Western world in particular, we are constantly bombarded by images of the ideal through the media, and this may contribute to the rapid growth of narcissism in society. For instance, some people try to live up to the ideal or pretend they fit in.

Although there is no one answer to the question of what causes narcissistic personality disorder, professionals agree that the sooner treatment begins, the better a person's chances for improved quality of life. In addition, since there are no born narcissists, it leads one to conclude that a person who develops narcissistic personality disorder and doesn't seek treatment remains one by choice. The narcissist is not bound by a chemical imbalance that alters moods; therefore, they choose to react the way they do. That then leads you to the conclusion that they know what they are doing. Yes, they know that they are hurting you. Yes, they are doing it on purpose. Yes, they can control it if they want to. Yes, they could stop if they wanted to. Because they know what they are doing, they are not a victim of a chemical imbalance or an emotional handicap. They are not at the mercy of their pathology or disorder, though they would have you believe it. They can change. But only if they want to!

There is no point feeling sorry for them, because that is exactly what they want and it doesn't fix their behavior. Sure, they had a dysfunctional upbringing. That warrants our empathy. However, there are people that have been repeatedly abused in their childhoods and still don't grow up to be narcissists who play cruel games with others.

You can only have so much pity for someone who has narcissism. I am sure if you are reading this, then you have given them more than enough love at the cost of your own health. You will need to figure out the line between being a Christian who helps and a Christian who is losing his or her own faith trying to save someone who doesn't want to be saved. However, hold on to hope. I believe you shouldn't give up until you have done all that you can. In the following sections, let me share with you where your boundaries need to be and where you should set the limits of your giving.

To-Do List

1. Narcissism can mimic other disorders, including histrionic personality disorder, attention deficit hyperactivity disorder (ADHD), borderline personality disorder, oppositional defiant disorder, and sociopathy. You can also have narcissism and still have another disorder also. Investigate these disorders before concluding your loved one has narcissism.

Do Narcissists Have High or Low Self-Esteem?

There are conflicting views on whether narcissists have high self-esteem. It would make sense that someone who feels others are envious of them would think highly of themselves. However, the traits of narcissism and high self-esteem are far more distinct than one would think.

A study done at the University of Southern Mississippi concluded that narcissists have low self-esteem. Narcissists feel superior to others but don't necessarily like themselves. In fact, narcissists' feelings about themselves are entirely based on others' opinions of them. Meanwhile, people with high self-esteem don't think of themselves as superior to others, and they tend to accept themselves regardless of what others think about them. People with high self-esteem perceive themselves as valuable individuals, but not more valuable than others. People with high self-esteem rarely become aggressive or angry toward others, because they are not affected by people's opinions. They do not need constant admiration, because they have established a healthy belief in their own value that doesn't require approval.

When narcissists receive the admiration they desire so badly, they feel proud and elated. However, when they don't get the attention they crave, they feel ashamed and may even react with anger and aggression. They don't have self-esteem without that fix of admiration they get from other human beings. Furthermore, narcissism and self-esteem have remarkably distinct childhood origins, and they develop differently over the lifespan. The person with narcissistic personality disorder has a list of symptoms and games they use to raise their self-esteem. Someone with a healthy level of self-esteem doesn't use games to raise it.

Regardless of whether your narcissistic partner has low self-esteem, don't let that or their sad childhood give them free rein to be abusive to you. The Bible says, "But we all, with open face beholding as in a glass the glory of the Lord, are changed into the same image from glory to glory, even as by the Spirit of the Lord" (2 Corinthians 3:18). If this person has been presented with Christ's message, they can't use their woes in life as a reason not to rise above them. They can be transformed if it is their will. Jesus said, "It is not the healthy that need a doctor, but the sick. I have not come to call the righteous, but sinners to repentence" (Luke 5:31–32). Narcissists are spiritually ill. Don't let the excuse of their circumstances become your excuse as well.

What Are Narcissists like as Parents?

Do narcissists' kids notice their disorder? I took to narcissist recovery forums to find out. Many children of narcissists describe the following experiences and things they noticed in their parents:

- They were self-centered and vain.
- They used people for their own good.
- They did whatever they wanted when dealing with their children and spouses.
- They wanted children to look great to their friends and colleagues. Children were most important when the narcissistic parent could brag about them—sad but true.
- Children couldn't get their emotional needs met from a narcissistic parent.
- Narcissistic parents were charismatic and always the center of attention, which took the attention off of the children.
- They didn't take criticism well.
- Their rage was truly scary.
- They were aloof and unsympathetic.
- They weren't around a lot. They got a lot of gratification outside the family.

Most said that their narcissistic parent didn't really know them because they were so self-absorbed. They were not interested in what their children had to say unless it affected them. They might have been talking to them but not listening.

The cold, hard truth is that whatever narcissists are doing to you in the relationship, they are also doing it to their kids. If they are giving you the silent treatment, then they are not above giving them the silent treatment. If they are disappearing to spend time on their hobbies or projects, then they are not only disappearing from you but from their family.

Narcissists are not above using their kids to get back at you. If they are ignoring you, they might spend time with the kids to make you jealous. If you threaten divorce, then they will use the kids to keep control and express their resentment. They might do this by stirring up emotions in the children and leading them to think you're not interested in spending time with them, thus getting them to feel victimized, like the narcissist does.

Children are the ultimate narcissistic supply, but they are treated in the same way any target would be treated. If they fail to meet the needs of their parent, then they are manipulated just like a partner would be. Narcissists don't have any special treatment reserved for their kids. They operate in the same mode, with the same games.

Narcissistic parents often damage their children. They may disregard boundaries, withhold affection until the children perform the way they want, or neglect to meet their children's needs, because their needs come first. Because image is so important to narcissists, they may demand perfection from their children or use their accomplishments to increase their already inflated ego.

Daughters of narcissistic fathers often describe feeling that they had to compete with siblings for time with their parent and never got enough. "As a young child, growing up, you got compliments on your looks, but as you got older comments were about your weight or your attitude." "You felt insecure about yourself. Like you were never enough." Statements like these indicate how narcissistic fathers made these daughters grow up to have insecurities in relationships. They felt like their partner wasn't committed and they might get dumped for someone else because they were raised to feel like they were not good enough.

Sons of narcissistic parents never feel that they can measure up. The narcissistic parent either competed with them or ignored them.

The narcissistic parent might be threatened by their child's potential or success because it challenged the parent's self-esteem. Consequently, a narcissistic mother or father might make a concerted effort to remain superior by putting the child down. This might include nit-picking, unreasonable judgment and criticisms, unfavorable comparisons, invalidation of positive attitudes and emotions, and rejection of success and accomplishments. Narcissistic parents make sure their children can't beat them. Therefore, sons grow up to feel second-rate.

Sons learn from narcissistic male role models how to manipulate and use people, especially women. They observe the dynamics in their parents' relationships and go on to treat their partners the same way. However, the appearance of a romantic partner in a teenager's life may be viewed as a major threat, and frequently narcissistic parents respond with rejection, criticism, or competition. In the eyes of some narcissists, no romantic partner is ever good enough for their kid.

Since a narcissistic mother or father often hopes that the child will permanently dwell under their influence, they may become extremely jealous at any signs of the child's growing maturity. As a teenager begins to show independence, activities such as choosing a career, making friends not approved by their parent, and spending time on their own are interpreted as slights that take away from the adoration the narcissist demands.

Narcissists do little to equip their children for life, meaning they give them no coping skills, no guidance in common sense, and no interpersonal relationship skills. They can't give what they don't have, right? They end up teaching their children that you either control or be controlled and appearances are more important than reality, plus a bunch of manipulative games. As you can see, the children of narcissists don't grow up normal. They become adults who either repeat bad behavior they picked up from the narcissist or feel as defeated as the narcissist's partner feels—not special enough. This seems to reflect the feelings of the narcissist's true self. Narcissists tend to make others feel the way they do inside. In the end, it takes an extremely strong and aware non-narcissistic partner to pick up the slack for the narcissist in order to raise the kids to have healthy self-esteem, morals, and relationship skills. Therefore, the non-narcissistic partner is cast into yet another role—the only responsible and healthy parent.

To-Do List

1. If you have kids in this relationship, the first thing you should do is write about how they are affected by the interactions between you and their narcissistic parent. Ask them how they feel the narcissistic parent treats them. Are you seeing symptoms of abuse in your children? Are they acting out or isolating themselves? Is their self-confidence dwindling? Are their grades poor? Are they talking back or using the same manipulative games as their narcissistic parent? When you look at how you feel, you can imagine how they might feel. Kids are observant about what goes on between their parents. Don't be so quick to say they are fine.

2. If you haven't already begun counseling or therapy, then this is when you start, because you need to be healthy so you can help your children. Make the call today! Remember, online narcissistic recovery forums are full of abused people. You need healthy people with perspective to see you through this, not abused people. Don't fall into the trap of telling your private business to strangers online. You don't need to tell your story to other abuse victims. What you need are solutions so you don't remain stuck.

3. I recommend that every Monday night you have a family night. It is not what you leave to your children that matters, but what you leave in them. This is a time to reconnect as a family. It is also a time for everyone to spend unplugged from computers and cell phones. Come together to play games or watch a movie. This is also the perfect time to have a spiritual lesson. You could read a Bible story or give a five-minute talk about a virtue. I wrote a book called *350 Questions Parents Should Ask During Family Night* for parents who want to ask their kids questions about issues that range from safety to morality.

   The point in doing this is to know where the kids are in their heads. In my family, we devote five minutes at the beginning of family night to family business. This is a time where everyone can vent their grievances or talk about upcoming events. This is when I find out if they are having problems at school, what is coming up in the week that the family needs to prepare for, and what problems need to be corrected in the house. By doing this, you are opening up an opportunity for dialogue with your kids, offering them attention, and producing a sense of belonging that can be helpful if one parent is self-absorbed. In addition, this is a great opportunity to create five-minute spiritual lessons that address bad habits your narcissist or family need to work on.

If the thought of starting a family night in your home is unfamiliar territory, don't be overwhelmed. There is a wealth of information on the internet to get you started. Just google "family night."

What Is an Enabler and What Do You Do about Them?

There wouldn't be such a thing as narcissistic abuse if there weren't people who enabled it. These are the people who sit on the sidelines and do nothing while the narcissist creates his or her drama. Enablers choose to remain neutral, often because they don't see the side of the person that their partner sees. The narcissist might be nice to them in social settings. However, they are not living with them, so they are not seeing what you're going through behind the scenes. However, we both know that abusing someone isn't fun if it's only a party of two. With a crowd, a narcissist finds unlimited potential for drama.

Narcissistic survivors have their own lingo for enablers who know about the narcissist's mean streak. They are called "flying monkeys." Yep, just like the ones in *The Wizard of Oz*. These enablers do the narcissist's bidding to inflict additional torment on you. They might spy on you, spread gossip, and build up the illusion that the narcissist truly is a victim and you are the perpetrator. Sometimes, if not always, the narcissist will turn on their enablers and use them as scapegoats. They have no loyalty to anyone if their needs are not being met.

My narcissist hacker had two "flying monkeys," a sibling and a hacker friend who did all his flirtation for him. He used them to play mind games with me and drop hints that he liked me, plus one even emailed me to let me know he was still interested if I would only leave my current relationship. This was the perfect cover-up for him so he could emotionally cheat on his wife. If she caught these people, all he had to say was, "I didn't do anything. Hey, maybe she misinterpreted what they were doing online. I never sent an email to her. She is a liar and mentally ill. Why would you believe her?" I am sure my narcissist hacker had that diversion tactic rehearsed just in case. Flying monkeys are used, but if they fail to do the narcissist's bidding or mess up in any way, they are blamed. It's the perfect setup for the narcissist.

The narcissist likes to keep enablers close, because they get an endless amount of attention from them when playing the victim role. For example, if you have complained that your partner is never around and is always busy, you can bet they have shared that story with an enabler so they can be the victim and you the insecure partner. Their addiction to attention makes loyalty impossible, especially when they have enablers in their life.

However, most enablers are not as sinister as flying monkeys. These are the people who have bought the victim stories. Most of the time they have only been shown the kind, loving side the narcissist wants them to see. For example, a narcissist's sibling might only know the tragic story of how they grew up in a dysfunctional household together and how they relied on each other to get through it. Maybe they had a parent with borderline personality disorder who went through extreme mood swings and was extremely cruel to them. You might dismiss the backstory that you as a partner didn't experience, especially if the sibling is giving excuses for the narcissist's bad behavior. However, you can't deny that the siblings might have trauma-bonded through their dysfunctional upbringing, so stating that the narcissist is behaving cruelly will be hard for their sibling to accept. Please consider that if the narcissism came about from a dysfunctional upbringing, there will likely be other siblings with toxic behavior as well.

Imagine having a parent who was always untrusting and moody, and who withheld love when you didn't behave the way they wanted you to. It's an awful way to grow up. When you are trying to describe your partner's bad behavior to their siblings, they might not see your complaints as valid. The enabling sibling isn't comparing your pain as a partner to a normal person's relationship. They are comparing it to what they experienced as a youth or in their own relationships. They might feel you have it better than they did and you need to stop complaining about their sibling. As cold as their opinion might be, you have to remember you're dealing with their distorted thinking because they were raised in the same household as your narcissist. Therefore, you might not receive healthy support from your narcissist's family to perform an intervention to get your partner the psychiatric help he or she needs.

There are also other reasons why enablers might not take your side. They don't want to lose the narcissist's friendship or cause discord in the family. Seeking support from enablers to try to change the narcissist is a losing battle. You can plan to do some sort of family intervention, but everyone has to agree to it. Because the formation of the disorder started in childhood, the narcissist's immediate family most likely won't be supportive. Besides, many times enablers are not able to see the flaws that you have seen in the narcissist's character (or even in themselves). That may be because you are closer to your narcissistic partner than they are. They are seeing the image the narcissist wants them to see. Or, to seek sympathy, the narcissist may have already started rumors about you being insecure or anxious. Telling enablers a different version of events will only lend credibility to the narcissist's story that you are paranoid or insecure. Sadly, your support will never come from the narcissist's enablers. Your support will come from people who trust and believe you. Sometimes this requires finding someone who doesn't know your narcissist so you can ensure they haven't been tainted by the narcissist's lies about you or the situation.

To-Do List

1. Enablers are secondary abusers. They are masters at overlooking red flags, blatant abuse, and the fact the narcissist is causing and not resolving any of the problems. Your best bet to avoid being talked about behind your back is not to discuss your problems in the relationship with anyone who would tell the enablers. If they approach you about problems in your relationship, politely tell them that your relationship is private and none of their business. And you are in your right to say that!

2. You can further set up a boundary with your narcissist by making the narcissist promise that no relationship problems are to be discussed with outside sources. However, getting your narcissist to keep that promise will be difficult, because narcissists are not above putting you down to other people or portraying you as the bad guy to get attention. The victim role is addictive to them.

What Are the Mind Games Narcissists Play and How Can You Avoid Them?

Narcissists are masters at playing mind games. They play to win and remain in control. They are poor losers and will often react with anger, then follow up with the silent treatment or disappear until you know your place. The only way for the other person to win is to not play! Every time we "go in," trying for decency, accountability, or sanity, things escalate and we end up even more confused and traumatized.

Now let's continue with the dance of the devil, unmasked and defined. Below are the manipulative games that your mentally ill narcissist will use on you. They might use all or some. Study them. Learn them and be ready to recognize them in your narcissist. When you find yourself in a fight with them, pause and label their games silently to yourself. Once you start labeling their games in your mind, you will not take things so personally. You will start to see them as symptoms of their mental illness rather than as stinging daggers. So let's look at the narcissist's games.

Silent Treatment

This is the most-used weapon in the narcissist's arsenal. When a victim tries to talk to a narcissist about their problems, the narcissist either responds with rage or refuses to say anything at all. Even the slightest of criticisms can start the silent treatment. As I mentioned before, narcissists are hypersensitive to any perceived slight. The silent treatment can go on for days or weeks, until you let their behavior slide or they convince you that you are the bully. Either way, they win, because they get all the attention they need without saying a thing. They do this to control, punish, test boundaries, and avoid issues of responsibility. Silence is their way of showing hatred and disdain or taking revenge for pointing out their flaws, because they don't have the maturity to talk through issues. They prefer to be in control of your responses by conditioning you not to speak up for yourself lest you suffer their silence.

Gaslighting

Gaslighting is a technique used to undermine your reasoning. Any time you confront them, you are called crazy. This is again a game of deflection. You are told that you are imagining things, that you don't know what you're talking about, and that they have no idea what you're talking about. They conveniently don't remember events or deny they happened. They might twist the truth about an event, stating you have forgotten what really happened or claiming you're making things up to cause problems because you suffer from anxiety, jealousy, insecurity, or whatever ailment suits their fancy at the time. If you truly do have a diagnosis such as depression or anxiety, they will use that to their advantage. Suddenly, you will be the one who has to seek therapy because your mental disorders have gotten out of control. Remember, people who tell you that you are being sensitive are saying it because they don't want to be responsible for your reaction when they mistreat you.

This happened to the wife of my narcissist hacker. On her social media, she posted several narcissism quotes and one that specifically said she was being gaslighted. Her husband had told her he didn't want anything to do with me, yet he was very much in my business by hacking my computer and cell phone. I am sure he was telling her she was being insecure. This likely made her feel like she was going insane. She didn't know what to believe. His wife should have asked him, "Why are you invading the privacy of someone if you want them to leave you alone?" Why she didn't ask that question led me to this conclusion: gaslighting suppresses common sense. You want to believe the narcissist's lies rather than be hurt by the truth. In addition, I think when you're in love with someone you would rather remain in denial because dealing with the anxiety that results from accepting the truth can be devastating.

The truth is that I never called this man or texted him. I didn't follow him in a car. When I did speak to him, it was for less than ten minutes and years passed between our conversations. There was no pattern of stalking or deranged behavior. Yet the narcissist portrayed me this way to cover up his feelings and triangulate his wife and ex. This shows how manipulative and cunning narcissists can be when they want you to believe their lies. They will take one thing, stretch it into something horrific, and back it up with exaggerated stories. Of course, you want to believe them because you're in love and everyone else is being told the same lies and believes them too. Do you see how easily you can be sucked into the warped stories about their exes and people your narcissist no longer associates with? The truth is that you don't really know the story of these people your narcissist is putting down, and your narcissist knows you're not going to go up and ask them for their side of events. Therefore, the narcissist has you fooled! Unless you talk to the other people in the narcissist's life, you are only going to hear one side of the story.

I ask you to see beyond the rumors and gossip that your narcissist has started about people. I have suffered greatly from the ugly smearing of my name by both my narcissists. I have prayed one too many prayers for the chance to set the story straight after I was slandered. Be smart enough to realize that hearing something doesn't make it so, and no amount of love for a narcissist can erase the truth about what they do behind your back.

Here are some signs that you are being gaslighted:

- **You walked in sure you were right and left barely knowing your name**. They project, divert, lie, and twist everything all around. By the time you're done talking to them, you are unsure you can follow their version of events. The truth is that people who lie go into lengthy stories and explanations. Someone who is truthful is short with his or her answers and doesn't get defensive.
- **The subject that you started with was not even covered**. They might not be a good liar or you have taken them off guard, so they need more time to prepare their lies. For example, you ask them where they were last night and the subject changes for no apparent reason.
- **The story you remember and the one that comes from their mouth are incongruent.** It's like you need a tape recorder with you at all times. This is because lies are hard to remember. The truth isn't.
- **You end up being the jerk.** You are the bad guy for not trusting them. This is when they get to enjoy your reaction to the drama that they are blaming you for creating.
- **You think they might be right and you're just crazy.** The narcissist knows your weaknesses and insecurities and will make sure you know them too. If you lack trust, they will say you are paranoid. If you blame them, they will say you are insecure. They want you to believe you are the problem.
- **They are way too angry for the inquiry**. As I have mentioned, someone who is truthful doesn't get defensive.
- **They try to get everyone involved by either mentioning other names or actually calling people in for their opinion**. This is

usually the elaborate liar tactic. The narcissist wants you to think you are the problem and brings in enablers to set you straight.

- **You end up apologizing.** They have an answer for every action they've committed, even if it doesn't make sense. They tell you that you are being insecure, which makes you feel guilty; therefore, you apologize.
- **You feel like you aren't good enough.** That is because they want you to be reliant on them. They can't remain in control if you are on equal footing.
- **You feel isolated and alone.** You start to feel like you are going crazy. Questions start to pour out of you like, "Why am I the only one who sees this in them?" or "Why is the problem always me?"

The Blame Game

Narcissists tend to internalize failure, feeling shame instead of guilt. People use shame and guilt interchangeably, but they are different. Shame is how we feel about ourselves, while guilt involves awareness of how our actions have injured someone else. Narcissists suffer from profound feelings of shame, which is why they seek so much adoration from people—to make up for it. This started in their youth, and with every failure in life, it has worsened. To avoid shame at all costs, narcissists externalize blame for all negative events. They feel someone else must be guilty, so they attribute blame to other people. This is when everything, and I mean everything, is everyone else's fault. If there was a fight, you can bet they are blaming you for starting it. Controllers and abusers never question themselves.

There is a debate whether narcissists really believe other people are to blame or if it's just a game to them. My conclusion is that it is both. They perceive everything as a slight against them. They are hypersensitive but will deny that is the case. Nevertheless, they probably do believe you are to blame as much as they are. However, they won't ever admit this. It comes back to cognitive dissonance. Cognitive dissonance is the mental discomfort experienced by a person who holds two or more contradictory beliefs or values. Narcissists don't like the discomfort that results from being confronted with information that contradicts what they believe.

As you can see, a lot of therapy is needed to lessen someone's narcissistic games. Telling your partner you love them and they are good enough is not enough to repair their deep-seated shame and low self-esteem. Immersing yourself in your faith will help with the spiritual illness, but counseling needs to go on so the narcissist's false self can be replaced with their true self.

Projection

This is when the narcissist blames you for the same behavior they have displayed. For example, they might accuse you of being rude when they are the one who behaves rudely. You might tell a narcissist that they are selfish, and in return they will say you are the one being selfish. They will give examples of your behavior. They might never have brought up their irritations before—most likely because they never were irritations. It's only that you've put them on the defensive and they need to turn the tables to get the focus off them.

There is also reverse projection, but this is more about you than them. This is when you project all your good qualities onto the narcissist. When they don't respond the way you expect, you become confused or hurt, question your reality, and believe you are to blame in some way. You have a dream of who they are because of a few nice things they did in the idolization phase, or you want desperately for them to be the dream partner you've always wanted. You now have a faulty image of who they are because you haven't seen their true colors—their manipulation. You don't see the abuse clearly. It's important to realize if you are doing this, which is why I want you to refer back to the list of traits you want in a partner and the list of traits your partner actually has. Do you see the inconsistencies between the dream you might have projected onto them versus the reality of who they are?

Table Tennis

Communication with a narcissist is a lot like tennis. Anytime you ask a narcissist to reflect about their behavior, they immediately hit the ball back over the net into your court. They do this because they don't want to take responsibility for their behavior. The difference between tennis and projection is that projection is when they accuse you of something they have done to you. In tennis, they bring up any and all the things you are doing wrong instead. As I mentioned earlier, narcissists have a problem with having to face their own shame. Therefore, they will avoid taking responsibility to prevent deep talk that gets to the heart of the matter—why they are doing what they are doing. They will always put up their defense mechanisms when you want to help them. They do this by deflection, which means changing the subject, leaving the room, throwing blame to change the conversation, or minimizing the seriousness of your concerns. It is an endless game of table tennis—back and forth—and no one wins.

Just Kidding

This game is often played when you find yourself giving up. Maybe you set up boundaries or have filed for a divorce or separation. Narcissists are notorious for either laying on the charm to win you back or the opposite: preparing to destroy your finances, reputation, and happiness because they fear abandonment and having to face shame or humiliation. They don't like to be alone, which is ironic because they often push the people closest to them away. In their fear, they might try to take you back through the idolization phase. They might tell you that they have changed or understand what you are experiencing and they will appear to mean it. What they have done is repeated the cycle all narcissists go through with the people they victimize: they idolize, devalue, and discard. The idolization period will last as long as it takes to make the situation calm down. In this phase, the narcissist tries to get you to let your guard down, but just when you think there is a genuine give-and-take in your relationship, he pulls a fast one—"just kidding!" They will start back down the path of belittling you, not taking responsibility, ignoring you, or distancing themselves the moment you are back to thinking they have changed.

Pop the Balloon

The rules of this game require them to throw words at you to pop your ego. They are insecure and anxious that you might leave them, become better than them, or not make them the center of attention. Therefore, they will cut down your accomplishments. They will even cut down your faith in God if they feel you are using "too much" religion to put them in their place. The game is for them to try to turn everything about you and everything you do into a complete failure. Extra points are given when they can take all the credit for anything good that has ever happened to you. They might be outright vocal with their abuse or covert with the use of eye rolls, scoffs, and half smiles when you talk about your accomplishments.

Sweet 16

Narcissists never let you reach maturity. Even if you are forty years old, you will still be treated like a teenager. They might shoo you away from doing the finances because they claim they could do a better job. They might not let you into the kitchen because they say you will mess up their meal. If you haven't figured it out already, they have cast you in the role of being helpless when it comes to homemaking. This is a game about control. They want you to be reliant on them. They want you to second-guess yourself because thinking for yourself might mean you would leave them or, worse, start standing up for yourself.

King or Queen of the Mountain

The king or queen watches the score and will one-up you if you get too close to the top of the mountain. They keep track of real or imaginary things you do, have done, or might do. This is their mountain, and no one is at the top except them. They rule with an iron fist. They make sure you know that they bring home the money or run the household. They pull out a laundry list of things they do for you. They feel justified to act as they want because they have something over you financially or skillwise. Their attitude is that you wouldn't make it without them. This attitude leaves a victim feeling inferior to their partner.

Poker Face

This is the game of constant bluffing. In fact, it happens so often that a victim doesn't know what is real anymore. A narcissist's positive attributes and accomplishments are made up or exaggerated to get other people to give them their fix of narcissistic supply, adulation, and accolades. They lie so often that it doesn't feel natural not to. They also make false threats to control people. For example, they might threaten that they are going to break up with you or separate from your marriage if you continue to press them for information about where they go or if you don't do what they want you to do. But if you call their bluff, they'll never do it; they're too afraid of being alone.

Duck Duck Goose

Before they discard you or you escape them, they will secure their other narcissistic supply. Even so, they will continue stringing you along or confusing you with statements such as "I love you" and "You are the only one I want." Finally, when you or they do the dumping, they are immediately with someone else. This might take you by surprise, and they want it to. They want you to be jealous and get upset. They want you to freak out; that way they can say how crazy you are. If they find out you tried to get answers, they may even claim you're stalking them or their new partner. Even if you were never in a relationship with them and refused to leave your current relationship so they could date you, they will paint you as mentally unstable and the one who had the crush. In the end, they have someone new to gaslight about your character while still receiving attention from you. Don't be so foolish as to believe they found someone new so quickly. That backup narcissistic supply has been around for a while!

Turning the Tables

These skilled manipulators have an arsenal of tactics at their disposal. They can push buttons to make you lose control. After a long time of suppressing emotions, a victim can get to the point of exploding. All your frustrations can come out ferociously in a single argument after being bottled up for too long. You find yourself on the offensive, which the narcissist uses against you. They say you are the abuser. You are the one losing control.

You are not the abuser! *Remember, having emotional responses to abusive situations does not make you an abuser.*

Dodgeball

This is the diversion and evasion game. You throw the ball and they dodge it like an Olympic athlete. When you ask your narcissist a question, instead of answering it, they may use diversion (steering the conversation to another topic) or evasion (giving an irrelevant and vague response). They might also try selectively forgetting. This happens so often you almost want to buy a tape recorder to keep track of all your conversations with them.

Passive-Aggressive Bullying

This is when the narcissist disguises bullying as helping. Advising, offering up solutions, and probing and questioning another person may be part of sincere attempts to help. However, these behaviors can also be attempts to belittle, control, or demean. Their advice might come with a condescending tone, scoffs, eye rolls, glares, or remarks that belittle your gender as incapable of doing the task without their guidance. They might include put-downs while offering the advice or boast that they could do it better. There is a hidden agenda with narcissists as they attempt to control their victims. They believe that they know best. This is their way of keeping one step ahead of you.

Hidden Agenda

The narcissist's need for attention, control, and supply is a twenty-four-hour, seven-day-a-week disorder. Every hobby, and every action, has a hidden agenda. That agenda is to get a high off the attention they receive, whether good or bad.

There is a hidden agenda in all things. For example, your narcissist's new interest in triathlons might be more than just an interest. His ex's new husband might be doing marathons and your narcissist is jealous of him. He still needs to be superior to anything his ex might have in her life. Therefore, he could be secretly competing to one-up her new husband—something you don't catch on to because he says he just wanted to try triathlons.

There is a deep delusion that most narcissists keep feeding. They all believe their exes still secretly want them. These fantasies are kept alive with actions. Maybe their offer to pick up their kids from the ex's house goes beyond just being a good parent. Maybe they see it as an opportunity to flirt.

Religious Guilt Trip

If you find yourself going through a separation, they might use religious guilt to keep you in the relationship. It could be as simple as stating, "The neighbors had marital problems, but they are still together and they have been through worse than us. So why are you giving up? Don't you believe in 'for better or worse'? Don't you believe in forgiveness?" Of course, taking advantage of your deepest beliefs is a low blow. The narcissist who pulls this tactic usually either doesn't go to church or attends for the social aspect only. They are hypocrites who know you're a kind, loving person who has faith. They play the religious martyr card to keep you on board a sinking ship.

The next phase of the religious guilt trip is called "forgive and forget." That is when you end up praying together over the matter. The narcissist hopes you will take the prayer and religious babble they have been giving you as true feelings, having you wrapped around their finger. They want control and the situation to be resolved. Usually, you're in the idolization phase again when this happens. However, after you have given up the notion of ending the relationship, in a few months you will be right back where you started—the devaluation phase. Religious guilt doesn't have to be centered on a breakup. They will use this game for resolving all sorts of issues in the relationship.

Pity Party

A narcissist paints a self-portrait of a person who is innocent in all aspects. They will tell one sad story after another to explain why they are at their emotional, financial, or social level. You will often see enablers willing to be taken in by this victim mentality. In addition, you will see a long line of exes who, according to the narcissist, are broken, cruel, crazy, or lost. This is often not true at all, or any issues are out of proportion. Narcissists are masters of illusion. They throw a pity party, while the truth is that they wreak havoc by mentally torturing, mistreating, and abusing those they fooled into loving them. Their starring role is as the victim. They don't like new screenwriters, like you, coming in and telling them they're wrong. They will be offended by the truth if you try to set them straight.

Triangulation

Triangulation is when the narcissist pits you against any other person who is willing to engage in their "victim-playing." The narcissist does this by smearing the character of one or both of you behind your backs. This enables them to preserve their false image and ensures they're viewed positively among the triangle. They adopt the role of prosecutor to assign blame for their misery. They tell lies about you to the rescuers, who are their family and friends. By clever seduction, through words and posturing, they entice their pawns to do the dirty work for them. Unaware that they are being manipulated by the narcissist's rendition of the truth, these pawns take up the cause by going after you (the actual victim). During this time, the narcissist gets attention by sharing their story. The rescuers (or enablers) become upset on the narcissist's behalf and try to rescue them. This results in the rescuers blaming you. Many things could result—anger, gossip, retaliation, or alienation toward you. Of course, what follows is that you get mad at the rescuers because you're innocent and have been lied about by the narcissist. Therefore, you engage in a battle with the enablers to get your truth believed.

For triangulation to work, the narcissist must keep the enablers and you from sharing information. Instead, they will usually pass on mean comments each of you has said about the other to fuel a rift. This tactic also provides the narcissist with the power of being the primary contact person and the one who transfers the information. Since everyone is communicating through the narcissist, the narcissist can further their agenda by putting their twisted spin on the information relayed between parties.

What does the narcissist do once the drama has started? They sit back and enjoy the attention they're getting. At any point they feel they're losing the narcissistic supply they get from you, they will become your rescuer by telling lies about their enablers. Of course, if you confront the enablers and they put the narcissist on the spot about it later, everything is denied: "My partner is crazy or insecure. I didn't say that!" In the end, this traveling back and forth around the triangle is how the narcissist gets attention or finds someone to blame for their misery.

Usually, the claims the narcissist makes about you are the truth about themselves (projection), while they continue to gaslight their rescuers. Defamation of character and destroying your credibility are their goals. This creates drama and gives them attention. If they cannot paint you as a liar because of your character, the narcissist will paint you as unstable, lacking in judgment, mentally delusional, or "damaged goods."

For example, my narcissist hacker told everyone I was mentally deranged, despite the credibility I had amassed as an author of self-help books and as a therapist. He was calling me a stalker while I published a book about child safety, which included a chapter on how to stay safe from stalkers. While he was talking trash about me, I was busy volunteering with the police department to help find missing people, and I was given an award by the police chief for rescuing missing hikers in the Sierra Nevada Wilderness. While I was rescuing human-trafficking victims in Cambodia, he was involved in illegal hacking. When I was in Florida rescuing endangered sea turtles for the Sea Shepherd conservation society, he was working to make people believe I was unstable. And when I spent every day at work treating critically ill patients at a trauma hospital, he was saying I was the immoral one. The truth was he couldn't hold a candle to the noble accomplishments I have done in my life, and he was probably jealous. I had a college degree, a great job, and a writing career. I made more money than him and could travel around the world. He had none of this, yet he thought he was superior to me, so he lied about everything in order to make himself look credible.

The narcissist believes they are the authority that determines reality. To them, your facts are meaningless and your logic is offensive. One might wonder how narcissists can live with themselves after spreading these appalling lies. Oddly, they do see themselves as victims in need of protection. They justify their vengeful behavior by telling themselves, "They asked for it and they got what they deserved for questioning me" or "She can't be trusted, so I need to get her before she hurts me." This paranoid attitude leads them to strike first. Even though you haven't done anything to warrant such a vicious triangle of drama, the narcissist has an image to maintain and can't go without a fix of the attention that comes when people see them as a victim.

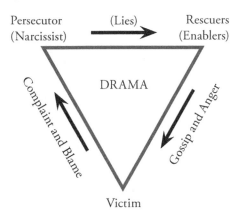

You may notice in the above triangle that both the persecutor and rescuer are on the upper end of the triangle. These roles assume a "one-up" position over the victim—you. You feel helpless and looked down upon. This causes you to continue in this triangle by doing one of four things:

1. Defend yourself by striking back.
2. Further submit to the abuse, thinking it must be your fault.
3. Try to convince the rescuers that the narcissist is not a victim, but a bully.
4. Leave the relationship.

No matter what you do to be heard or believed, the very people who could intervene have become persecutors themselves. This doesn't only happen when you have done something that hurts the narcissist. They also will use this triangle to keep their partner in a state of jealousy or insecurity. For example, they might tell their partner that a third party (a friend or someone attractive they both know) has been flirtatious with them. This is meant to keep the partner insecure and foster a fear that they could be easily replaced. It also gets them to try harder to please the narcissist. Lastly, it creates rivalry between you as the partner and the person they say likes them. This drama fills the narcissist with much-needed attention while also giving them control.

Emotionally healthy individuals don't enjoy hurting someone by sharing comments that others have said about them, but a narcissist takes pleasure in it. For example, the narcissist will mention to their partner that a family member made a cruel comment about them. Then they will pretend to be supportive of their partner's anger and appear to defend them. Not only does the narcissist get to delight in the hurt expression on their partner's face, but they also get to swoop in like the hero. This creates chaos and is a powerful fix of supply for the bored, drama-driven narcissist.

In my case, my narcissist hacker orchestrated triangulation. He had the perfect target—me. He tarnished my name with a smear campaign and made sure no one would believe the truth: that he was attracted to me (for more about smear campaigns, turn to the section "What Is a Smear Campaign?"). This game worked for him. One night I ran into him at church. At the time he was dating his soon-to-be wife. He again told me that he would date me if I would get a divorce. I told him I couldn't make that guarantee. He asked me to not leave the church but to keep coming as long as I was separated from my husband. I asked him, "Why would I do that? You are already in a relationship with someone else." My question angered him, and he stormed out of the church. He had weird views on morality. In his opinion, it wasn't immoral to hack my computer and listen in on my private moments, but it was important that I get a divorce so he wouldn't look like an immoral man. Does this make sense to you? His logic baffled me. What followed was him telling everyone that I would not leave him alone and he was being stalked. He lied because I hurt his ego and I called him out on his unfaithfulness to his girlfriend. He not only got to play the victim in his fantasy, but he was able to keep his soon-to-be wife insecure by fostering fear that she could easily be replaced because of how desired he was. Moreover, it created drama, which gave him tons of attention.

Drama Queen or King

Narcissists like to provoke emotions in their victims to get a reaction. Whether negative or positive, it doesn't matter. The narcissist lives off drama. The routine nature of everyday life bores them. If they are not getting enough narcissistic supply from others, they resort to baiting. They know your buttons and which ones to push to stir up drama.

It is hard to imagine that someone *wants* conflict in their life, *but narcissists thrive in chaos.* They will continue to aggravate a victim until they snap. The narcissist will then sit back, feigning surprise at how angry, passive-aggressive, and volatile the victim is. Of course, the victim will feel bad, apologize, and absorb the blame. Essentially, they are shamed for losing patience and behaving the way the narcissist does every day. The narcissist wins by getting attention and control by becoming the victim.

Double Standards

Narcissists are notorious for having double standards. They seek out the trophy wife or husband and expect you to live up to that title so they look good. However, they don't live up to being the kind, loving partner you want a relationship with. To the narcissist, their behavior is justified for their gain. Narcissists operate by imposing a set of expectations on people. Usually these are rules they can't live by behind closed doors. However, this double standard works for them in two ways. When you live by the rules, all the people who know you will think your partner is a great person. If you screw up, they use it against you.

Minimizer

The narcissist rarely tells the truth. They would rather deny their behavior until the end because there is nowhere for you to go with your anger if they didn't do what they are being accused of. However, on occasion, they might admit to something only to trivialize the situation. If they ever confess to an emotional affair, it won't be called that. They might say they only talked to someone once or twice. The conversation was benign. They might admit they found the person attractive and would have dated them if they were single. What the narcissist leaves out are major details, like the fact that they looked up their new target on social media every day to find out more about them. In my case, he hacked my computers and listened in, in order to know what he was missing out on. The conversations might have been brief but more intense than the narcissist describes. The narcissist minimizes the situation and sets the victim up to underreact by hiding that there is anything to be concerned about. The result of minimizing is that you mistrust and question your own perceptions and emotional experience, which means you're being gaslighted.

Disappearing Act

Narcissists disappear. This can be for a few hours, a few days, or even weeks. This is their self-centered way to avoid dealing with people. It may be to spite you, or it could be that they have a new narcissistic supply and find it more gratifying to be around. The narcissist I was in a relationship with did the disappearing act a lot. When he wanted an ego boost, he ran to his church friends. He gravitated toward what gave him attention—his adoring fan club. Narcissists are always seeking new supply to feel good. This could be a competitive sport, hobby, club, meetup, activity, or even checking in on people from past relationships or maybe checking up on that guy or girl they are attracted to that you don't know about.

Sabotage

Because narcissists fear abandonment, they will make sure you don't leave them even if they see you are dissatisfied with their behavior. They will keep you from anything else that is important to you, including friends, family, going to college to obtain a degree, or a better job that requires traveling. They might make disparaging remarks about people who support you. This could also target people of the opposite sex who they fear could take you from them. It could even mean intentionally getting you pregnant so you won't leave the relationship. They are selfish individuals.

Narcissists might not participate in things that matter to you if they clash with what the narcissist wants to do at that moment. Vacations or free time are usually spent doing what they want to do.

Initially, it is almost impossible to not react to a narcissist's cruel and disproportionate behavior, where the punishment does not match the supposed crime. I understand your frustration. If you are like me, a passionate advocate for fairness who has specific beliefs about life and how people should be treated, then staying quiet will be hard to do. For a born rescuer who hates injustice, to sit back and shut my mouth when something is blatantly cruel, unfair, or ridiculous takes more patience than I usually have.

Maybe you feel like I did. In my relationship with my narcissist, I thought I was doing the right thing by fighting back. I was standing up for me. However, I soon learned that a million things could be spoken without words—with silence. It not only gets the point across, but it can deescalate the situation if you do it right. The worst thing you can do to a narcissist is ignore them. Remember, they are energized by drama, conflict, and inflicting trauma. So why give them ammunition during the battle by reacting to their bad behavior?

I know some of you out there are saying, "No way am I not going to say something back!" Well, if that is the case, you are giving the narcissist what they want, which is drama and attention, and you are creating your own trauma. I am not telling you to give them the silent treatment for days or even hours. I am telling you to disengage. For those who want a more spiritual reason for deescalating narcissist drama by remaining quiet, let's look to the Bible.

When should you keep your mouth shut?

- In the heat of anger (Proverbs 14:17)
- When you don't have all the facts (Proverbs 18:13)
- When you haven't verified the story (Deuteronomy 17:6)
- If your words will offend a weaker brother (1 Corinthians 8:11)
- If your words will be a poor reflection of the Lord or your friends and family (Peter 2:21–23)

- When you would be ashamed of your words later (Proverbs 8:8)
- If your words would convey a wrong impression (Proverbs 17:27)
- If the issue is none of your business (Proverbs 14:10)
- When you are tempted to tell a lie (Proverbs 4:24)
- When you are feeling critical (James 3:9)
- If you can't speak without yelling (Proverbs 25:28)
- If you have to eat your words later (Proverbs 18:21)
- If you have already said it more than one time so that it becomes nagging (Proverbs 19:13)
- When you are tempted to flatter a wicked person (Proverbs 24:24)

Proverbs 21:23 says, "Those who guard their mouths and their tongues keep themselves from calamity." I know it is not fair to listen to someone verbally abuse you. However, I will tell you what is fair: not listening to it! The following are rules of thumb when dealing with a narcissistic bully:

- Stop playing the victim by reacting to it. They can't enjoy themselves if they see you are unfazed by it all. By now, you should know that tears don't work for very long before they are right back at it. You need to become emotionally numb. Sometimes shifting your perspective about them makes it easier. Remember that they're mentally ill. If you have to imagine that nonsense comes out every time they open their mouth, then do so. Their verbal garbage is backed by paranoia, fear, and illogical conclusions. Don't get upset by their disorder's childish tantrums. Seriously, let it roll down your back. Satan knows how to push buttons. Put on your armor of God and let it bounce right off you.
- Don't bully back. You are the mature one. They want any excuse to turn you into the bad person, so don't let them.
- Walk away. There is no fight or drama if you disappear. Go visit a friend. Go into another room. However, don't engage. Let them rage in a room by themselves. You don't need to stick around and be abused.
- Don't give them a place to go with their slams and digs. For example, if they make a joke at your expense, laugh with them—one of those "you're so stupid" laughs if you want—but don't say anything more. Alternatively, if they make a sarcastic or fake comment, thank them in an unemotional tone followed by silence. Just don't overreact. That is what they want. Direct the

conversation. If they want to play the blame game, ask them why they fell in love with you in the first place. You may get flustered with the different things they throw at you, but do your best to be prepared and walk away if you must.

- If they are rude, pretend that you didn't hear them. Correct them later after the heat of the fight is over.
- If they harp repeatedly on the same accident or mistake you made, tell them you don't care about that anymore. You've forgiven yourself, learned better, and moved on.
- If you do something embarrassing, keep your cool so you don't give them any fuel to harass you with.
- Refrain from wanting to win the conversation. You don't need to be right, but act right, which means you ignore what they say, leave the situation (if necessary), and don't take their nonsense to heart.
- Pick your battles (King of the Hill).
- Set and commit to boundaries.
- Gather the facts (this might be where the spying comes in, for times when confrontations will need to be backed up with solid proof). There are many apps you can download off the internet to place on your spouse's cell phone undetected, so they can't delete text messages or emails if you suspect cheating.
- Try to get your narcissist to therapy. Tell your therapist which of these games he or she is playing with you. Talking about this openly in couples therapy can help lessen the games.

Applying these tactics doesn't make you a doormat. It makes you smart! You can't win with a narcissist. If you verbally bash them, they will hit back harder with verbal or emotional abuse. Remember that as the mature person in the relationship, your job is to deescalate the situation and bring back sanity to yourself and others. This is what a good parent would do for a child who is out of control, and yes, it is the same thing! I am not telling you to allow disrespect. If your child called you a bad name, you would stand up for yourself and tell them that was disrespectful. The same goes for your narcissist. However, they are a little too old for the "time-out" chair. So calmly stating what their bad behavior is and how it is disrespectful, followed by disengaging from their drama, is the best tactic. Let them have a tantrum in their room by themselves if they want. Grab the car keys and go have a good time shopping or golfing. You are too mature to carry on with fighting. Get it?

I can't emphasize enough that you have to change yourself to live with a narcissist—or at least deal with them if kids are involved. And by all means, don't fight in front of the children! If a fight breaks out, throw the kids in the car and leave the situation until your narcissist cools off. I know living with a narcissist can be frustrating because they know how to push all your buttons. However, if you picture God standing right beside you the next time they try to lure you into a fight, maybe you will be able to rein in your anger. Because in reality, God is with you. He knows what you are going through. He wants you to turn the other cheek and walk away from it—defuse the situation. Don't fight the devil with the same tactics the devil uses! I guarantee that when you stop focusing on the content of these fights and look at how the narcissist uses these games, you will begin to see the pattern. You will begin to see the mental illness, not the fight. And you will know how to outwit them.

Before we go any further, I want to address physical abuse. If you are being physically abused, then you need to get out of the relationship. God doesn't reside in a person who physically abuses someone. This is a deal breaker, and God wants you to leave. If they hit you, throw things at you, or threaten physical violence, then they have crossed the line. I hope you have not let your dignity stoop so low that you endure the evil acts of physical abuse. This isn't a wake-up call just for the women reading this book. Men can be physically abused as well. I hope if this has happened to you that you realize that nothing justifies it. *A person who is physically abusive to you is a person who doesn't love you.* Being a strong son or daughter of our Heavenly Father requires your swift exit from that type of abusive relationship. Also, to uphold your boundaries, you want to leave the situation if they threaten suicide in the event that you separate. A person who makes that threat is ill and manipulative. There is nothing romantic about someone killing themselves. It doesn't mean that they love you so much they couldn't go on without you. It just means they are sick and they don't care about you, themselves, or God's commandments.

The Other Dance Partners—Narcissistic Supply

If you are lucky, the only narcissistic supply the narcissist will have is a bunch of friends or a group of acquaintances on Facebook. You run into trouble when the narcissistic supply comes from his or her ex or people they refuse to admit they are attracted to. Whether the narcissist is just a big flirt or a full-blown adulterer, he will always be on the prowl for new supply. He is in a perpetual state of comparison shopping. This means you are never safe within the relationship. Let me repeat that: you are not the only thing sharing your narcissist's attention! **Whether you are aware of it or not, you are in a constant state of competition with every potential replacement.** If your narcissist's friend has a spouse who is better looking than you are, you can almost bet that your narcissist is annoyed not to be the one everyone is envious of. That hurts to hear, but narcissists want to be envied and are shallow with their love.

Warning signs of cheating:

- They might shut down their phone every time someone enters the room.
- They might only go online when you are asleep.
- They might insist on picking the kids up from their ex's house without you.
- They might not acknowledge your relationship in public or not set their status on Facebook to "married" or "in a relationship."
- They might frequently bring up the accomplishments or looks of other people whom they admire.
- They use social networking to provoke jealousy and rivalries while maintaining their cover of innocence.
- They bait previously denounced exes with old songs and inside jokes.
- They are not where they say they are.
- They spend less time at home than they did at the beginning of the relationship.
- They spend a lot of time talking about their exes or other people who like them. They say it was in the past, but they don't seem to keep it in the past. It's as if they can't let go of them.
- There is always drama surrounding them.
- They adopt different personas for different people—transforming their personality to match their audience. However, sometimes it's as if they have forgotten who they are around. The mask slips.

- They resort to hacking to listen in to the house of someone they are attracted to. They tell you that person won't leave them alone, but strangely they won't leave that person alone because they are invading their privacy.

It is not uncommon for narcissists to use flirtation to get narcissistic supply. This might be the case, rather than a true desire to get back together with their ex. Once the attention is returned, the narcissist abruptly changes directions. They end the flirtation by blaming the victim for "misunderstanding" their intent. They further hurt the victim by shaming them, saying they are in a committed relationship. It is a sick game that narcissists like to play, and, of course, they never own up to the fact that they are cheating. They are doing it for attention and control.

If they don't cut off the flirtation, then you have problems. Remember, narcissists are bored in long-standing relationships, and it isn't beneath them to flirt.

To-Do List

1. Pull out your notebook. I want you to define what cheating means to you. Be as specific as the examples I gave above.
2. Sit down with your partner and ask, "Can you define what cheating means to you?" Let them define it without interrupting. After they have had a chance to share, bring out the list you wrote for step one. Share that list with them, and make sure you both agree on the definition. If they don't agree, you have a definite trust problem. This is the point when you say, "I believe that is cheating, and if you do it, you will have broken my trust. If you break my trust, I am going to _____." Fill in the blank with your action plan. This might mean separating. If someone really loves you, then they will not want to hurt you. Don't compromise on what cheating is. When you compromise, then you are sinning. You need to abide with what the Bible says, or you are not standing for what is true and right as a son or daughter of our Heavenly Father should be. Sharing with your narcissist what the Bible says about cheating is helpful in making your point (Matthew 5:27–28; Proverbs 19:1; Galatians 6:7–8).

Does the Narcissist Feel Remorse or Guilt?

The many survivors I have talked to on narcissistic abuse recovery boards all say the same thing: their loved one never appeared to feel sorry. They might have said the words begrudgingly after being shown the evidence, but something was always lacking—they don't mean it. Survivors all say the same thing: that narcissists are inconsiderate of people's feelings. The real truth is that they do consider your feelings. Your feelings are exactly what they are trying to affect. They are watching your reactions and determining if they have you back under control and attentive to them again. Your hurt feelings are their pain-killing drug.

No one hurts someone intentionally unless they are seriously wounded inside. Many victims use the term "psychologically raped" to describe the lack of remorse and abuse by the narcissist. The victim fully trusted the narcissist's false self and bonded with that individual, only to be betrayed to feed the narcissist's fix.

Can the narcissist feel any remorse? There is a difference between feeling regret and feeling remorse. Regret has to do with wishing you hadn't taken a particular action. It can lead a person to feel sorrow, grief, hurt, and anger—but these can be because of the damage the action caused to him or her, not necessarily for any other person who was hurt by the behavior. Narcissists can feel regret. They might even confuse it with remorse. However, remorse involves admitting one's mistakes and taking responsibility for one's actions. It leads to confession and true apology. It also moves the remorseful person to avoid doing the hurtful action again. On the other hand, regret only leads a person to avoid punishment in the future.

Sadly, narcissists can learn not to get caught the next time, but they rarely learn not to hurt other people's feelings or cross other people's boundaries. The problem is that they think everything they do is actually caused by others. They are in denial about their disorder. Denial was first described by the Austrian psychiatrist Sigmund Freud as a psychological defense mechanism, which means it is a way to cope with the anxiety of dealing with everyday conflicts. When someone is in denial, they reject facts that are too uncomfortable for them and insist that they are not true despite sometimes overwhelming evidence. More simply stated, denial is lying to oneself and believing the lie.

Narcissists constantly deny to themselves that they are at fault, and this is why they do not feel guilty. *Narcissistic personality disorder wouldn't exist without denial as a main symptom.* Instead of taking responsibility for their own feelings or actions, they typically feel angry with you for reacting negatively to their harmful behavior.

Deep inside, the narcissist knows that something is amiss. They do not empathize with other people's feelings. Actually, they hold them in contempt. They cannot understand how people are so sentimental. The things narcissists do seem coldhearted, but they are not robotic. They mourn and grieve, rage and get infatuated. However, this is precisely what sets them apart: this rapid movement from one emotional extreme to another and the fact that they never occupy the emotional middle ground.

The narcissist is especially emotional when weaned off their drug of narcissistic supply. Breaking a habit is always difficult—especially one that defines (and generates) oneself. Getting rid of an addiction is doubly taxing.

Emotions the narcissist experiences arise in reaction to slights and injuries, real or imagined. Their emotions are all reactive, not active. They feel insulted—they sulk. They feel devalued—they rage. They feel ignored—they pout. They feel humiliated—they lash out. They feel threatened—they fear. They feel adored—they bask in glory. They feel envious—they plot revenge.

As you can see, the narcissist is in need of therapy that goes beyond the Bible and prayers. They are mentally ill. A trained professional should be helping you in the process of rehabilitating them.

Did My Narcissist Ever Love Me?

Yes, but only to the extent that they know what love is, and their concept of love is superficial. It's not the love you can build a healthy relationship on. The type of love that narcissists experience is called *limerence.* Limerence (also known as infatuated love) results from romantic attraction to another person and typically includes compulsive thoughts and fantasies and a desire to have one's feelings reciprocated and thus form or maintain a relationship.

In other words, the state of limerence is much like being high on a drug. When a narcissist falls in love with you, they can be the most romantic person you could ever imagine. They'll gaze longingly into your eyes and say you are the one they have been waiting for, that they want to spend every moment with you, and that you are special. However, it's not you they are seeing. What they see instead is a reflection of themselves that you show them by reciprocating. You make them feel good about themselves by giving them attention and letting them know how wonderful you think they are. You're basically nothing more than a mirror of the person they pretend to be.

It's common for teenagers and young adults to have a "crush," but it's a temporary state. Infatuation only lasts an average of one or two years (about the length of an average engagement). However, this isn't real love; it is more of an obsession. You're projecting what you want to see in someone rather than seeing what is really there. After the newness wears off, it takes mature love to deal with the differences in relationships, the boredom that comes with familiarity, and the responsibilities of building a life together. The narcissist can't advance from this state.

Once you begin to show human flaws and imperfections, you are no longer mirroring the narcissist as they want to be mirrored, and that's when the abuse and manipulation will begin. You move from being a person they admired to someone they use for narcissistic supply. You now serve a role.

Many survivors have described feeling like they were living with a person who wanted to have all the benefits of being in a relationship without the emotional responsibility. That's why their marriages and relationships usually don't last long. The truth is that the narcissist's version of love is the following:

- The desire to have you devote yourself to them without outside interference
- The desire to have sex
- The desire to impress others by having you as their partner
- The desire to possess and control you
- The desire for financial security
- The desire not to be alone

After the newness has worn off in a relationship, they will still expect admiration from their partner, and if they are not getting it, they seek supply elsewhere or punish the partner with games until they get the supply they need to feel fulfilled for that moment. They may seek outside narcissistic supply even if you are giving them admiration. They are addicted to it.

If a narcissist has discarded you and moved on to someone else, don't feel bad. This is a cycle. Infatuation doesn't last, and the next person will go through the same experience as you have.

What Is a Smear Campaign?

When we dump a narcissist or a narcissist dumps us, one of the first things they do to make themselves feel better is embark on a smear campaign. Running a smear campaign provides the narcissist justification as to why you were never worthy of their presence to begin with. By getting "the word out" about how horrible their ex was, the narcissist feels pumped up and vindicated about how the relationship ended.

Narcissists can do this in response to rejection even when their victim wasn't in an official relationship with them. Both of my narcissists subjugated me to smear campaigns. As a victim, no matter how many times you articulate the truth to others, you find it difficult to get people to believe you. This is because the narcissist has prepared to smear you long before you knew about it. They have zoned in on your flaws and made other people aware of them well in advance. They are not smearing you at the last minute. They have calculated this from the get-go. They know you might have the benefit of truth, but they are not going to let you ruin what they have spent years perfecting—their false self or any future relationships they have with others.

Most of us who've been involved with a narcissist have been targeted by a smear campaign at one time or another. If a breakup is on your horizon, you might be worried about it in advance. After all, breaking up with a narcissist isn't like any other breakup on the planet. If there are mutual friends, coworkers, or children involved, there will always be fallout, but it's not nearly as insurmountable as it appears. In fact, by making one amazingly simple switch to our reaction, we can change the dynamic of the smear itself. The key, my friends, is to say *nothing at all*—not a single word. Believe me, there will be power in your silence. However, if you overhear anything about yourself, simply say, "I don't understand this untrue gossip. I only wish him the best. Would you pray for him?" Put it back on the gossiper, and invite them to take the high road with you. This tactic paints you in a better light than telling the gossiper off or putting down the narcissist.

To-Do List

1. If you are in the middle of a smear campaign, stop feeding the firepit of hell. Satan will keep on raging and let the narcissist tell lies about you. Your job as a son or daughter of our Heavenly Father is to be righteous. Live joyfully and walk away without bitterness. Have you ever heard the phrase "Fake it till you make it"? Maybe you feel rage and want revenge. I beg you to stop or you will ruin much of your reputation fighting gossip. If you already started the gossip with friends or family, put a stop to it today. Set a goal not to bring up your narcissist's name in any conversations with people.

2. If the gossip started at church, consider changing times you go to church (this holds true for other community events as well). I didn't want to do this because all my friends went to church at the same time I did. However, over time, my church attendance lost its purpose. I was supposed to be feeling peace and learning from the sermons. Instead, it became the only time I could gossip with people to get my point across that my narcissist was the jerk in the relationship, not me. I actually made it ten times worse for myself. Finally, I switched times and was able to begin healing, because I could finally hear God's messages for my life. He was telling me to turn the other cheek and let it go.

What Is Hoovering?

There is a term for how narcissists linger after a breakup: *hoovering*. This is when the narcissist tries to pull their partner back into the relationship after a period of separation. This can happen weeks, months, or even years after the relationship ended. They act like nothing happened and they can pick up where they left off without any work on their part. They will keep one foot in the door of your life to have control. They might continue to text you, email you, or have you as a friend on social media. They might tell you that they want you back, but this isn't entirely true. What they want is your attention, sex, or money. None of the responsibilities involved in the relationship are of interest to them. They might want to use you for financial reasons or as a crutch until they find someone better. Remember, they don't like to be alone. Maybe they need you for triangulation to keep a new spouse jealous. For whatever reasons, narcissists don't go away! Here are some signs of hoovering:

- They get in touch with you for pointless or made-up reasons or just to strike up conversations.
- They contact you on birthdays or other holidays even though the relationship is clearly over.
- They reach out to your friends or family for information about you.
- They want to return something to you but don't want to mail it—they have to give it to you personally.
- They find out about personal loss or difficult situations you're going through and reach out to say they are there for you if you want to talk or need a friend to lean on.

The reason hoovering works so well is the victim has hope. Victims want to have closure. They want to hear the things they have been waiting to hear, such as how much the narcissist cared for them or, better yet, how sorry they feel. They want to believe the narcissist has turned their life around and genuinely feels remorse for how they treated them. The problem is that they don't feel any of that. However, they will tell the victim what he or she needs to hear to give them one more shot—which is probably number ten in a long line of reconciliations the victim already gave them.

Can Narcissists Change and What Can I Do to Help?

I truly want to give you hope. However, changing a narcissist is not something you alone can accomplish. It will be up to them. Let me repeat that. *There is nothing you can say or change about yourself that will make them love you more.* They have disordered thinking and are mentally and spiritually ill. Some narcissists want to change when they lose most of their narcissistic supply or their image is tarnished. This is when they are at their lowest point and are more willing to see how their actions have caused them to push away people in their life.

However, it is hard to get them to this point unless a large amount of their inner circle shows that they disapprove of their behavior.

People with narcissism have learned to ignore, suppress, deny, project, and disavow their vulnerabilities (or at least try to) in their attempts to shape and reshape who they are in their interactions. Change means opening up to the very feelings they've learned to avoid at all costs, allowing the vulnerability back in. It's not that people with narcissism can't change; it's that it often threatens their sense of personhood to try. *Therefore, they don't want to change.* Their failed relationships often confirm, in their minds, that narcissism is the safest way to live. The sad irony of the narcissistic condition is that, in an effort to protect themselves, narcissists inevitably invite the very rejection and abandonment they fear in the first place.

Narcissists know what they are doing is wrong, but they don't seem to get how the behavior is not protecting them and how it is making their life worse. Chronic narcissism's negative consequences may include the following:

- Financial, career, or legal trouble from rule breaking, gross irresponsibility, careless indulgence, or other indiscretions.
- Quitting a job out of boredom or irritation with coworkers.
- Damaged personal and/or professional reputation.
- Loneliness and isolation. Few healthy, close, and lasting relationships.
- Family estrangement, including kids distancing themselves.
- Divorce, separation, or breakups.
- Relationships that are cut off when others feel let down, disappointed, lied to, used, manipulated, violated, exploited, betrayed, ripped off, demeaned, invalidated, or ignored.
- Missed opportunities from a lack of true substance and/or connectedness.
- Addictions to sources of supply (drugs, gambling, porn, affairs, hacking, etc.).

Despite a history that often shows a pattern of problems, the narcissist won't take responsibility. They can't deal with shame. Therefore, they are reluctant to see that they are the cause of problems in a relationship. If you are lucky enough to get them to a therapist, they can be manipulative and can easily turn the therapy session around to another blaming situation where they try to convince the therapist they aren't the problem—you are. Therefore, it will require a therapist with a strong knowledge of dealing with narcissistic personality disorders to make gains with the narcissist in therapy. Requesting that your narcissist join you in couples therapy would be a better approach than telling your narcissist that he needs therapy alone.

You might believe that giving unconditional love will help your narcissist. However, you have to accept that narcissists don't want unconditional love. Unconditional love requires openness and honesty. It requires facing fears, feeling uncomfortable emotions, and being open to change. In the narcissist's mind, these are things to be avoided at all costs. That is why every time you think you are getting somewhere, you come face-to-face with an impenetrable wall that they want to stay behind.

The key, then, to a narcissist changing is to break the vicious circle—to gently thwart their frantic efforts to control, distance, defend, or place blame in the relationship by sending the message that you're more than willing to connect with them, but not on these terms; to invite them into a version of intimacy where they can be loved and admired, warts and all, if they only allow the experience to happen. This will require the help of a trained therapist. Doing this by yourself will almost surely bring about the narcissist's resentment. It seems the more you get to the heart of the matter, the further they push away using their games.

Not only will you need to rely on professional help, but you will also need to rely on a higher power and support system. This requires something more than simply attending church. However, attending a church is important because you are fighting a person with immorality issues. Once you find a church, you will want to join a marriage enrichment program.

I joined Re|engage, a marriage enrichment program used in many nondenominational churches. Marriages in any condition can benefit, whether you are struggling to get along, your marriage is broken, or you simply want to grow closer as a couple.

Re|engage meetings are held once a week for approximately two hours and have two major components: large groups and small, closed-group sessions. Both groups examine God's design for marriage and apply principles from the Bible to guide couples toward growth in their relationship with each other. In the small, closed group, you read from a book on marriage each week at home with your partner and then come together the following week to discuss that chapter. If you want to speak freely about what is happening in your marriage, you can become part of a small, closed group. A closed group consists of six other couples, which makes the atmosphere more personal. Obviously, nothing spoken about in the group is made public. These sessions are free to attend, and you can attend even if you are not nondenominational. Don't worry—they are not interested in recruiting you to their church. The whole program is strictly about reconnecting couples who are having marriage difficulties as well as helping those who are not having problems to strengthen their relationship.

I joined Re|engage simply to learn how I could improve my marriage. I joined a closed group, and over a six-month period, I made lasting friendships and improved my marriage. I think this is the perfect environment to help a narcissistic partner become more vulnerable and open.

If your church doesn't have this program, take the book *Reconnect, Reignite, Resurrect* by the Re|engage program to your pastor and see if they can start one or if you can start your own. The book alone is a great resource for married couples in recovery or even for unmarried couples. You can find out more about the program and how to get the book at marriagehelp.org.

The best thing about the program is that you and your spouse can go through it as many times as you want. After I went through the program, my husband and I kept in touch with the people in our small group. Their friendships helped strengthen our marriage because of the bond we all formed through sharing the trials in our marriages with each other. Our small group continued meeting once a month as a Bible-study group long after the Re|engage program was over.

The next step you need to take after you have secured a therapist, religious faith, and a marriage enrichment program is to prepare yourself. This will require setting up boundaries and being firm with them. We will talk more about this later.

To-Do List

1. Visit your church and see what marriage programs they have. If they don't have any, then look closely at other churches in your area. Nondenominational megachurches usually have these types of programs. Like I have mentioned, you can even start your own program by ordering the Re|engage program's book at marriagehelp.org.

Can Medication Lessen Narcissistic Traits?

Although no psychiatric medications are approved for the treatment of narcissistic personality disorder, patients often benefit from the use of medications to alleviate symptoms associated with it. These include antidepressants—specifically, selective serotonin reuptake inhibitors (SSRIs)—to deal with depression and antipsychotics to regulate anger and mood shifts. However, be advised before you run to a physician for a prescription: antidepressants are only going to make them feel better if they are depressed. They may not feel true depression but simply use the victim card for their gain, to blame others, and to have control in a situation. Also, an antidepressant doesn't cause a narcissist to stop playing their manipulative games.

Antipsychotics and mood stabilizers can be used if the narcissist cycles from rage to depression. Again, this might lessen occurrences, but it only works on chemical imbalances. There is a marked difference between someone who has a mood disorder and someone who doesn't. Chemical imbalances are to blame in mood disorders, but narcissism is a personality disorder; therefore, narcissists often shift to anger or rage for no chemical reason. Changing the chemicals in their brain is not a solution for having someone love you more. It only lessens depression or anger. Again, it doesn't stop them from playing games. In fact, if you give an unhappy narcissist antidepressants, then all you really have is a happy narcissist playing games with you. This is where cognitive therapy comes into play to change behavior. However, as we have discussed, to reach the point of therapy, a narcissist has to want to change.

Reclaiming Your Right as a Son or Daughter of God

"To be or not to be, that is the question."

—William Shakespeare, *Hamlet*

For me, the hardest part of recovery from narcissistic abuse was accepting that my perceptions of these narcissists were not real. I had projected wholesome traits onto them based on only the acts of goodness I had witnessed. But a few glimmering moments aren't the whole picture.

When it came to both my narcissists, I had a vision of who I thought they were, behind all those mind games and anger. In the last section, I spoke about the dreams people have, not unlike fairy tales. We want to believe that this person is the princess or knight in shining armor we hoped to meet ever since we first watched Disney movies as a child. When they don't behave like this, our minds fight to keep the fairy tale alive. So you project all of your best traits onto that person—because you expect to find them there, right? The dream can be so beautiful that you ignore and minimize every bad thing your narcissist does. You sweep it under the carpet because you don't want to see them as anyone other than who you want them to be.

Eventually, in the discard phase, you are forced to wake up. And unfortunately, when you finally do, you realize that you have lost your health, spirit, and dignity. At that point, you might feel like I did—ashamed and angry. That's what I experienced with both my narcissists. I had lost all my boundaries and self-respect because I wanted to believe my narcissists were people they were not.

I admit that I am a sensitive soul and a born fixer. I like to look for the best in people, and I want to believe that everyone can change. However, this empathetic nature also turned me into a doormat.

When I was in a relationship with my first narcissist, I knew how badly he was treating me. I saw how arrogant and egotistical he was. However, everyone seemed to like him, so I second-guessed my own intuition. I let him cross boundaries because I didn't want to lose him. I felt that if I kept trying, I would stumble across the right moment or words that would somehow soften his heart, and then he would see my pain and ask for my forgiveness. This thinking came from a part of me that was still a little girl who had a big heart and no strong boundaries.

I would love to tell you that I walked away from that relationship with my head held high. I would also love to tell you that I had enough self-respect not to allow this man to walk all over me. But I can't lie. I loved that dream of him so much that I couldn't let it go. When someone you love says goodbye, you often stare long and hard at the door they closed and forget to see all the other doors God has left open in front of you.

In my situation, all my dignity left me when he ended the relationship. Rather than trust in God, I fell apart. I did the very thing a narcissistic abuse victim *should not* do, which was try to reason with him. This only added to the gossip among his enablers and made me appear to be someone with low self-esteem rather than who I really was—an abused woman who wanted to know why he wanted to marry me one week and then didn't the next. I was confused, frustrated, heartbroken, and clueless as to what I had done wrong.

To keep one foot in the door of my life, he cruelly left me dangling, saying, "If it is meant to be, it will be." This was simply a hook to make me wonder if he was having second thoughts about us. In his mind, it was his way of not ending the relationship (hoovering). When I became engaged to my husband, the narcissist tried to win me back, but it was obvious he didn't love me. He loved the game and the need to control me.

I would love to tell you I learned my lesson from that monstrous boyfriend, but I didn't. I went on to make more mistakes with my narcissist hacker. I made up a dozen reasons for why he did what he did to me—all of which excused his behavior and shifted the blame onto the women in his life, rather than him. His ex and wife wanted to know if he was unfaithful. Yet a part of them wanted to believe in the "dream" about their loved one, which meant believing my narcissist hacker's outrageous and laughable claim that I was a stalker who was going to hunt them down and kill them in their sleep. They were pathetically insecure. Therefore, they chose to keep tabs on me by hacking my home computer system and cell phone. The ridiculousness of their perception and unwarranted actions had me baffled for a long time. Were they really that naive? Why would they accept the preposterous over the simple truth staring them in the face—that he was disloyal?

However, I wasn't much smarter than these two women, because I also bought the dream. I thought he was a kind Christian man who wouldn't think of hurting me in this way. Naively, I bought into the assumption that these two women were the only ones doing the hacking and he wasn't participating in it. If he tried to stop them from their criminal activity, then he would be admitting that he cared for me. I know. Dumb, right? In my mind, I made all sorts of excuses for his bad behavior and minimized my trauma by telling myself that he wasn't a part of it. I learned later that he was the one who was participating and more than likely introduced the idea for doing this to the women in his life to prove he was faithful. Yet the reality was that he wanted to know more about me by listening in and hurt me at the same time because I didn't divorce my husband.

I naively believed the hacking would last for a month, until these two women felt vindicated. I was wrong. Instead, it lasted for years. In fact, their hacker friend still likes to look through my computer files and listen to my phone calls. He likes to post snippets of my private phone calls on his website. He is smart enough to leave my name off of his website so he can avoid the police asking him to take down his cyberbullying page. He also deleted the emails he sent me off my computer system before I could photocopy them for the police.

Should you ever feel that your narcissist is spying on you in this manner, here is how you can tell if they are listening in to your cell phone:

1. While on the line you might here popping or excessive static, humming, or clicking.
2. You might get unusual text messages.
3. The battery life of your cell phone drains faster than it should and you have to charge it often.

4. You have apps open that you didn't open and cell phone charges you didn't make.
5. The battery might feel hotter than usual and you haven't been using your phone.
6. Files might be moved or open on your computer system and your passwords might be changed.

By the time this book is published, I will have endured four years of having my computer system and cell phone hacked. It could go on forever. Sadly, there is nothing the police can do about it, unless I can catch the person logging on to my computer and capture their IP address, which requires someone with hacking skills. There are people in the community who possess this ability to help people who are being hacked. However, they usually charge a large fee and even then hackers have ways of disguising their IP address. Changing cell phones or computer systems doesn't remedy the problem. They just use their hacking skills to rehack you. Antivirus software won't prevent hackers, either. I had reputable antivirus software on my computer, and the hacker was still able to hack my computer.

I am a good person who unfortunately was taken advantage of by a bad person. I naively wanted to believe he didn't want to hurt me. It wasn't until much later, in therapy, that I woke up from this delusion and accepted that an ungodly man who didn't have any respect for the women in his life was abusing us all. This wasn't a little joke or prank to get even with me. This was a sickness and a violation of my civil rights, punishable by time spent in prison. He was a toxic, egotistical liar and a sick, perverted criminal. He was lying to his wife and his ex about his feelings for me, and he covered his tracks by telling them that I was the one who had a problem. I bought in to the Christian façade he had created for himself. I believed he was capable of feeling guilt, compassion, remorse, and empathy. He wasn't.

It took me a while to wake up from this false perception I had about my narcissist hacker. In therapy, I learned to accept reality. He was a cruel man and the one who orchestrated the whole event. He wasn't leaving me alone. Nor did he care that he had invited sociopathic strangers into my private life by asking them to help him hack my cell phone and computer. He wasn't doing anything to stop his hacker friends from learning my passwords or looking at my financial files online. He didn't care that they took money from my accounts or were rifling through my computer files to learn more about me on a daily basis. His actions went far beyond the behavior of someone who liked me. This was someone who felt entitled and was punishing me for not being single. So if he couldn't have me single, he did the next best thing—he used me. He used me to boost his ego by telling everyone that I liked him and that he was a victim because of it. This got him a lot of attention from his ex and wife. I was also a source of entertainment for him. He could dial in at any time and listen into my phone conversations, which made him feel in control of me. He enjoyed the power that came from knowing my business. I am sure he thought, "Why do I have to wait for her to get a divorce so I can date her? I can listen in and find out everything about her now. If I want to know what she is like in bed, all I have to do is overhear her intimate moments through the speakerphone on her cell phone. I don't have to chase after her. I already have the best part of her—her privacy."

I spent a lot of time in therapy trying to figure out why I had been physically attracted to someone so abusive and why I made so many excuses for him. I eventually found the answer in my upbringing. I grew up with toxic family members. I constantly made excuses for their bad behavior to lessen the trauma their actions and words caused me. My dismissal of bad behavior had become a long-standing habit. As a result, my definition of normal behavior had become skewed. I was drawn to the things this person had in common with me. I also felt comfortable talking with him. However, this was not a healthy version of comfort. Rather, his games were sick and twisted but familiar. That is why I overlooked his abuse—because his cruelty felt normal. I had allowed too many people to cross my boundaries for the sake of calling them my family. He was no different from the other people I let linger in my life.

I hope this revelation helps you if you find yourself wondering why you go back to someone every time they prove to be so mean, or if you have a pattern of attracting toxic individuals into your life. Maybe the narcissist represents the toxic mother or father in your life and you are living out the chance to win back their love by enduring the abuse. On the other hand, maybe that individual represents some part of your life where you felt you had failed. Maybe your constant attempts to mend this relationship have nothing to do with love, but rather a second chance to win a battle you lost in the past. Furthermore, you could have a rescuer personality, making you the kind of person who likes to save lost souls, and your narcissist is simply a stray dog you brought home to nurse back to health. Maybe you're waiting on them to thank you. Who knows? But it's worth investigating.

When I look back on the abuse I suffered, I feel ashamed, because I turned my back on common sense. I didn't have strong boundaries that said, "If someone does evil things to me, then I shouldn't make excuses for them or minimize their bad behavior." I didn't live by a set of rules that taught others how to treat me. I realize now that these men desired me *but didn't value me.* And somewhere during the abuse, I stopped valuing myself too, because I put up with their behavior. I forgot what it means to be a daughter of our Heavenly Father. It means that I shouldn't excuse bad behavior or accept disrespect from others just because they have a mental illness or had a difficult upbringing. Why should I hold them to a lesser standard than myself? They still have freedom of choice, and they can choose not to do bad things.

Maybe you are in a relationship with your narcissist and have reached a turning point, just like I did, and have finally decided that this is not who you are or how you want to live. Or maybe you are no longer with your narcissist and you feel like you've sacrificed your worth and wasted emotion on someone who didn't care. Sometimes the hardest battles in life are between hanging on and letting go. I understand your pain. I know that you have suffered, or you wouldn't be reading this in search of answers.

I want you to know this: Jesus Christ wants you to reclaim your right as a strong son or daughter of our Heavenly Father. "For I know the plans I have for you," declares the Lord, "plans to prosper you and not to harm you, plans to give you hope and a future" (Jeremiah 29:11). How this person has treated you is not okay! But despite what you have been through, you mustn't set up camp inside your own pain and lose faith in what God still has in store for you. The only down-side of having a good heart is that you're constantly looking for angels inside demons. And they wonder why the good know so much pain!

It's important to remember that Satan will try to use us to do bad things. And if he can't, then he will use our negative emotions to keep us in a place of bitterness and victimization. This means we stay trapped and miserable. Matthew 16:26 reminds us, "What good will it be for someone to gain the whole world, yet forfeit their soul?"

What keeps so many victims of narcissistic abuse trapped in the past is how we view things that have happened to us. All of us are going to experience major events like death, marriage, growing old, raising kids, and making career choices. But life is determined by how we interpret those events—what we decide these things mean to us, and what we plan to do about them.

It's easy for us to blame events in our lives for our problems. *I am unhappy because I lost my job. I am overweight because those people were mean to me.* This process of assigning blame is not unlike how the narcissist blames others. In the same way, we say *I am hopeless because of the abuse I suffered.* It is not the abuse that keeps us tethered to that part of our lives, but our interpretation of it. We can't gain the momentum we need to move away from the past unless we see the positive things we can take from those experiences, rather than focusing on the negative. What frees us is shifting our negative emotions into positive ones, gathering new resources to dig our way out of our grief, and changing our value system.

But most of all, we need to learn self-reliance. To be self-reliant is to be responsible for all your actions and what you know. You have now been educated about the games that narcissists play. Therefore, from this point on, every step in your recovery is *your* choice. Blaming another person will not get you to a place of healing. Who is accountable for your soul and happiness? You guessed it—YOU! To be self-reliant is to be responsible for your own spiritual healing. To achieve this, you need to have a strong understanding of why you shouldn't stoop to the level of your narcissist's games—or forever remain the victim.

I understand what it means to cling to the label of victim. It helps you feel like you're in the right. "He or she did me wrong." "It wasn't my fault. They need to pay for it." "I have the right to hate them. They deserve it." We often say things like this when we are hurt. Unfortunately, we also stop asking ourselves how to get out of this angry state, and we become too comfortable in our own victimhood. The victim mentality is about believing that your well-being is based on *what is happening to you.* However, nonvictim thinking is when you know that your well-being is based on *how you respond to what is happening.* This slight shift in perspective can help you walk out of that victim role and become a thriving son or daughter of our Heavenly Father. I understand how stubbornly people can cling to labels. But you need to trust that God has a better life ahead of you that doesn't include the sad place you have been dwelling in for so long.

Change requires courage. However, courage doesn't happen when you have all the answers. It happens when you are ready to face the questions you have been avoiding your entire life. There are life lessons to be learned in your pain if you only do the work to see them, so you can change this label of victim to learner. Throughout this book, I will continue asking you questions so you can learn from your circumstances.

So let me ask you one of the most important questions in your recovery: who are you? Beliefs about your identity create boundaries within which you live your life. This is not limited to whether you are a person with low self-esteem or a confident person. What we believe about ourselves could be internalized by buying into our narcissist's opinions of us. Maybe you consider yourself overly sensitive or an over-reactor because your narcissist told you so. It is one thing to be anxious over what your narcissist is doing to you and another to think of yourself as an anxious person. You have to be careful with the labels you create for yourself, or you will let others label you. After a while, they will begin to define your experience, change what you notice about yourself, and cause you to make choices about what you will or will not do. This new identity changes the way you live. Once you decide who you are, those attributes become consistent in your behaviors. Because of both narcissists, I became stuck in the stage of victimization. That became my identity for a long time. Since they weren't around for me to vent my anger at, I turned to God. I wanted to know why God didn't give me a huge prompting from the Holy Ghost that would have warned me about these individuals before I bought into their false image. I prayed constantly for both of these narcissists to change and for answers as to what to do, but nothing was happening. Over time, I felt like all my disappointments had untethered me from trusting in God. He didn't seem to be giving me the answers I needed. I grew impatient and I wondered if he was listening at all. However, I didn't give up all my hope. For solace, I turned to the Bible and there read countless stories of people who, like me, had gone through tough times. One story that helped me was that of Joseph.

A long time ago, Joseph's father Jacob doted on him. In fact, he showed too much favoritism to his son, attracting so much envy and jealousy from Joseph's brothers that it almost resulted in murder. Joseph's own brothers sold him into slavery. Can you imagine the betrayal he felt? However, when Joseph was made a slave in Egypt, he still lived as a son—a son of our Heavenly Father. Instead of becoming bitter and seeking retaliation for his circumstances, Joseph entrusted himself to God, as evidenced by his behavior. Despite his circumstances, he lived righteously according to God's word and retained his dignity. He was presented with four difficult tests, and he passed each of them with flying colors. He passed the test of betrayal by forgiving his brothers. He passed the test of sexual temptation by fleeing Potiphar's wife and going to prison for his righteousness. He passed the perseverance test when he was forgotten after giving a dream interpretation to the cupbearer. In addition, he passed the stewardship test when he refused to take revenge on all those who had betrayed him and became a faithful steward over the resources of Egypt.

Joseph lived eighty-one years after being elevated from the prison cell. He could never have passed those tests had he not lived as a son of his Heavenly Father. He had a strong sense of boundaries; he didn't commit adultery, and he obeyed God's laws. He knew who he was, and this is why he was successful in his trials.

> But God sent me ahead of you to preserve for you a remnant on earth and to save your lives by a great deliverance. So then, it was not you who sent me here, but God. He made me father to Pharaoh, lord of his entire household and ruler of Egypt. (Genesis 45:7–8)

When God delivered Joseph from prison, he took him to the pinnacle of power. Many of us have been taught that Joseph was second in command to Pharaoh. Actually, Joseph was placed over his entire household. He may not have had the title of Pharaoh, but from a spiritual position, Joseph oversaw the entire nation. A closer examination of scripture tells us two very important things about his advancement. The purpose of Joseph's deliverance was "to save the lives of his brothers" for the sake of a new nation and for Joseph to "spiritually father Pharaoh." How could a thirty-year-old father someone possibly twice his age? It is because it was a spiritual relationship. Joseph never lost sight of who he was. He never lived as a slave or victim. In his heart, he knew he was a son of our Heavenly Father. This is why he did not succumb to the temptations that come with power, influence, and wealth.

He remained a steward of God's purpose on the earth for the nations of Israel and Egypt.

I share this story with you because even Joseph had no idea that his trials would lead him to a different status in life if he only remained true to the principles of what it meant to be a son of our Heavenly Father. He suffered, not unlike how you are suffering. He had to overcome his own smear campaign when he was accused of adultery by Potiphar's wife. It was bad enough that his own brothers betrayed him and he was sold into slavery, but he also had to deal with a false story made up by an unrighteous woman. I admire Joseph's strength to endure it all.

God's desire is that we all become more like his son, Jesus. "I will be a father to you, and you shall be my sons and daughters," says the Lord Almighty (2 Corinthians 6:18). However, before you rush off to make a list of rules that tell people how to treat you, let's define what a son or daughter of our Heavenly Father is. What good does it do to tell you to set boundaries if you don't know why you should have them? You need to know who you are and what you will and won't put up with in your life.

If you don't know your worth and trust that God will provide someone better for you, then you are likely to let your narcissistic partner, or the next person you form a relationship with after leaving them, cross those boundaries because of your own desperation to keep your dream alive. It is time to wake from this dream and embrace the discomfort of reality. The person you care or cared for is spiritually and mentally ill. They do not love you in the way that you love them. However, here is the promise when you accept this reality: it might be uncomfortable at first because of your fear of losing someone or standing up for yourself, but as you rebuild your faith in God, it will get better. You have a new chance to attract the right person into your life and create a version of yourself that God would be proud of.

God is working for you right now. Heaven is holding conversations about you. Angels have been assigned to you, so be at peace! If God could close the mouths of the lions for Daniel, part the Red Sea for Moses, make the sun stand still for Joshua, open the prison doors for Peter, put a baby in the arms of Sarah, and raise Lazarus from the dead, then he can certainly take care of you! Just like he delivered the

Israelites out of Egypt, he is going to deliver you out of this abuse. Trust him.

Living as a son or daughter of our Heavenly Father will help you reclaim your respect and dignity. And I mean *living*! It is not enough to say you are one. If you are to survive narcissistic abuse, you are to *live* as one. What you plant in your soul is what you will harvest with your actions. "You were bought at a price. Therefore honor God with your bodies" (1 Corinthians 6:20).

The following sections of this book will be your guide to forming the blueprint of your life—the new, stronger version of you! You might be thinking, "Wait a minute! I have been going to church and living righteously." If that is the case, then you are on the track to healing. However, what I have noticed in survivors is a shaken faith and anger. They had minimal boundaries, which meant fewer of the attributes our Heavenly Father wanted for them. In the many survivors of narcissistic abuse that I have met, God's intended attributes were replaced with what the narcissists wanted them to believe about themselves. Wherever you might be in your spirituality, you're in pain or you would not have sought out this book. Stay with me. Let's reclaim your identity and make it impenetrable so nothing like this can ever happen to you again.

You have been walking in hell for a long time. It is time to get to the other side. It is said that some people are built by the fire. I say you are the fire. You are a radiant light. Don't ever let anyone put out your light because they are blinded by it. You need to cancel all the opinions your narcissist had about you. Their words are not reality. It is time to listen to what God says about your potential. To be a healthy son or daughter of our Heavenly Father, you need to work toward being emotionally and spiritually mature. This requires you to have the courage and desire to face the truth about yourself and your relationship instead of denying it. Even if you are no longer in the relationship or were simply used as narcissistic supply, these pages apply to you as well. Emotional and spiritual maturity are things God desires for all of us:

> So Christ himself gave the apostles, the prophets, the evangelists, the pastors and teachers, to equip his people for works of service, so that the body of Christ may be built up until we all reach unity in the faith and in the knowledge of the Son of God and *become mature, attaining to the whole measure of the fullness of Christ.* (Ephesians 4:11–13; emphasis added)

Growing into God's Vision of You

It is time to establish a strong identity. From here, you will know what your boundaries are and defend them to your dying breath. Let's hope that your choice to become a Christian wasn't made because you *kind of* wanted to be good or you wanted to meet people to hang out with. Let's hope you call yourself a Christian because you want to follow Christ's teachings and be an example of the goodness of his life's mission. Even if you are not a Christian, the things I am going to touch on still apply to you, so don't let the Bible scare you away from spiritual healing. There is a message in this book for you as well.

Let me ask you this: How are you doing when it comes to being a son or daughter of God? Have you been a doormat in your relationship, or have you been God's warrior? The beginning of this chapter starts with Hamlet's famous line, "To be or not to be, that is the question." So let me be direct with you. Do you plan to be a victim for five more years, or do you want to be a strong individual who isn't stuck in the past? I can guarantee if you continue to dig the same hole in the same place in your life, eventually you will be standing in a grave. Isn't it time to step into God's role for you?

Here are the characteristics of a son or daughter of our Heavenly Father to help you determine if you're on the right track. You might be saying, "Yeah, I know how I am supposed to be. How does this help me get over the sadness?" Well, if you really applied these attributes, you wouldn't be reading this book. You would have either left your narcissist or learned how to stand up to the abuse because of your strength and faithfulness in God's plan for you. God's desire for you is to be a person of dignity. There is no dignity in narcissistic abuse. I guarantee that if you know your worth, you won't sacrifice your needs to keep someone in your life.

Do you have any of the qualities below? If you are going to move away from calling yourself a victim of narcissistic abuse, you are going to need to acquire them. This is the identity that your God wants from you:

- **You are motivated to seek God without him prompting you.**
  "But seek first his kingdom and his righteousness, and all these things will be given to you as well" (Matthew 6:33).

Sons and daughters of God put him first in their lives because they know that God is the source of all their joy. Furthermore, they turn to God without prompting from other people. God didn't design your life so you would constantly fall down, but he does hope that you will be brought to your knees. Daughters and sons of our Heavenly Father pray often. In religion, they find guidance and moral support. They pray with their partners, narcissistic or not, and their children. They actively seek God through the spiritual people they associate with and the wholesome books and movies they read and watch. If you're not hungry for Christ, then you are probably too full of yourself.

- **You are more concerned about spiritual growth than how you rank next to other people.**
"Seek good, not evil, that you may live. The the Lord God Almighty will be with you, just as you say he is" (Amos 5:14).

Sometimes people don't practice what they preach; they take the easy road and compromise regularly instead of doing the hard spiritual work of living out their faith. As a result, their entire effort becomes focused on looking good on the outside and desiring people's attention instead of desiring to please God. As much as this book is about the narcissistic qualities of your partner, I want you to recognize any narcissistic qualities you have in yourself. It's only fair, right? Do you live only the image of a Christian? Simply put, are you a fan instead of a follower?

I am here to tell you that God is tired of being "admired" and not obeyed. Your love for him must extend beyond religious posts on social media and church attendance to walking with him when the service is over. Author Ron Smith observes profoundly, "There was a time when people went to church, heard the truth and wept over their sins. Today people go to church, hear a motivational speech and ignore their sins."

My narcissist hacker's sibling was public with her love for Christ. Her Facebook page is full of Christian quotes. However, this didn't keep her from playing mind games with me online. She approved of the hacking that was going on. One of the people involved stole money from my financial accounts. She might not have been the one that stole the money, but she is guilty for allowing it to happen to me. I was being abused, and she didn't care. What she did wasn't very Christian, and it is a shame that she believes that Jesus Christ approved of what she was doing. The lesson to gather from my sorrow is this: let your Christianity go beyond wearing a cross and social media posts. Let's hope that when you decide to define what being Christian means, it won't be the superficial things but a change in character—showing kindness, love, compassion, mercy, and empathy.

If you are more of a fan, then I want you to consider renting the Not a Fan series of videos produced by Pastor Kyle Idleman. I stumbled across his series on YouTube after my narcissistic abuse. I was moved by the storyline in the series. Its message hit home. I needed to go from the comfortable position of being a fan to being a true follower. This meant I had to stop telling people I believe in Christ and start showing them I believe in Christ. Please take the time to check out the series on YouTube or his website, notafan.com. It will kickstart the new you!

Sons and daughters of God know that if they make the effort to care for their insides (their heart, their emotions, their guilt, their faith), then their outward actions will be right too (Matthew 23:25–26). Therefore, you are not in this world to impress others but to love others. You live by a higher law—God's law. When you do, this also means that, as a couple, you are not just caught up in the house, finances, children, and hobbies. You have built your life around spiritual growth, so growing spiritually is a frequent topic of conversation in your home.

- **You search for the truth.**
"For we can do nothing against the truth, but for the truth" (2 Corinthians 13:8).

When you're in a bad relationship, it's easy to be in denial. Who likes problems? No one! Pushing away the issues, trivializing, downplaying the seriousness of behavior, or outright ignoring it in hopes it goes away are often done when a person is in pain. Anxiety happens when you realize that the person you are with is not helping you spiritually grow and emotionally feel secure. However, biblically, truth is freeing (John 8:31–32) and you will actually be stronger internally and spiritually when you don't have to hide what you really think and feel (Psalm 32:1–6).

So what does it mean to search for the truth? Besides reading your scriptures and learning about your partner's disorder, it can also mean choosing not to live in denial about how badly someone is treating you. You stop minimizing bad behavior out of fear of them leaving you. You don't stay and suffer in silence because of the fear that you won't find better. You are truthful to yourself about why you have let things go on as long as they have. You also don't let them gaslight you because you don't want to know the truth and would rather stay in your imaginary fairy tale. If they are being unfaithful, you investigate and find out the truth somehow, some way—but you don't give in to ignoring their lies. You live in truth, and that means waking up and rejoining reality!

- **You admit the truth to God.**
  "I know also, my God, that thou triest the heart, and has pleasure in uprightness" (1 Chronicles 29:17).

  Sons and daughters of our Heavenly Father understand that time spent with God is an important time to confess and admit our own sins and lies, not just vent our feelings about what isn't going well in our relationships. You are not like the narcissist who is puffed up and arrogant. Sons and daughters of our Heavenly Father are humble. They take responsibility for what they have done wrong. They understand that God can lift away the guilt they feel about their choices through repentance.

- **You practice spirituality daily.**
  "But strong meat belongeth to them that are full age, even those who by reason of use have their senses exercised to discern both good and evil" (Hebrews 5:14).

  Sons and daughters of our Heavenly Father are not only spiritual warriors on Sunday, but every day of the week. I think the answer to many of the decisions you must make regarding your narcissistic partner or ex can be drawn from this question: what would Jesus do? No, Jesus wasn't a doormat, nor did he plot revenge. Yes, he might have become angry because of people's unrighteousness. That is only because he knew they were capable of being much better than how they were living. I am not asking you to get mad at your narcissist and pick a fight. Get mad at the behavior and see it as something you won't tolerate in your life anymore. Choose to take a spiritual approach to dealing with it. I will tell you more about how to do that later in this section. You may not see the effects of your decision until much later, but the

Bible promises that those who constantly work at being righteous and honest will reap the benefits.

- **You hear God's voice.**

"For as many as are led by the Spirit of God, they are the sons of God" (Romans 8:14).

Sons and daughters of our Heavenly Father understand that to be led by the Spirit of God is to submit to his influence, suggestions, and control. They understand that nothing is a coincidence. They don't take random encounters with people lightly; they believe God is loving and in the business of answering prayers. They are not going to only pray for help. They are going to look for what God sends their way. This could be a person, book, opportunity, sermon, or other spiritual message.

When I was in my relationship with my narcissist, I prayed a lot. However, that is all I did. I didn't have the right to say God was silent when my Bible was closed. How many times have you prayed hoping it was a telephone and God was going to pick up the line and start telling you what to do? That isn't how he works. Yes, sometimes you feel a prompting. However, many times God answers through other people. Therefore, it is important as a son or daughter of our Heavenly Father to get out there and meet people. Make yourself available for blessings. Look for that person, place, or thing that has the answer you have been praying for. God wants you to find it, but he is using your circumstances to make you strong by seeking it. "To him the porter openeth; and the sheep hear his voice: and he calleth his own sheep by name, and leadeth them out. And when he putteth forth his own sheep, he goeth before them, and the sheep follow him: for they know his voice" (John 10:3–4). Sometimes we pray for things but have no intention of acting on the answers we get. Be active about your prayers!

- **You are bold as a lion.**

"The wicked flee when no man pursueth: but the righteous are bold as a lion" (Proverbs 28:1).

A righteous son or daughter of our Heavenly Father has true courage. It is the kind of courage that comes not from physical strength, but from spiritual strength. They don't fear the future because they know that God has gone ahead of them and prepared a way. Therefore, they don't stay in a relationship because they're afraid to be alone. They know that is a wrong reason to stay! They either leave because of their courage to go it alone (trusting that God has a better plan) or they stay because they feel they're making *progress* with a partner who *wants* to change with them. Notice how I emphasized "progress." When you are in love, you can easily find the smallest thing the narcissist did and call it progress as an excuse to not leave the relationship. You have to be real with yourself. If your partner doesn't give you the silent treatment after one fight, but does after twenty others, then that isn't progress. That just means you're lucky one time. If your partner doesn't want to change, then you have to accept that they can't help you spiritually grow as a person or together as a couple. Therefore, it's time to leave the relationship because you trust God is going to send someone who can help you spiritually grow.

Sons and daughters of our Heavenly Father also safeguard their dignity by having strong boundaries. This comes from understanding they have standards in alignment with a Christian life. The people in their life rise up to their level rather than requiring them to lower themselves to be in their company. Even if they have low self-esteem, they will fake it until they rebuild it. This comes from saddling up despite their fear and holding firm on how they expect to be treated.

- **You have a contrite spirit.**
  "For all those things hath Mine hand made, and all those things have been, saith the LORD: but to this man will I look, even to him that is poor and of a contrite spirit, and trembleth at my word" (Isaiah 66:2).

  A contrite spirit is in total opposition to a proud, haughty, self-confident, self-righteous, and narcissistic one. With firm boundaries, they don't give in to their insecurities or sacrifice their dignity for peace. A son or daughter of our Heavenly Father is deeply affected by sin. They wish to *do* what is right, rather than *be* right. They are a humble person who knows judgment is not theirs, but God's. They understand that their righteousness isn't an invitation to come down hard on their narcissist by calling them an evildoer and shaming them into defensiveness. They're calm, kind, and humble, but they are firm on what they believe, and sin is something they won't tolerate. Therefore, they have created strong boundaries that are in line with how Christ expects them to be treated.

- **You are faithful.**
  "These shall make war with the Lamb, and the Lamb shall overcome them: for He is Lord of lords, and King of kings: and they that are with Him are called, and chosen, and faithful" (Revelation 17:14).

  To be faithful is to be trustworthy, true, and someone who can be relied on. It also means to keep the faith and trust in the promises of God. Sons or daughters of our Heavenly Father might not see the answers to their prayers immediately, but they know to have patience because God has heard them. He is walking with them through their narcissistic abuse. He is using other people, books, sermons, articles, music, and pastors to answer their prayers. They trust that God knows what they have suffered and is preparing a way for them out of the abuse.

  They are the type of person who seeks God in all their decisions, rather than letting their emotions dictate their actions. Therefore, a true son or daughter of God isn't going to let this one person out of the millions they could be with destroy their spirit. They believe their birthright is to be happy and fulfilled. They know this because they live the saying "Those who leave everything in God's hands will eventually see God's hand in everything."

- **You are godly.**
  "But know that the LORD hath set apart him that is godly for Himself: the LORD will hear when I call unto Him" (Psalm 4:3).

  A godly person demonstrates love toward God and man with great desire, ardor, and zeal. "My little children, let us not love in word, neither in tongue, but in deed and in truth" (1 John 3:18). A son or daughter of our Heavenly Father does not wage war with the narcissist who discarded them. They let it go! They live the way God wants them to. They know their worth and have values. They are graceful and live by a code of conduct of the highest integrity. Therefore, they associate with people who also have these attributes.

- **You don't practice deceit.**
  "Jesus saw Nathanael coming to Him, and saith of him, Behold an Israelite indeed, in whom is no guile!" (John 1:47).

A son or daughter of our Heavenly Father is sincere and upright. They're never crafty, deceitful, or hypocritical. At all times, they are what they profess to be. They do not abuse someone because they have been abused. They stand above that level of evil. They act in a way that is Christlike and well above the narcissistic games of their partner.

Their outward appearance matches their authentic self. When faced with a smear campaign, they don't stoop to the same games as the narcissist. They have standards that are always maintained. The high road is always their destination.

- **You are humble.**

"Better it is to be of a humble spirit with the lowly, than to divide the spoil with the proud" (Proverbs 16:19).

Like Jesus, the son or daughter of our Heavenly Father is meek and lowly in heart. They are not arrogant or thinking they're superior to others as the narcissist does. They are not self-righteous, nor do they believe they are better because they are a Christian. They don't categorize people into good or evil. They don't judge a person, but the behavior. They are humble and see individuals who are struggling just as they do. They don't let other people's bad behavior pull them down to the same level. Therefore, they do not try to go after other people for revenge.

- **You are merciful.**

"Blessed are the merciful: for they shall obtain mercy" (Matthew 5:7).

The scriptures tell us that God is full of compassion and abundant in mercy. Likewise, a son or daughter of our Heavenly Father is affected by the sufferings of others. They are inclined to help and comfort all those in misery and grief. Their life is full of service to others because they see that in Jesus Christ's ministry to his people. They look for ways they can contribute in their community or church.

They are willing to forgive others, but they also know that constant forgiveness for the same offenses without changing the situation is not what God wants them to offer. Rather than dwell with them, he wants you to walk away from people who show no remorse.

- **You are obedient.**
"As obedient children, not fashioning yourselves according to the former lusts in your ignorance" (1 Peter 1:14).

A son or daughter of our Heavenly Father lives the commandments. These are their rules for being a decent human being. They don't step away from them to meet their wants or needs. They trust the rules God gave them because they know their life won't be better morally without God's guidance. They also expect those who share their life to live by those same rules. If their narcissistic partner can't help them spiritually grow, then they are not meant to be in their life. Therefore, they let the narcissistic person go because God didn't intend for them to be a parent to their partner. He wants a team working together in righteousness to do his will. He doesn't want two people fighting and not working together as one. He wants healthy parents raising his future generations.

- **You are watchful.**
"Blessed are those servants, whom the Lord when he cometh shall find watching: verily I say unto you, that he shall gird himself, and make them to sit down to meat, and will come forth and serve them" (Luke 12:37).

A son or daughter of our Heavenly Father is vigilant and discerning of the times in which they live. They contribute to the betterment of the world rather than being of the world. They understand that their relationship is not about two people acquiring stuff, but two people growing spiritually through life experiences and lessons. They are forever mindful of the example they set for their children and family members. Therefore, they watch their language. They don't put themselves in situations that would make other people wonder about their values. They know God has a plan for their life and Satan has a plan for their life. They are wise enough to know which one to battle and which one to embrace.

- **You have self-confidence and dignity.**
"Strength and honor are her clothing; and she shall rejoice in the time to come" (Proverbs 31:25).

Christians attain self-worth and esteem by having a strong relationship with God. Their sense of dignity comes from their participation in Jesus's mission. They know they are valuable because of the high price God paid for us through the blood of his son, Jesus Christ. Anything that separates them from the person and mission of Jesus Christ is sinful, and thus it is beneath their dignity. That means if they enable a narcissist's bad behavior by being a doormat, they are most certainly distancing themselves from the fullness of being a true son or daughter of our Heavenly Father. They are honest with themselves by accepting the truth that their constant attempts to prove their worth to their narcissist go against what it means to have dignity.

In conclusion, I know this list of characteristics can be overwhelming. It is a lifetime of work to rise to the challenge. However, it is a necessary list to look at because you are not meant to be a victim. You are so much more than that! Somewhere along my road to recovery from narcissistic abuse, I prayed to the Lord and told him that I didn't want to remain a victim anymore. This is not who I am; it is who I was. I am letting it go. The abuse happened to me, and I can't go back and change what I said or didn't say or how my narcissist escalated it into unneeded drama. I can't erase the faulty picture of who I was in the minds of the people who were poisoned by my narcissists' lies. I can't undo the embarrassment I felt for being gullible about my narcissists' true character. I can't erase the time wasted on them. Starting today, I can only choose to no longer be a victim. Victimization is not how my story ends. I am not going to let two evil men out of a million righteous men in the world write the ending of my life story, nor am I going to let them control my happiness any longer. This is my wish for you. You are the author of your own story, not your narcissist.

Now that you have reviewed what a son or daughter of our Heavenly Father is, it is time to see where you are lacking. From that, you will get a clearer picture about what needs to be fixed before you institute a set of boundaries to safeguard your worth.

To-Do List

1. Define who you are. I am not asking for a list of physical characteristics or career status. I want you to write down your strengths and weaknesses. Then ask yourself: has my narcissist changed the view I have of myself?

2. After you do that, I want you to write a description of the person you want to be. What would you look and feel like? How would you act?

3. Write down the spiritual attributes you are lacking.

4. Write down what your belief system is. This should take a page to write. I am not asking you to write simply that you are a Christian. I want you to define what Christianity means to you and why you choose to follow that belief. Do you follow the commandments? Now take a long, hard stare at what you have on paper. Are you a follower of Jesus Christ or mostly a fan? Do you live this when it suits you or is it something you do daily? There is a difference between believing and doing. You can believe in Christ all you want, but it means nothing if you don't do what he has asked of you. Now write down how your narcissist has changed your beliefs.

5. Are you building a Christlike lifestyle or looking for a shortcut by staying in this abusive relationship? People stay in abusive relationships for lots of reasons; sometimes this is because of hope, and other times it might be out of fear of being alone. Write down your reasons. Do they line up with the attributes of a son or daughter of our Heavenly Father?

6. If you are struggling with an attribute, write a list of five goals that will help you strengthen yourself in it. For example, you might not have faith in God. You could make it a goal to read the scriptures every day, attend church every Sunday, attend a Bible-study class, go on a church service project once a month, or volunteer in a position at your church. After you have written your five goals for this month, I want you to write five more goals for the year, such as reading the entire Bible, going on at least five service projects, implementing all your boundaries, and not giving in once.

7. Earlier, I asked you to list the traits you want in a partner. I want you to flip to that section in your journal. Go through the list and see if it matches the attributes our Heavenly Father would want for you in a mate. I also asked you to list the traits your partner possessed. I want you to write their spiritual attributes beside that list. Are any of these things close to the attributes God wants for you? It is my hope that by now you understand why I am asking you to do this. I want you to see what you are missing and what God wants for you. (As you write about the above attributes, think of this not as a list of righteous objectives that only Christians possess. *Virtues are human traits known by all faiths.*)

What Is Your Next Move?

During your recovery, I want you to be a gatherer of references. Don't settle for the saying "Bad things happen to good people" and then wallow in bitterness. Go out there and find the stories about the people who learned lessons from their abuse and came to an epiphany, people who can say, "I understand why I went through it, and now I can grow from this!" As I read books on narcissism, I gathered references from people who moved beyond being a victim to becoming a thriving, happy human being. Each had found new references to get themselves unstuck.

Part of the process of moving out of the narcissistic abuse victim mentality is knowing who your authentic self is and living it. This is different from God's identity for you. It is the extra part of what makes up your personality. The authentic self is the you who can be found at your absolute core. It is the part of you not defined by your job, function, or role. It is the composite of all your skills, talents, and wisdom. It is all of the things that are uniquely yours and need expression, beyond what you believe you are supposed to be and do. Your authentic self is not driven by circumstances, opinions of others, or negative emotions. It doesn't make decisions based on fear, ego, or what other people want from you. It realizes that the person who broke you is not the person who knows how to fix you. Therefore, you stop looking to the narcissist to make you feel whole.

To be authentic is to feel at home in your body and true to our sense of values. It means possessing the confidence to know we are enough. We can be true to our own personality, spirit, or character despite external pressures. When you're not living your authentic self and God's identity, you find yourself feeling incomplete, as if there is a hole in your life. You may have found that it's easier to fulfill the roles your narcissistic partner, friends, or family expected of you rather than becoming who you really want to be. Living this way robs you of the energy needed to be what God wants you to be in life.

When you live a life that has you ignoring your true gifts and talents while performing the assigned role your narcissist wants you to play, then you are living a fictional self. The fictional self sends you false information about who you are and what you should be doing with your life. Relying on information from the fictional self means putting your trust in a broken compass. Restoring your attributes as a son or daughter of our Heavenly Father will put you more in tune with who you are. When you do that, you can begin creating a blueprint for your life.

There are two things you need to repair after narcissistic abuse—your life resume and your life blueprint. The life resume is who you are. This includes the attributes of a child of our Heavenly Father that I listed before. It also includes your boundaries and authentic self. A life blueprint is our model of how life should be.

Let's talk about your life blueprint first. Motivational coach Tony Robbins said, "We all have a story in our head. It's the one we grew up with. It might be something along the lines of work hard in school, be a nice person, find the ideal mate, get a house with a white picket fence, start a family, and live happily ever after." In essence, it is that dream most narcissistic abuse victims cling to about their partners. It is the way it should be. When people are unhappy, you can always bet that their blueprint doesn't match their life.

When life doesn't go as planned, Tony says we have three choices:

1. Blame something.
2. Change your blueprint.
3. Change your life.

Some people opt for a fourth option, which is "do nothing." The reality is that blaming someone else is the option most victims choose, and so does your narcissist. It is easy, but there is no happiness there. The second choice narcissistic abuse victims make is to change their blueprint. After the narcissist has worn down a victim's self-esteem, the victim begins to believe this is the best their life will ever get. They believe the lies they tell themselves or the narcissist tells them, that there is no one else out there for them who is any better than their narcissistic partner. Many victims would rather believe a lie because *the truth requires change.* Change can be a scary thing, so instead they change their blueprint or the definition of their fairy-tale ending. Sadly, they overlook the option God has given them, which is number three—change your life.

My friend, you won't see your worth and you won't be able to move toward the destiny God has in store for you unless you change your perspective. You need to realize that you have all the control over how you feel and how your life is going to turn out. Your narcissist doesn't have that power unless you give it away.

So are you living your authentic self and blueprint? Let's find out. With each question, be honest about how it is now and not how you wish it would be.

To-Do List

1. What is your blueprint? You wrote about the attributes you wanted in a partner. Now write about what you want for your life in all the following areas: spiritual, health, friendships, career, financial, life mission, family. It is time to get real about what you want. If you want a large family, write it down. If you want a partner you can trust, write it down. Be specific. The more specific you are, the more boundaries you will be able to write later.

2. Now it is time to contrast that blueprint with the life you are actually living. Does your life match up with the blueprint in these areas? If not, what's missing? Make sure you write this down carefully, because you will review your list when you set your boundaries.

3. This is the time to explain the trauma that you have been through. I have waited until now to have you write it down because I want you to contrast it with all you have written in your blueprint. Let it all pour out of your soul. Leave nothing out. Express every emotion. This is your version of events. Include who, what, where, when, why, and how. List how long this has gone on and who the enablers are. List how you tried to resolve the situation. Include what worked for you and what failed. Don't forget to write how this relationship, or being targeted by a narcissist for supply, has changed you.

4. Write down five things this person did to you that took you further away from being a son or daughter of our Heavenly Father. This is a list you will want to keep somewhere so you can see it often.

5. Look at the list of five negative things. Sometimes we learn from our mistakes and wish we could go back and change the outcomes. If you had known then what you know now, what are five things you would have done to change what happened? Don't forget to use the attributes I listed about a son or daughter of our Heavenly Father to help determine how you would react.

6. What you have gone through is stressful and traumatic. However, it is up to us to get out of this state of victimhood. Could you have

prevented any of it? Be honest. If you could go back in time, what would you have done differently? How can you apply this today?

7. List the enablers of your narcissistic partner. Journal about the parts they played in your life. Have you distanced yourself from these people?

8. Sometimes, people besides your significant other have played a role in the problems in your relationship. They could be another man or woman your narcissist had an emotional or physical affair with. Do you blame them only and not the narcissist? If so, why? Do you truly believe that people outside the relationship have control over your partner's affection? Because I need to wake you up if you buy into this falsehood. **If they care for you, there is no other person.** They are a grown-up who made choices. The cold, hard truth is this: they made the choice to cheat. I know that hurts to hear, but I'm sharing it with you to wake you up to the reality of infidelity. Infidelity is not a minor relationship problem; it is grounds for divorce if there is no remorse and it continues. So take the time now to write what happened and how you feel about it. How has it changed you?

9. Who are the people who have supported you and helped you the most to this point? I want you to remember this list for later in this section. Do these people also have the attributes of sons or daughters of our Heavenly Father? I can't emphasize enough how important it is to have a healthy support system. If you have people in your life who just want to hear your sad story because they like drama and negativity, then you're sharing your pain with the wrong people. It is healthier to share your hurt with a trained psychologist or pastor. I recommend both, one to give spiritual advice and the other to give psychological advice. In addition, having a close friend is always comforting. However, take a close look at who you get your advice from. Sometimes loved ones project their fears onto their friends. For example, someone might say, "You don't want to get a divorce because you're older and you're not going to find someone else. All the best people have been snatched up. It is better to ignore what he does. Men make mistakes." That advice sounds awful, doesn't it? However, I have heard women recklessly giving this advice, which is untrue and based on their own insecurities. On the list you've made of friends, mark those who are healthy and truly helpful. Also, make a list of those you told your story to who shouldn't know your business. Sometimes when we are vulnerable, we share private stuff with people who are not close enough to truly care about us. Let that list

be a reminder to start instituting a boundary that states, "I will not tell my private problems to strangers or acquaintances." This will be your first boundary to put into action. More will follow.

10. Sometimes a person's games can overshadow all the great things that happened during your relationship with them. This one and only time, write about the five greatest things that happened while you were together. If you weren't together, list the five greatest things that came about because you knew this person. I want you to tell me five great things that made you want to become a better person. In a nutshell, what did they do to help you grow spiritually? The reality is that your dream might be focused on the superficial. That means you may be clinging to them because they are good looking, give you physical satisfaction, have money, or make you look good to others. These are not reasons in alignment with what God wants of you. They are benefits, but they won't take you in the direction of being a righteous son or daughter of our Heavenly Father. Also, don't list that they gave you children. The children are as much yours as theirs, and just about anyone can become pregnant or make someone else pregnant. Consider who has raised those children afterward.

11. Take your journal to your counselor and psychologist to discuss your blueprint and the abuse you experienced. Together you can get further help with writing goals to make your blueprint happen.

12. Write your life resume. What do you have to offer? What are your talents? What are great qualities in your personality? Isn't it time you raised yourself up? So go on and brag. Why wouldn't someone else want you?

13. If you are no longer in the relationship with the narcissist, I want you to ask yourself this question: how is this person going to affect my life in ten years? It may be surprisingly little! Time has a way of healing wounds. Therefore, I want you to make a list of all the things you want to accomplish in ten years. This should be your bucket list and get you excited about the future.

So far, you're doing marvelously! Now let's get to the even tougher questions. I want to know how you feel now because of all that you have experienced. Has your abuse crippled you or empowered you to change? Let's face it, in a relationship with a narcissist, things they do and say eat at us. Sometimes you can be stuck because of anger, unable to move forward by either letting go or setting boundaries.

Sometimes you can spend your entire relationship trying to convince them they are being abusive. This validation never comes your way, and trying to get it only keeps you stuck in a situation that is going nowhere. If this is the case, let's get real and write it down. It's time to deal with it once and for all. You need to move on by setting boundaries and goals that are not based on past hurts.

To-Do List

1. Look back at the list of five negative things this person did. What are you still angry about and unable to get over? For example, are you so fixated on your jealousy over your partner's affair that you've focused on getting back at the other man or woman? Sometimes you have to take a step back to see clearly. Instead of focusing on this other person, how about seeing the ungodly characteristics of your partner who betrayed your trust? That takes precedence over anyone outside your relationship. Fear, low self-esteem, and trauma have a way of making a person lose their perspective when it comes to what they truly need to be angry about.

2. Are any of your narcissist's character traits keeping you from moving forward or pushing you to take steps that move you further away from being Christlike? Have you been pulled down to your narcissist's level? Have their games and manipulation taken you in a direction that doesn't resemble the person Christ wants you to be?

3. I want you to write what you consider abuse to be. Define it.

4. After you have finished your definition, I want you to write down how you think Christ defines abuse. The Bible regards abuse as sin because we are called to love one another (John 13:34). The Bible strongly condemns those who take advantage of or abuse others (Exodus 22:22; Isaiah 10:2; 1 Thessalonians 4:6). Being in denial will never gain you happiness. In the next section, we will talk more about what our Heavenly Father wants for you.

Why Do Men or Women Stay with Abusers?

Why do people stay with toxic partners? There are many different reasons. It could be as simple as finances or low self-esteem. I don't know you. So you tell me. What is your reason? Even if you are no longer in the relationship, why did you stay so long?

Doesn't it make sense that you should have good reasons if you are going to stay in a relationship with someone who is mentally and spiritually ill? Yet many people who stay don't have a well-thought-out reason. In fact, when it comes to our fears and dreams of how things should be, a few of us hang on a lot longer than we should. I stuck around with my first narcissist because my life's blueprint consisted of living the fairy-tale ending. My drive to find Prince Charming was so intense that I wanted to put a square peg into a round hole. I was trying to make a doomed relationship work for the sake of a fake dream. Because that is what it would have been. Everyone would have seen us as a cute couple, but behind closed doors, it would have been something completely different. As sons and daughters of our Heavenly Father, it is time to stop making excuses for our narcissists' behavior and start having faith!

If you are not in the relationship anymore, don't gloss over this section. You need to know why you put up with as much as you did. So pay attention, because wrong reasons tend to repeat themselves in future relationships.

Maybe you want your relationship to work out. If that is the case, then don't let any of the following be your reason for staying. The only reason you should want to stay in the relationship is because your narcissist is willing to admit they are mentally ill and agrees to seek treatment. In addition, they should be attending a faith-based church with you and any marriage classes your church provides. This is the *only* reason to stay, because God wants you to have a spiritual relationship, not an abusive one.

Some of you might be saying, "Hey, wait a minute! Isn't staying for the kids' sake a good enough reason?" Listen, if the children are learning manipulative abuse from their father or mother, do you think you are doing them a spiritual service by staying? It is not what you leave to your children that matters; it is what you leave inside of them. God has entrusted their spiritual growth to you. They are observing the abuse you receive and learning to consider whether they can get away with the games the narcissist uses. Don't let unnecessary guilt make wrong choices for you. You are a son or daughter of our Heavenly Father, and you have spiritual giants to raise, not abuse victims or abusers.

I understand that narcissism is on a spectrum. Some don't have it as bad as others. However, when you get to the point in your abuse that you need to find a book for answers, it's likely you have already thought about leaving. Even if you are dead set on remaining with this person, take the time to look at the fears that keep people stuck in abusive relationships. You need to learn if you are in love or simply anxious.

Here are reasons narcissistic abuse victims don't leave:

- **Fear**

  You may be afraid of what will happen if you leave the relationship. Your fears can range from thinking you will never find anyone new to love to worrying how your narcissist will react. Here is the truth: many narcissists get downright mean if they feel abandoned. They might say that you will never get full custody of the kids or that no man or woman will want you. These are evil statements from a mentally and spiritually ill person. They may indeed try to make these threats come true. However, a strong son or daughter of our Heavenly Father doesn't shy away from evil; they stand up to it!

  Don't let fear cause you to stay and be abused. God is calling you to be a person of courage. The Bible is filled with examples of individuals called by God to perform acts of courage that they are reluctant to take on. For example, Gideon is the poster boy for fear. When God first commanded him to rescue the Israelites, he was hiding in a winepress to escape his enemies (Judges 6:11). Throughout his entire story, Gideon constantly tested God by asking him to perform signs. First, he had God consume an offering of food he presented to an angel (Judges 6:20–21). Next, he petitioned God to send morning dew only onto a piece of fleece he laid out (Judges 6:37–38). Finally, just for good measure, he laid out the fleece again but asked for the exact opposite to happen (Judges 6:39–40)!

  Gideon was afraid, but when he finally put his trust in God and obeyed, the Israelites were freed from seven years of oppression. There will always be moments in life when we are worried about giving ourselves over to God, but the truth is that we can trust him with our tomorrows. Obedience does not require us to be fearless; it only asks that we have the faith to follow God in difficult times.

- **Belief That Abuse Is Normal**

  If you don't know what a healthy relationship looks like, you may not recognize that your relationship is unhealthy. This can happen to a person who has too many toxic connections with people (perhaps from growing up in an environment where abuse was common or through previous bad relationships with family, friends, and exes). However, if you are reading the pages of this book, then you know your relationship is or was not normal. Therefore, there is no excuse for how you were treated.

  Don't buy into the belief that all relationships go through rough times like yours. They don't! Good relationships are not something only lucky people have. I am married to an emotionally healthy man. He would never play the manipulative mind games depicted in this book. And guess what? I have met more godly men like him who are available and looking for a godly woman. I have also met godly women looking for a godly man. They are out there if you are willing to look for them. Maybe you have limited your perception based on your friends' or your own bad relationships or watched too many reality TV shows. It is time to distance yourself from the warped mentality that games are to be expected and disloyalty is normal. If you find yourself rationalizing the abusive games a narcissist plays, then you need deep therapy along with the narcissist.

- **Embarrassment**

  Maybe it is hard to admit that you have been abused. Maybe you feel you have done something wrong by becoming involved with an abusive partner. Maybe you worry that your friends and family will judge you. First off, you did nothing wrong. Narcissists are like con artists. They portray a picture of perfection to the masses, but behind it is a very different kind of person. What you also need to keep in mind is that you don't want to be anything like the narcissist. Therefore, you have to stop caring about what other people think.

  It is not weakness to leave a bad relationship; actually, it takes courage. If someone asks why you left the relationship, don't be weak and say the relationship didn't work out. Be strong! Tell people that you have boundaries and trust God is going to provide you with someone who is worthy and will respect you. Isn't that the truth? If you must care about what people think, then let them see your faith, not your embarrassment. That earns respect and admiration! The people who love you will be there to help you through it. The people who want to gossip about you are the ones who have no life and low self-esteem; they love to hear your problems so they don't feel as bad about theirs. Don't let this be a reason for staying.

- **Low Self-Esteem**

  Some of Satan's most powerful weapons are psychological. Fear is one. Doubt is another. Anger, hostility, worry, and, of course, guilt top the list. *However, the most deadly weapon in Satan's arsenal is low self-esteem, since it has such a pervasive effect on every aspect of our lives.*

  If you don't love yourself, how are you going to love another? How are you going to raise confident children? How are you going to teach people how to treat you?

  Would you want your son or daughter to go through what you are going through now? How would you counsel him or her? Why is it that people often live by double standards? Trust your Heavenly Father and what he thinks of you. The real you is the person God sees, not the image you project (Proverbs 23:7). The truth is that you will never rise above the image of yourself in your own mind. In developing a healthy self-image, we must base it on what God's word says about us.

  You have a birthright as a son or daughter of our Heavenly Father. This means you are to have healthy self-esteem.

  Consider the following facts:

  » God created you as a unique person in his image. His creation gives you worth (Genesis 1:27).

  » God loves you. God is a loving Heavenly Father. His love gives you a sense of belonging (Jeremiah 31:3).

  » God planned for you. God wants your heart to be his throne. His plan gives you significance (Psalm 139:16).

  » God gave you natural abilities and spiritual gifts. His gifts give you competence (Ephesians 4:7).

  » God's son, Jesus, died on the cross for your sins. His death makes you acceptable (2 Corinthians 5:16–18).

  If you are using low self-esteem as an excuse for your wrong choices, stop doing it! Because if you truly feel that this is the best you're going to find in a mate, then you are right. What you think is what you reap. Yet narcissism is not God's best for you.

- **Immature Love**

  Maybe you are staying in the relationship because you hope the abuser will change. This was my reason. If a person you love tells you they'll change, you want to believe them, right? The problem with this thinking is that words are meaningless without action. Moreover, as you might already know, narcissists are good at putting you back through the idolization phase to keep you hooked, but eventually the devaluation phase will come. It always does! Most narcissists are not invested in changing in the relationship because they don't see what they do as a problem.

  I had a friend in a narcissistic relationship. You can't imagine how frustrating it was to hear "He loves me" as the justification for her bad choice in a man. Her definition of love was way off the mark. He was constantly jealous and untrusting of her. He even called and asked to speak to me on the phone because he didn't believe she was out with a friend. When he got mad at her, he would call her names. Sadly, she was caught up in the dream of what she wanted him to be rather than the reality of what he was. She cared about this dream so much that she allowed her abuse to continue. I finally was able to get her to admit the fear behind letting go of her fantasy. She told me there were no good men left for someone her age. This is what was left over, so she couldn't be choosy. In her mind, all she had to do was to wait it out. Maybe something she said would eventually sink in with him and he would treat her better. She was wrong and continued to be abused.

  This dream is so strong in people that they will deny, ignore, rationalize, justify, and ultimately go back to that most pathetic defensive position: "But I love them." What is that supposed to mean, anyway? You love being manipulated, lied to, and disrespected? The reality is that most narcissists don't change, because they don't feel like they have a problem, and very few even see themselves as narcissistic. After they call a psychiatrist and go to therapy for months, then you might have something worth hanging on to. However, in the meantime, if you are using "I love them" as an excuse without a real definition of what healthy love is, then you will need to seek therapy yourself.

Below is a list describing healthy love versus toxic love:

1. In healthy love, development of self is your first priority. In toxic love, obsession becomes your first priority.

2. In healthy love, you have room to grow together and individually. In toxic love, you want security and find comfort in sameness; intensity is seen as proof of love, when it might be fear, insecurity, or loneliness that you feel, not love.

3. In healthy love, you have separate interests and maintain other meaningful relationships. In toxic love, you have total involvement in maintaining the relationship, your social life is limited, and you neglect old friends and interests.

4. In healthy love, you encourage each other's mental and spiritual health. You also feel secure in your own worth. In toxic love, you are preoccupied with your partner's behavior and fear your partner changing.

5. In healthy love, you have trust. In toxic love, narcissists are jealous and possessive, fear competition, and protect supply.

6. In healthy love, you compromise, negotiate, or take turns at leading. You solve problems together. In toxic love, there are power plays for control, blame games, and passive or aggressive manipulation.

7. In healthy love, you embrace each other's individuality. In toxic love, you have a dream of who your partner should be and try to change them to fit your own image.

8. In healthy love, your relationship deals with all aspects of reality. In toxic love, the relationship is based on delusion and the avoidance of what is unpleasant.

9. In healthy love, both partners' emotional states are not dependent on each other's moods. In toxic love, you expect your partner to fix and rescue you.

10. In healthy love, you have a healthy concern about your partner while being able to let go. In toxic love, you are obsessed with their problems and feelings, and your self-esteem can plummet because of their disapproval.

- **Cultural/Religious Reasons**

    Maybe you are staying because of religious reasons. Religious grounds for divorce vary in different cultures, and only you can make the best decision for you. However, I have some points I need you to consider. Let's look carefully at what the Bible says about divorce. The Bible only explicitly allows divorce for two reasons. Jesus proceeded to state one exception in which case divorce is permissible: sexual immorality on the part of one's spouse, that is, in context, adultery (Matthew 19:9). In such a case, however, divorce is not mandated or even encouraged—forgiveness and reconciliation should be extended and pursued if at all possible. But divorce is allowed, especially in cases where the sinning spouse persists in an adulterous relationship.

    Paul adds a second exception, in instances where an unbelieving spouse abandons the marriage. This would typically be the case when one of the two partners is converted to Christ at some point after marrying and the other person refuses to continue in the marriage (see 1 Corinthians 7).

    However, I see other areas not mentioned in scripture. For example, if a husband is beating his wife, that would certainly seem to violate the 'one flesh' union. If he were beating himself, we'd recommend psychiatric help; if he is beating his wife, who is supposed to be one flesh with him, he is certainly not treating her as one flesh.

    Now, I don't want to let that be an excuse for people to opt out of their marriages—someone saying, she abuses me (because she doesn't laugh at my jokes) or he abuses me (because we had an argument). But there does come a point where discretion is the better part of valor. Some people are too ready to grasp for that point; others wait much longer than they should. Jesus told those persecuted for his name to flee from one city to another to escape persecution (Matthew 10:23), and sometimes the apostles did so (Acts 14:5–6). It is heartless to make someone remain in an abusive situation.

    The Bible displays a concern for justice and is concerned with protecting the vulnerable, it also teaches that believers can glorify God by bearing up under unjust suffering. This calls for wisdom and balance: Certainly we should do everything we can to protect victims of abuse while at the same time respecting the marriage bond and not dissolving it lightly.

Christian counselor and author of *The Emotionally Destructive Marriage*, Leslie Vernick, believes that "chronic hardness of heart" is grounds for divorce when there is a serious sin issue, a serious breach of the marital bond, a serious trust breakdown . . . and there is no repentance or willingness to look at that and how that's affected the marital bond and the bond of trust. This would seem to fit the criteria for a narcissistic relationship. While some biblical interpreters may not agree with her conclusions, Vernick draws upon Moses's allowance for divorce cited by Jesus in Matthew 19:8 to support this viewpoint.

In her work with people who are experiencing such situations, Vernick first counsels a wake-up call conversation with their spouse, followed by separation if the husband or wife fails to turn from their sin. A separation of this sort, undertaken with the support of wise counsel, clarifies the destructive consequences of sinful habits and could have the potential to lead to eventual healing and restoration.

Vernick emphasizes that there is a difference between a difficult or disappointing marriage and a destructive marriage. She points out that we must not seek divorce simply because we are not getting everything we want out of our marriages: if we have such high expectations, no one can live up to that.

There are varying viewpoints on divorce by several scholars and church leaders. As sons and daughters of our Heavenly Father, our role is clear: we are to spiritually grow and help others. However, if that isn't happening because of our partner's emotional abuse, then we are to seek out all options before divorcing or breaking up. I encourage you to seek counsel from your pastor about programs you can participate in to improve your relationship. I already spoke of the Re|engage program. Seek out other programs in your community. You might even consider buying relationship DVDs to watch as a couple. I recommend Tony Robbins's excellent *Ultimate Relationship Program*. You can get all his motivational programs at tonyrobbins.com and sometimes find his DVDs on eBay. The point is to leave no stone unturned. When you leave a relationship, you should have tried *everything* so there are no regrets later. This book is your everything. Do the things in it as your last attempt before deciding to break up.

If you have separated but still feel there are things you could have done, then consider talking with a counselor before reestablishing your relationship. Make sure you are emotionally prepared to set boundaries and are making the right decision to reconnect with your partner.

- **Pregnancy/Parenting**
  Maybe you feel pressure to raise your children with both parents together, even if that means staying in an abusive relationship. The flaw in this plan is thinking the narcissist's actions don't affect the children. Go back and read about the children of narcissists in the first section of this book. They are affected! By staying in a relationship with a narcissist, you become the psychologist for your kids. They could grow up to have low self-esteem or solve problems like the narcissist, with manipulation or games.

  Yes, one home is easier for children; however, you are responsible for raising them to have attributes that reflect those embraced by sons and daughters of our Heavenly Father. They need good role models. They will pick up on how you are treated. The question is this: do you want to teach your children that you are weak and should take abuse in life, or do you want to teach them what a warrior for Christ really looks like?

- **Lack of Money and Nowhere to Go**
  You might not be the breadwinner. Maybe you stayed home with the children or you live in a part of the world where apartments are expensive to rent. Whatever the situation, don't let this be your reason for staying. Find a way to live in dignity. Don't become so proud that you stay because you like the expensive things your narcissist buys for you. Sons and daughters of God don't sell themselves cheap! Nice houses and fancy cars are material reasons to stay. God wants you to rise above the temptation of money. Jesus said, "No man can serve two masters: for either he will hate the one, and love the other, or else he will hold the one, and despise the other. Ye cannot serve God and mammon" (Matthew 6:24). "Therefore take no thought, saying, What shall we eat? Or, What shall we drink? Or, Wherewithal shall we be clothed? For after all these things do the Gentiles seek for your heavenly Father knoweth that you have need of all of these things. But seek ye first the kingdom of God, and his righteousness; and all these things shall be added unto you" (Matthew 6:31–33).

  I believe many people stay in abusive relationships because the change in lifestyle becomes more overwhelming than they can handle. A woman might think, "I have to live in a cramped apartment with my kids, and then what? What if I don't meet someone else? What if I never have that cute home I can decorate and raise a family in? What if I can't get a better job to support myself? What if I can never afford nice things?" These are real fears when you divorce in a place with a high cost of living.

On a narcissistic abuse board online, I met a woman named Carla who came up against this very problem. She didn't have family or a network of friends to let her live with them. She was on her own. She was an office manager at an air conditioning company and made a modest salary. It was barely enough to afford an apartment's rent in California and still have money left over. She put herself on a low-income subsidized apartment waiting list. It took one year before an apartment became available. She stayed with her abuser and waited out her time. She said it was hard to stay and pretend she cared when in reality she was biding her time until she could get her finances together. When the apartment became available, the rent was $800 instead of the $1,200 monthly starting price for a one-bedroom apartment. A stipend made it easier to pay for utilities, and she had a little bit left over to take the kids to the movies on occasion. She then applied for scholarships and Pell Grants so she could go back to school at night and get a better job. She found a way out of her situation, doing what was needed rather than giving up on her future happiness.

Today, Carla says she is glad she left. She had faith that God would provide, and he did. Three years after she left her narcissistic relationship, she met a man who was everything her ex was not. He was godly and showed her respect. She married him. She told me times were tough after she left her narcissist. She recalls the difficulty of being in that one-bedroom apartment and going to school. There were moments when she wanted to run back to the abusive man she left. She had periods when she felt lonely and negative about her future. However, during those times, she doubled her efforts to break free of the rut she was in by being active in her church and attending singles activities to make new friends. Eventually, through trusting God instead of following her fears, she got back that cute home and the material things she had once enjoyed. Her faith in God is what pulled her from the abuse and out of dwelling on the past.

The point of sharing this is to let you know you can change your future. It happened for Carla. It can happen for you! You don't have to live in a disappointing marriage or relationship. God loves you regardless of your choice to stay or leave. He won't abandon you during the storm. He is preparing all the right things to bring you to victory and happiness in your life if you trust in him.

- **Stupid Forgiveness**
Sometimes victims stay because they believe everyone deserves a second chance. Yes, God tells us to forgive, but he doesn't tell us to stay and take an abuser's put-downs. Sometimes, we cripple people who are capable of walking because we choose to carry them. Often, we love too much and don't allow people to grow through consequences. God doesn't tell us to let evil continue. Please don't take the scriptures and twist them around to cover up the real truth, which is that you are afraid to leave. Many anxious victims do this so they don't have to deal with change—when change is the one thing that would set them free.

In addition, you shouldn't let your narcissist use the scriptures to manipulate you. Narcissists don't have a problem with saying, "You have been on my case for a long time. When are you going to forgive me like it says in the Bible?" Yet this comes from a person who hasn't shown real love for Christ by living righteously in a long time. It is manipulation at its best. Furthermore, don't get to the point that you say, "Well, he cheated on me, lies to me, plays games, and doesn't want to change, but I will forgive him by staying because I am not perfect either." Forgive others, but *don't put up with their sin.* If your narcissistic partner will not rise to a level of decency and respect toward you, then they have hardened their heart and turned away from God. This would meet the criteria for divorce as described by Leslie Vernick before. Remember, if you have to convince a narcissist to stay, then they have already left.

- **Trauma Bonding**
This is when you stay because you are holding on to the elusive promise or hope that things will be different. You may be addicted to the hope of the idolization phase returning and are in denial about the three phases the narcissist cycles you through: idolization, devaluation, and discard. You have become willing to

tolerate anything for temporary payoffs such as more attention, kind words, and moments of happiness.

I have spoken about the most common reasons why people stay in abusive relationships. Now it is your turn to be brutally honest with yourself. Again, if you are no longer in the relationship, you can still take this time to understand why you stayed as long as you did. If you are still in the relationship, now is the time to look seriously at why you're staying.

To-Do List

1. What are or were your reasons for staying in the relationship? If you cite superficial things you like about your narcissist, be prepared to write all the spiritual things you like as well. I want you to be mindful of what you love in a person. Maybe your priorities are out of sync.

2. If you felt your reasons for staying were legitimate, write down why, and be explicit. Was your partner repentant? Are or were they going to counseling and putting into practice what they learned?

3. If you keep using one of the excuses to stay in your relationship because you think it is a valid reason, I want you to make an appointment to see a counselor or psychologist. If you are actually doing the exercises in the to-do lists, then you should be seeking additional help beyond this book. Present your reason to a trained professional and work with them to heal yourself. You shouldn't excuse bad behavior. If you feel stuck, you might be complicating things because of fear. You need someone to listen to you and help you through this. If counseling is too expensive, visit a pastor at your church. The point is to seek help from someone who can spend more time with you than what this book provides.

4. If you are planning to stay in the relationship, then again my advice is this: the narcissist should be required to see a trained psychologist and a psychiatrist for medication that might lessen the narcissist's symptoms, plus cognitive therapy. You are to attend marriage or couples counseling, whether or not you are married. You should also attend church together regularly and all marriage or Bible classes you think would help your partner get back on track spiritually.

5. If you suffer from low self-esteem, then write down five things you can do this week to raise it. The first thing on your list should be to search for books on the topic or use Google to find videos and

websites. No excuses. Do the work instead of making low self-esteem an excuse for the rest of your life. Your self-esteem problem can be fixed. It is not incurable, but it requires your effort to heal. In addition, I want you to look to the source of your low self-esteem and write about that. Is your narcissistic partner making it worse?

6. If finances are your reason to stay, then this week I want you to formulate a plan. Look into loans, Pell Grants, scholarships, subsidized living, cheaper apartments, roommates, and new jobs. Don't just say there isn't any money to move out on your own. Talk to your pastor and tell him your situation. Maybe he knows of a church member who could help you. Exhaust your resources. If you don't have resources, then start making them. Join groups on Meetup.com so you can get to know people. Find a different church. Look at government programs. There is no reason you can't leave a situation.

7. If you're struggling with leaving a marriage because of religious reasons, then research, starting with the points I cited before, and then talk to your pastor or bishop. Be smart and ask more than one source. You will be surprised by how many people disagree. In the end, it is your decision. God asks that you live spiritually and raise your kids spiritually. If you have become less like a daughter or son of our Heavenly Father by being with this person and they don't plan to change, then you know what you must do—leave.

8. Define what real love is. After that, I want you to write why you love or loved your narcissistic partner. Leave out time spent together or kids. I want to know why you would choose to stay with them out of all the people in the world you could be with. What makes them so special? Specifically, what Christlike qualities make them special? Now list all your partner's non-Christlike qualities. Which of these things have made you a worse person? (For example, have you started cursing because they curse? Did you stop attending church because they don't go? Are you irritable when you never used to be?)

9. If you think you are experiencing trauma bonding, I want you to write down what you are hoping for when your narcissist puts you through the idolization phase. Instead of saying that you hope they will change, write specific things they must do to show they are committed to changing. Now review this list and write down things they could do that would cause you to leave the relationship (for example, cheating on you or verbally abusing you in front of the children).

Wasn't This Relationship Ordained by God?

When my narcissist hacker's wife caught on that her husband was being disloyal, she filed for a separation. Shortly after that, he worked his narcissistic magic and manipulated her into believing he was worth keeping, so they reconciled. What followed was a slew of quotes posted on her social media page that suggested she credited God for them staying together. One came from Isaiah 14:27: "All the forces of darkness cannot stop what God has ordained." Sometimes Bible verses are taken out of context. There is nothing in the Bible that states soul mates exist. Other similar soul mate–related quotes followed on her site. At the time, I tried to figure out the mindset of the women in my narcissist's life. Why would either of these women think that this disloyal man was their soul mate, especially one that was abusive to them and was violating the law by hacking my computer and cell phone? What I gleaned from the pathetic quotes that they posted openly on their social media sites was that, like most narcissistic abuse victims, they had bought into the dream. And, of course, when you have a dream about your narcissist, then the belief in soul mates is sure to follow. The truth was his wife was not his soul mate; she was the next woman he found to abuse. Sadly, she wasn't much different from other people who want to believe in destiny. Who doesn't want to believe that God had a hand in them meeting their loved one? There is nothing wrong with believing that God is leading your footsteps. However, it is quite a different thing to believe that he created only one person for us out of seven billion people on this earth, and out of those people he intended us to be with someone who was abusive.

This issue has been heavily debated within the Christian community, often in the context of differentiating between God's perfect and permissive will. Sadly, most Christian believers seeking God's will in their relationships begin with the wrong question, focusing on the superficial similarities they have with another person rather than the spiritual qualities that will help them grow as a person. If each of us had a predestined soul mate, would the Bible feature so many passages that help us to evaluate potential romantic partners? No—scripture is clear, telling us we must make wise choices and use our discernment to find a mate who is both godly and suits us as a unique individual.

We can't believe in destiny, as it would be contradictory with the principle of free will. If we make our choices, then we can't be bound to a determined future. God knows what comes in the future because God isn't bound to time as we are. In short, destiny is a result of cause and effect, which is a result of time. Maybe God had a hand in you meeting, but to say you were given a soul mate would be buying into superstition.

Eventually, I came to understand the notion of soul mates as adolescent fantasy: a narrow vision of the world wherein God is some mysterious matchmaker. It still is a commonly held belief that God has one—and only one—person in mind for each us; all we have to do is find each other. It is nonsense that a special someone who was made just for you is the reason you keep going on bad dates, keep second-guessing your choices, and keep yourself in a constant state of hopefulness.

It is a commonly held belief, too, that each bad date is one date closer to The One; it's just a matter of time. In the meantime, the idea of The One demeans everyone else who steps into the picture. It's the same reason why I dislike the term "best friend": there can only be one best friend and every other friend can only be second best. Why create hierarchies?

Another flaw in the concept of soul mates is the belief that we are missing our other half. As part of people created in God's image, our souls are perfect and whole unto themselves. They do not need to be mated to any other person's soul to feel complete.

So if the idea of a soul mate isn't scriptural, where does it come from? The Greek philosopher Plato is the one who popularized the idea when he posited a story in which humans originally contained the qualities of both genders within one body, but were later split into male and female by the gods—split in both body and soul. Each human would then long for the "other half" of his or her soul. He went on to say that when an individual finds their other half, the two enter into perfect understanding with one another and are made complete in utter joy.

Rather than following the themes of Plato's dramatic story of soul mates, follow the word of God and dedicate yourself to the mate you've *carefully* chosen. Notice how I emphasize the word *carefully*? It should be a decision of wisdom rather than emotion only. Let their spiritual qualities be the things that bind you to them, not the superficial. The Bible warns us against thinking of love as a mere emotion—it's far more than that. It's a willingness to work for the good of another, to work with their faults and to be selfless, loving our mates as Christ loved the church. This should be something one would expect in a soul mate, if you believe in that concept. However, with narcissists, it doesn't fit, because their bad behavior doesn't bring out the best in us or make us more spiritual people.

I met Mark on one of the narcissistic abuse recovery boards I was frequenting online. He and his wife have been married for two years, and he said they are well suited: they can spend hours talking and laughing, are attracted to each other, get along with each other's friends and families, and agree on faith, politics, and financial matters. But he told me that the "glow" had worn off. She had taken him from the idolization phase into the devaluation phase in the second year of their marriage. She had become bored and begun to belittle him, following with the silent treatment when he complained. He gave and gave in the relationship and she did little in return.

"She was supposed to be my best friend. She was the one who said she could never hurt me, but she has. I thought she was my soul mate, my everything, but I made a mistake," he said bitterly.

"That's why you have friends and family too," I said. "She should be your wife, not your everything. She should also be someone who is helping you grow as a person spiritually, not putting you down and distancing herself."

The constant search for our missing half seems to produce nothing more than disappointment, disillusionment, and frustration. We should not be trying to fill our hearts by acquiring another person, but through living God's commandments and focusing on our life purpose. During that process, if we meet someone who can make it even better for us, then maybe God had a hand in it. The truth is that the Bible does not contain any passages that indicate that "The One"—your soul mate—exists at all, and although God may have specifically created Adam and Eve for one another, we live in a fallen world in which no individual, or relationship, is perfect.

So if we let go of the soul mate notion, are we simply settling for second best and making do in life and in love? No! Look for someone you admire, someone who values you, someone you respect, someone who treats you lovingly, someone who appreciates family life and lasting commitment, someone who shares similar life goals, someone who communicates well, especially in conflict, and, of course, someone you feel an attraction to and spark with. Look for someone according to the scriptural guidelines we have discussed.

That there is only one right person for you is a nice idea if you think you have or will meet that person. But what happens when years pass and "The One" still hasn't crossed your path? That view could cause anxiety, fear, and doubt. I believe God cares about each of us with respect to finding a suitable mate, and though his design involves just one person at a time, it could involve more than one in a lifetime if one outlives their spouse or divorces. The idea of there being one and only one person seems like an impossible and unfair game for God to create for us to play. There are seven billion people in the world. It is reasonable to believe there are several people who could be a perfect match for you.

If you choose to believe in soul mates, then I suggest considering this bond as something that doesn't come to you at the beginning of a relationship, but rather something that is developed over time as you discover who that person truly is. It is a process of growing together spiritually.

In conclusion, the term *soul mate*, when stripped of all its mystical prose, is just another way of saying "this person fulfills me." Some people, however, would swear on their mother's life they were supposed to be together. Who am I to take that away from them? Yet when it comes to the cruelty of narcissists, ask yourself, do you have to constantly prove your value to them? Wouldn't a soul mate know that already? Is your other half supposed to be an abuser? Let's hope your answer to that last question is "no."

What Happens to Victims after Prolonged Exposure to Narcissists?

If you decide to stay in your relationship, then we need to talk about all the things that can affect the health of a narcissistic abuse victim. One of those things is PTSD, which results from persistent psychological trauma within an environment in which the victim believes there's no possibility of escape. You might envision a soldier having PTSD when they return from war. However, it isn't a diagnosis only for military personnel or sexual abuse survivors. It most definitely can develop if you stay in a narcissistic relationship for too long. Now, I know what you're thinking. If you tell someone that you are suffering from PTSD as a result of a narcissistic relationship, they might roll their eyes and think you are being overdramatic. This is because they equate trauma to something physical. They expect to see you looking disheveled and covered in bruises from your narcissistic partner. However, we both know that is inaccurate. Psychological abuse isn't something you can see. Moreover, it is the most damaging of injuries, because it takes much longer to heal.

Narcissists are sinister and practiced at playing mind games. They control and dominate their victims by gaslighting, pathological lying, undermining, downplaying, and many other emotionally destructive methods. You shouldn't need to prove physical abuse to skeptical people to get empathy. Proving that you have been emotionally abused results in more emotional abuse from other people. Sadly, we live in a society where appearances are everything. People put more weight on how things look on the outside than on how they really are. Therefore, don't try to tough it out without seeking help because a few people diminished your symptoms out of their ignorance about narcissism. What narcissists do to victims is traumatic.

Let's look at the symptoms of this disorder. According to the National Center for PTSD, a division of the U.S. Department of Veterans Affairs, these are things you might be experiencing:

- **Reexperiencing aggressive acts and comments made by the narcissist.** You might find yourself thinking about these events repeatedly. You may have nightmares. You may feel like you are reliving the event in your mind. This is called a flashback. You may see, hear, or smell something that causes you to relive the event. This is called a trigger.
- **Hypersensitivity.** This may manifest as trouble sleeping, being frightened easily, difficulty concentrating, and outbursts of anger. Small criticism can seem large to someone who has been abused. You might distance yourself from people who are critical because of stress.
- **Feeling keyed up.** You might be in constant fight-or-flight mode, preparing yourself for the next drama or fight your narcissist is

going to start. You might have chronic anxiety about them leaving or being disloyal. This in turn leads to physical and emotional fatigue, which later manifests as illness in the body. You might develop adrenal fatigue and have hair or weight loss.

- **Negative changes in beliefs and feelings**. The way you think about yourself and others changes because of trauma. You may not have positive or loving feelings toward other people and may stay away from relationships. You may forget about parts of traumatic events or not be able to talk about them. You may think that the world is completely dishonest and no one can be trusted.
- **Repetition compulsion**. This involves reenacting traumatic events in an attempt to gain closure. This is why we often reabuse ourselves after our abuser has left. You might be looking up quotes or Pinterest pins about narcissistic abuse too often. You might spend too much time on narcissistic abuse recovery forums or Facebook pages to get validation. Alternatively, you might be stalking the narcissist online to see if they are with a new partner. In essence, you're trying to gain closure from a mentally and spiritually ill individual, and it isn't going to happen this way.

If left untreated, disorders such as PTSD, depression, and anxiety can lead to other symptoms and conditions that affect all areas of life:

- Inability to handle stress
- Eating disorders
- Drug and alcohol addictions
- Weight gain or loss
- Damaged relationships
- A negative outlook on life
- Depression
- Specific anxiety disorders such as panic attacks and phobias (for example, agoraphobia among victims who were stalked or hacked)
- Crippled self-esteem
- Loss of career and loss of desire to be productive
- Diseases such as cancer or autoimmune disease, with victims of abuse having higher incidences of certain types of cancer
- Suicide

One type of treatment doesn't fit all for those who suffer from PTSD, but there are various ways to get through the disorder and get rid of the symptoms that plague and disrupt your life. These include the following:

- **Traditional Talk Therapy.** Talking it through is sometimes the best way to treat the disorder. Counselors and psychologists who are specially trained in PTSD treatment can usually help someone find closure for the traumatic incident that has caused such a lifestyle change.
- **Cognitive Therapy.** This type of therapy helps a PTSD patient realize that the events that took place weren't their fault and helps alleviate feelings of guilt.
- **Coaching.** When the person suffering from PTSD is otherwise mentally stable, a good life coach can help them learn new coping techniques for dealing with the symptoms. This can work together with or independently from traditional therapies.

Don't despair if your psychologist or counselor didn't give you this diagnosis but you think you have PTSD. If you are being treated with medication for depression or anxiety, you are getting the same medications they give to people with PTSD: antidepressants (selective serotonin reuptake inhibitors) and antianxiety medications (benzodiazepines).

In addition to these medications, I would also ask your doctor to do lab work to rule out adrenal fatigue. James L. Wilson, PhD, the author of *Adrenal Fatigue,* writes that symptoms include the following:

- Trouble getting out of bed
- Chronic tiredness, even after you wake up in the morning
- Trouble thinking clearly or finishing your tasks

Prolonged stress and lack of sleep can contribute to adrenal fatigue. If you are feeling drained of energy, it wouldn't hurt to have your doctor check your thyroid, B_{12}, and iron levels to see if this is the culprit. If you have a serious lack of energy and your lab results are coming back normal, I would push your doctor for a consultation with an endocrine specialist to rule out hypothyroidism, which can result from stress.

The lesson is to push for answers about your health. If you are still in the relationship with your narcissist, then getting your health under control is important! Don't wait several months, because by then it will be too late. Get the lab results now! Whether you are still with your narcissist or not, you will need a strategy to combat stress. This will involve a healthy eating plan and exercise, along with vitamin supplementation. Below is your homework.

To-Do List

1. The first thing you should do is find a therapist who will help you deal with someone who has narcissism. Then begin working on your emotional health.

2. Write down any symptoms you might be experiencing because of prolonged exposure to narcissistic abuse. Make an appointment with your doctor to get lab work done. Ask them to check your blood pressure, iron, vitamin D_3, magnesium, sodium, cholesterol, potassium, and thyroid levels. In addition, do a routine physical exam.

3. Get a gym membership or start a daily walking routine. Whatever you choose to do, make sure it involves moving. I try to get in ten thousand steps a day to keep in shape. The endorphins from exercise will combat the stress you are feeling. They will help lower blood pressure and cortisol levels, plus elevate your mood. This is vital to your recovery.

4. To combat stress, you will need to eat a healthy diet. You want food with healing properties, such as fruit and vegetables. I recommend ordering author Tony Robbins's weight-loss program *The Body You Deserve*. That program, along with Weight Watchers, helped me reach my desired weight.

5. Put a reward system in place. For example, if you walk five days a week for a month, treat yourself to a forty-five-minute back massage. Whatever you do, make the reward something easily attainable. You need to pamper yourself. Giving yourself a reward makes it easier for you to stay on track with your health goals. It will also help you combat the stress associated with narcissistic abuse.

6. Don't be afraid to ask for antidepressants. It's almost impossible to live with a narcissist without developing depression. If you don't want to take antidepressants, then you might consider natural alternatives such as herbal supplements (fish oil, B-complex vitamins, 5-HTP, theanine, vitamin D, St. John's wort, SAMe, zinc, folate).

7. Meditate! It is crucial in your recovery that you have breaks from the pain by refocusing your thoughts. Make meditation a part of your recovery. There are many meditation cell-phone apps on the market. I use the Android app Calm. Every evening, or when I feel particularly

stressed during the day, I do one of the breathing exercises in the app. This does wonders for clearing my head. I also bought a Fitbit Charge 2 and do the breathing exercises that come along with it.

Where Is God in All This Misery?

Helen Keller said, "Self-pity is our worst enemy, and if we yield to it we can never do anything wise in this world." Grieve, yes, but stay there, no! Sometimes we yield to self-pity; we lose faith in God. So where is God in all of this abuse? He is walking beside you. God sometimes allows things to get dark in our lives to help us grow and teach us about himself. Some things we accomplish in darkness cannot happen in any other setting. If you feel like you're in a dark place, know that God has not abandoned you. You are not wandering aimlessly in the dark. He sees the path you are on. "For the ways of man are before the eyes of the Lord, and he pondereth all his goings." (Proverbs 5:21).

After God performed many miracles to deliver the Israelites from their enemies, they continued to doubt him. God took them to the wilderness and tested them. He let them go without water for several days. God knew they needed water and could have given it to them, but they didn't ask for it. They didn't pray. Instead, they complained. Therefore, they failed his test. He wanted them to rely on him for everything. When Moses cried out to God on their behalf, God said if his people would listen to him, he would meet their every need. Finally, they listened and obeyed. They got the water they needed. And they were content for a while, until another crisis happened—of course, they ran out of food and God once again had to remind them to trust him and pray.

Does this sound familiar? Can you think of anyone who wants to get to the promised land but doesn't do what is necessary for the trip? I have talked about the importance of being a strong son or daughter of our Heavenly Father. Would it make sense if you run into enemy territory and get shot at? If you know the narcissist's evil ways and choose to engage in their games, you are going to get hurt. Common sense, right? Therefore, if we open ourselves up to the consequences of not living God's way, we shouldn't be surprised if the enemy abuses us. We've left the protection of God by not instilling boundaries, by not standing up for ourselves, by allowing the narcissist's bad behavior to continue unchecked, and by not leaving if our spirituality is dwindling.

I believe we are all like the Israelites. We each walk through our own wilderness, trying to get to that happy place—the promised land. The wilderness is where we are forced to leave behind the familiar, the comfortable, the old us, and the bag of tricks and coping strategies that worked for us before. The wilderness is where God takes us to get Egypt out of our hearts. Your narcissistic abuse was Egypt and your narcissist the Pharaoh. God wants to get the hunger for what is comfortable and easy out of your heart. It isn't because he wants us to suffer. It's that he doesn't want us to depend on the comfortable. He wants us to depend on him.

When you are in the dark, there are many reasons why God doesn't show the plan he has for you. If he did tell us the future, it wouldn't be much of a walk of faith. Another reason is that the full magnitude of what lies ahead can be too much for us to comprehend. I think too many of us get in God's way by thinking too small about the future or not thinking there will be one at all. On the other hand, some of us remain stuck by becoming too fearful at God's silence.

God didn't send the Israelites to the promised land directly. He led them on an indirect route through the wilderness because he needed it to take longer. If they had gone another way, they would have ended up in a war with the Philistines, and many would have gone back to Egypt because it would have been better than the possibility of dying. How many times have you said to yourself, "Maybe it is better to stay and put up with my narcissist's behavior because the fear of the unknown makes me uncomfortable"? That is not what God wants of us. He wants us to continue living in dignity and remain faithful.

Bad things happen to good people. However, your job as a son or daughter of our Heavenly Father is to not set up camp in your pain and turn bitter. God wants you to move out of victimization to become a thriving human being who has overcome the worst, learned from it, and looks forward to the blessings he brings. This can become hard to do if you have a negative attitude and have lost hope, but you can gain strength from many people in the Bible. Ruth and Naomi are perfect examples of women who went through stressful trials but remained faithful. And guess what? They more than thrived; they went on to have great blessings because of their obedience and faithfulness. These are the things you can learn from both of them:

- **Don't Let the Past Hold You Back**

  Ruth's home nation is Moab, a place and people that the Israelites looked down on. At the beginning of the book, she has lost her husband. She also lost her husband before having a child, and some believe she may be barren. She decides to live with Naomi, her mother-in-law. She may have had moments of self-doubt and wondered, "How am I going to support myself? Who is going to love me now? Will I ever meet someone?" She was human; it is natural to have anxiety during change.

  As she embarked on her first journey to Israel, she must have been nervous, and her pain must have been immense. Ruth had many reasons to shrink into a shell and live in obscurity. However, she didn't. Ruth didn't allow her past to hold her back, but she put her faith in the belief that there was still life to be lived. She knew that it was best to move forward in that confidence.

  You have a purpose regardless of the relationship you are in or the relationship you left behind. Although your confidence might waver, your calling does not. As a son or daughter of our Heavenly Father, you must pull it together and move forward, because God has blessed you with a calling in this life. Staying rooted in the past serves no purpose; it only brings pain. Jesus told his followers, "What I do thou knowest not now; but thou shalt know hereafter." (John 13:7). So don't be afraid to let go of the past. The phrase "do not be afraid" is written 365 times in the Bible. That is a daily reminder from God to live every day fearlessly.

- **Have Faith**

  For such a young believer, Ruth showed remarkable faith—Faith that there was still a purpose for her ahead, faith to believe that God was who he said he was and would provide for her and Naomi. You might not be able to see what God is doing, but trust that he is moving things into place for you. Your tears are not ignored or forgotten. When you've done everything you can do, that's when God will step in and do what you can't. That might mean he will soften your partner's heart, or that might mean God is working behind the scenes to prepare a better future for you once your relationship is over. *You must realize that faith is not about everything turning out okay. Faith is about being okay no matter how things turn out.* Therefore, you must not distance yourself from God during the low points of your life, but hold close to him. This can be accomplished by trusting that there is a greater power in the universe that has your best intentions in mind. To trust God in the light is nothing, but to trust him in the dark—that is faith.

- **Be a Person of Good Character**
  The true character of a person is not defined by what they do in front of a crowd, but instead by what they do when no one else is around. Ruth had no idea her story would be showcased for millions to read, yet she showed incredible character in obscurity. She showed exceptional respect and honor to her bitter mother-in-law. She worked hard in the field to provide food for Naomi and herself. Ruth proved to be a woman of integrity, and finally she met Boaz, a good and righteous man whom she married. Everything she did revealed great character, and God honored her.

  Martin Luther King Jr. once said, "The ultimate measure of a man is not where he stands in moments of comfort and convenience, but where he stands in times of challenge and controversy." Resist the temptation to take revenge or stoop to the level of your narcissist because of your pain. Instead, rise above it so people don't buy into the way he or she portrays you. Stand as a light for all to see!

- **Believe Redemption Is Possible**
  Ruth had no reason to believe she had earned anything, but she believed God was everything she needed. Ruth believed God would provide, and in that place of faith God did miraculous work. He took a poor, hurting outcast and healed her, provided for her, and brought her a great love with Boaz. Redemption is possible in your life. No matter where you come from or what you've been through, God has a plan for you that far surpasses all of that. If you think you've blown God's plan for your life, rest assured that you are not that powerful! You have to let go and trust God.

- **Leave a Legacy**

  Perhaps one of the best parts of Ruth's story is the legacy God established through her. God brought her and Boaz together, and they conceived a child. That child would be in the lineage of Jesus, the savior of the world. Ruth, a Moabite, was made part of the lineage of Christ. If you commit your life to God and you keep firm to your calling, there is no limit to what God can do through you.

It wasn't an easy life for Ruth. She grew up in a nation of sinful people. She suffered the loss of her husband. She followed Naomi to a foreign land and lived in poverty—all very difficult circumstances, to say the least. However, we can see God's fingerprints all over Ruth's story, and there is no doubt he was at work the entire time. It was a long and difficult journey, but it ended with redemption. Ruth started out empty, but she ended full!

Maybe you have decided to stay in your situation. If you do everything I have advised, then the situation might improve. However, if it doesn't, then you have tried all that God wants you to do. Be sure in your decisions so that ten years down the line you can say you chose your life and you didn't settle for it. If you decide to leave, have faith that God is leading your footsteps to help you. He will guide you to a better future. If your narcissist left you, then take heart, because God is with you now.

Let's look at Ruth's mother-in-law, Naomi. Not only did she suffer the death of her spouse, but she also suffered the deaths of her two sons. I am embarrassed to tell you I used to read the book of Ruth and think in my arrogant little way that Naomi needed to get over it. I thought, *God was with her, and he gave her Ruth as a companion and later made her the great-grandmother of King David, so what is the problem?* She had every right to be hurting, just like you are hurting now. And it was not fair for me to be so unfeeling about Naomi, because I knew how the story ended, but at the time she did not. That brings us to this one eternal truth: you don't know how your life is going to end. You have the power to make it turn out good or bad. Your happiness is not in another person's hands, so don't think your narcissistic partner has that much power. It is important to stay positive and remember that both you and your Heavenly Father are going to create a better future for you. However, that won't happen unless you learn to leave the label of "victim" behind. Solomon reminds us, "To every thing there is a season, and a time to every purpose under the heaven. . . . A time to weep, and a time to laugh; a time to mourn, and a time to dance" (Ecclesiastes 3:1,4).

I am not asking you to sidestep your trauma. You have to go through it to get where you're going. If you're going through hell, keep going. Trust me, you will get to the other side. So allow grief to take its course, knowing that you won't be in this place forever. God is leading you to the next chapter in your life, just as he did for Naomi and Ruth.

Naomi and Ruth are not the only ones to suffer in the Bible. Look at Jesus and his disciples. When God called Paul, he told him all that he would suffer for his name (Acts 9:16). And, oh how he suffered—stonings, shipwrecks, sharp pain, slander, and beheading. And, of course, what about Jesus? He suffered the most. He experienced firsthand the greatest human trial imaginable. He endured being betrayed by one of his apostles, deserted by his closest friends and followers, falsely accused, mocked and abused, spit upon and reviled, beaten unmercifully, and publicly condemned by the very religious leaders whose job was to stand for God's law. He was turned over to foreigners to be executed in the worst form of death, tormented and shamefully hung naked before jeering crowds on a cross. Jesus has suffered as you have suffered. He did not tell us that life would be fair, but instead it would be worth it!

Maybe you are like me. I look for answers as to why things happen to me. Did God allow this to take place in my life? Alternatively, do things just happen and God is there to help when they do? We must approach suffering practically and relationally. As human beings, we are part of a suffering world, and therefore we should say, "Why not me? Who am I to be spared?" Jesus was not. Paul was not. Most human beings are not. However, as children of God, we can go on to ask, "Why me, Lord?" in a more positive way. We do that when we ask God to help us find the good we can dig out of the bad. Within every adversity lies a sleeping possibility. Therefore, look for those possibilities! Maybe instead of asking how you can get this person to treat you better, you can ask why you are letting yourself be treated that way. Is there not a lesson here that will make you into a stronger son or daughter of your Heavenly Father? It's likely that when God doesn't change your circumstances, it's because he is concerned with changing *you* within your circumstances.

After my narcissistic abuse, I wanted to steer clear from heartache. I cut myself off from the world and stopped socializing. That was the wrong direction to go with my pain. Now I realize that hurts can draw us to God, to others, and finally to ourselves—to our best selves. We never know who we really are until we are tested. Paul says, "I know what it is to be in need, and I know what it is to have plenty. I have learned the secret of being content in any and every situation, whether well fed or hungry, whether living in plenty or in want. I can do all this through him who gives me strength." (Philippians 4:12–13). To choose to live is to choose to learn, because life is one long lesson.

It is not time to wallow in sorrow over what has been done to you, but rather to leave the victimization phase behind. Let me tell you a story you all know, but with a different perspective. Jesus was close friends with Mary, Martha, and Lazarus. They had shared many meals together. Lazarus got sick, and it became evident he wasn't getting any better, so out of desperation, Mary and Martha sent word to Jesus that he should come quickly and heal Lazarus. Jesus loved Mary, Martha, and Lazarus, yet the Bible tells us that when he received the message, Jesus stayed where he was for two days. That one sentence would make a good sermon. God's timetable is not our timetable. How many times have you prayed that Jesus would come fix your relationship? Jesus lingered where he was, but then he said to his disciples, "Our friend Lazarus has fallen asleep, and I must go wake him up." Jesus may linger, but he hasn't forgotten us. In this case, I think he lingered to prove a point.

On his arrival, Jesus found that Lazarus had already been in the tomb for four days, and that's a significant point because some Jews had a belief that after three days the soul would depart from the body. The four days may have been a statement that Lazarus was dead. We're told that Mary and Martha met Jesus, weeping, and said, "If only you had been here earlier, you are too late, Lazarus is dead." And what did Jesus do? He went out to the tomb and told them to roll back the stone to open the grave. After that, he said, "Lazarus, come forth!" And before their very eyes, Lazarus walked out still wrapped in his grave clothes. Jesus said to them, "Unbind him, and set him free." What we see here is that Jesus is all about raising people up. So instead of staying victimized and depressed over your situation, listen to him calling for you to rise.

Jesus has a resurrection for you! He wants to bring you out of that tomb, whatever it is that imprisons you. He wants to set you free from your grief and anything that holds you back, and he has the power to do it. If you hear his call and respond in faith, he will raise you up and give you a new start, a new chance, a new life, a new hope, and a new meaning. But do you even notice his call? Are you sitting around waiting for your narcissist to change? Are you only praying? God wants you to look deeper into yourself for answers and take notice of the things he is bringing your way to rescue you.

Notice what happens when Lazarus comes out of the tomb. Jesus turned to his family and friends and asked them to unbind him and set him free. Most of us don't stop to think about this. Jesus performed the miracle, but he relied on others to take part in it. Certainly, Jesus could have taken the tomb clothes off Lazarus and set him free himself, but he didn't! He included other people in performing his miracles and he still does. Maybe you are ignoring advice from others to leave or you're not really changing your reaction to your narcissist. Have you considered that instead of you waiting on God, he is waiting on you? Consider changing your prayers. Instead of asking God to change your partner, you could ask to see the help God brings your way more clearly. Maybe these people have been prompted by God to assist you. So many of us look for the big miracle when we pray. How about looking for the small things God sends your way? Maybe he is sending articles, TV sermons, contacts, or situations to help you heal. Maybe the advice someone gave you is God's message. Take the time to recognize those small acts going on around you. God's love is to be found in the small things people tend to overlook.

Remain steadfast in your faith. Don't hope for signs of his help, but expect it. If Lazarus hadn't obeyed Jesus, he would still be in the tomb. If his friends and family hadn't obeyed Jesus, Lazarus would still be confined to his grave clothes, walking around like a mummy. However, by the grace of God, through the power of Jesus, and with the help of friends and loved ones, Lazarus was set free!

When you find yourself wandering in the wilderness, ask these two things: "Why am I in the wilderness?" and "Lord, what is your goal for me in this trial?" Look for clues God is leaving you and for the people who will help you overcome the things you have gone through. God is always trying to give blessings to us, but our minds are usually too full to receive them. Remain ever vigilant and open to your surroundings, because he is walking with you and wants you to find the bread crumbs he leaves on the trail to lead you out of the wilderness and into the promised land. Lastly, remember that before you ever had the problem, God already had the solution!

To-Do List

1. Write down what you are asking of God in your prayers. Is it for your partner to change or for you to change? I can guarantee God is trying to change you first. However, you have to understand that he won't interfere with freedom of choice. You must do more than want to change; you must take action. Don't wait on God to do the dirty work of removing someone from your life. He is waiting for your strength, dignity, and courage. The same is true if you decide to stay in the relationship. God is waiting on you to set your boundaries and do everything required before considering divorce. He is waiting on you to stop wallowing and rehashing your problems with others while doing nothing to change them. You have to take action as a son or daughter of our Heavenly Father instead of waiting for someone or something to change your circumstances.

2. Write down the advice you've been given by friends or church members. Have you tried any of it? Have you been looking for answers or simply wanting validation? This is important to know, because how much validation does one need? If you believe you're in a relationship with a narcissist, then let this book be your validation. If that is not enough for you, then speak to a therapist for that validation. The question is this: what are you going to do now that you know you are being abused?

3. Have you distanced yourself from our Heavenly Father because he has not answered your prayers in the way you want? Does distancing yourself make it any easier to receive his blessings and help? Sometimes we need to be reminded of what God has done for us. List the things in your life that you feel were given to you by God. These could include your health, your children's health, and good parents. Start a gratitude list in your journal to change your perspective about your circumstances.

4. How can you strengthen your faith in God? List three things you can do this week. They could include attending Bible classes or attending church services if you have become inactive. In addition, instituting family prayers and reading scriptures invite faith-seeking practices into your relationship. Starting a family night on Monday evenings or attending a monthly church service project is a great start.

What Does Your Life Purpose Have to Do with Narcissism?

Christ says, "And we know that in all things God works for the good of those who love him, who have been called according to his purpose" (Romans 8:28). We have all been blessed with talents and gifts that God intends us to use to help the world become better. If you are in a relationship with a narcissist and have been beaten down by games, you are forfeiting your life mission or at least hindering it by not being the best version of you. How can you be the best version of yourself if you don't have strong boundaries? The answer is that you can't.

A life mission has these three attributes:

1. It positively benefits you.
2. It removes suffering and brings joy to others as well as yourself.
3. It requires you to engage in an area you find intrinsically interesting and where you have strong abilities.

The Bible teaches that God uniquely shaped each of us for a purpose. This world is not here for you; you are here for it. When you get to heaven, God is probably going to ask you two questions: "What have you done with my son Jesus Christ's message?" and "What did you do with what I gave you?" God gave you gifts and talents not for your benefit but to bless other people. In John 17:18, Jesus says, "As you sent me into the world, I have sent them into the world." He is talking about you having a mission and a purpose. Every believer needs both a ministry in the church and a mission in the world—a ministry to believers and a mission to unbelievers. You can perform these in many ways, like being an example and helping others or by pursuing a hobby focused on service. It could be as simple as spending time helping the needy or something larger like using your music talent to create a song whose proceeds go to charity. There are endless ways to use your talents to help others.

If you want God's blessing on your life, you must care about the thing that God cares about most: bringing lost children back to his flock. I am not saying you have to preach the gospel to them. Kindness, charity, and compassion are all ways to serve by example.

Don't fall into the habit of constantly praying for blessings for your relationship when you are not doing anything that gains blessings. How many times have you prayed for things when you did nothing to further God's glory? Remember that sometimes God doesn't change your circumstances because he is trying to change you.

The greatest blessings I have received came from helping God's ministry. Connections I needed seemed to be right there. If I was praying for help in an area of my life, I would meet someone at church or during a service project. If I wanted to learn why something turned out the way it did, I would get an epiphany while on a medical mission, because people in similar situations shared their trials with me. Through these experiences, I have gathered that God wants to use people to help you, but you need to make yourself available to feel these promptings and you need to be doing things to receive blessings. That is not to say God only gives when he gets. However, he is like any healthy, loving parent. He won't spoil you and ignore bad behavior. Sometimes he uses tough love. Therefore, it most certainly doesn't hurt your case to be charitable and draw closer to him while you are going through your storm. Show him you want to change by your actions, not just your prayers.

During the abuse from my narcissist hacker, I spent a lot of time at the Upper Room, a soup kitchen in my hometown. Working there dissolved the anger I had for this man. I visualized my narcissist hacker as being no different from the messed-up and addicted lost souls who walked into that dining hall every evening for a meal. I also learned what happened to me was not the worst thing in the world compared to other people's lives. Eventually, this insight helped bring me to a place of acceptance and forgiveness. I don't think I would have gotten there unless I put myself in servitude so I could see God's wisdom clearly.

When you make changes in the world, you will make changes in *your* world. The trickling-over effect of blessings changes your circumstances. You don't have to be in a place of influence, celebrity status, or spiritual greatness to make a difference. The smallest, most unrecognized person can make an impact. Author Richard Nelson Bolles writes in his book *How to Find Your Mission in Life*, "As the stone does not always know what ripples it has caused in the pond whose surface it impacts, so neither we nor those who watch our life will always know what we have achieved by our life and by our Mission. It may be that by the grace of God we helped bring about a profound change for the better in the lives of other souls around us, but it also may be that this takes place beyond our sight or after we have gone on. And we may never know what we have accomplished, until we see him face-to-face after this life is past."

Usually there are seven signs that show you have found your calling:

1. It's familiar.
2. It's something other people see in you.
3. It's challenging.
4. It requires faith.
5. It takes time.
6. It's more than just one thing.
7. It's bigger than you are.

Parenthood is an important purpose, but it shouldn't be your only purpose. You have an assignment from God himself. It goes beyond the role of father, mother, wife, or husband. When we see these roles as our missions, we are in trouble because they may or may not stay with us. If we lose the role because of death or divorce or other loss, we would lose the mission and our life purpose. But your true calling does not change, as it would if it were defined by roles, jobs, or results. We may not understand what it is or even define it well, but it is God's purpose for your life as a believer. A worldly relationship just focuses on the material things in life. A spiritual relationship focuses on helping one another grow and better this world through your actions.

You don't have to be perfect to have a life mission. You are a special being who has been given talents, skills, and blessings. Do you seriously think that God doesn't want to use you? Look at the unlikely individuals God used to do some of the greatest things in the Bible. Noah was a drunk. Abraham was too old. Jacob was a liar. Leah was ugly. Joseph was abused. Moses had a stuttering problem. Gideon was afraid. Peter denied Christ. Naomi was a widow. The Samaritan woman was divorced. David had an affair and was a murderer. Lazarus was dead. Should I go on? God wants to use you to do something great. Don't let one person's abusive mind games keep you from your greatness!

When you are not living your life purpose, you can bet you're not experiencing the greatest joy possible for you. When you take on the label of victim, it is hard to be humble about life because pain causes us to feel like God owes us something. Victimization leads a person to become focused inwardly, which takes them far away from their life purpose. Over time, prayers can become lists of wants rather than needs. Mother Teresa once said, "I used to pray that God would feed the hungry, or do this or that, but now I pray that he will guide me to do whatever I'm supposed to do, what I can do. I used to pray for answers, but now I am praying for strength. I used to believe that prayer changes everything, but now I know that prayer changes us and we change things."

As a son or daughter of our Heavenly Father, I ask you to ask yourself what is really important and then have the courage to build your life around your answer. Narcissistic abuse should not be the focus of your life. Why would you let one person take you away from what you are meant to do? Your time is yours, not your narcissist's. Don't let them steal your time by causing you pain and anxiety. The games and fights you have been through are a distraction from something more important that you need to accomplish with your time—your life mission. Remember when I talked about Satan's will for the world? Distracting you from your life mission while you battle emotional abuse is part of his will.

Paul was extremely passionate about his purpose. He says in Acts 20:24, "However, I consider my life worth nothing to me; my only aim is to finish the race and complete the task the Lord Jesus has given me . . ." And what is this task? To serve others. God has given you a mission in this world. You're not here just to take up space; you're not here just to strive after your own personal goals. You were not meant to be fighting every day for a person's respect, loyalty, and love. You were not meant to live in a state of depression for years because a narcissist discarded you. Nor were you put on this earth to constantly give one person adoration to boost their self-esteem. You are meant for more than that! You are an example to your own children or future children and to others. People learn how to treat you from what they see you put up with. Trust me, you don't want any of your children to grow up and be in abusive relationships because they saw you do it, so it must be acceptable.

Your partner is your helpmate. They should be someone who can help you grow and contribute in this world. They should support you in your life mission (whatever that may be), not distract from it.

To-Do List

1. What are your talents? Don't become fixated only on what you can see, such as music, art, dancing, or writing. There are less visible talents God has planted in you. Some people are great communicators, listeners, problem solvers, planners, or managers. Be specific—you are allowed to brag here! Ask relatives and friends for input if you need help.

2. What are you passionate about? Write about cooking, music, counseling, or other interests.

3. How can you combine items from the lists above to make a difference in this world?

4. What have you been passionate about but set aside because the problems in your relationship took precedence?

5. If you choose to remain in this relationship, what are your partner's talents? How could you combine them with yours to better the world? For example, my life mission is writing. My husband's talent is his great managerial and people skills. I struggled to figure out how we could combine the two. Then it made sense: I have ADHD and needed someone to keep me focused. He uses his managing talents to keep me on track so I can get my writing done. Then, when I get the royalties for my book, we use that money to go on medical missions, where he continues using his management and people skills. This is our life purpose. It isn't elaborate, like curing cancer, but a life mission doesn't have to be. Our small contribution brings us great joy and fulfillment, especially doing it as a couple. It strengthens our marriage.

Creating Personal Boundaries to Safeguard Your Dignity

If you are completing the to-do lists in this book, then I am proud of you! Now we're going to work on establishing boundaries. First, what is a boundary? It is a line in the sand that represents what you are willing to do and what you will not do. Boundaries are not like a fire alarm with the notice, "Break glass only in emergency." You don't wait until they are crossed to say you don't like what is going on. Also, boundaries are not consequences. Boundaries are principles woven into the tapestry of your character. They are the foundation of your integrity. Boundaries are about taking responsibility for our own lives as sons and daughters of our Heavenly Father. God has great plans for your life that don't involve unhappiness and depression! He doesn't want you to live a life that is semi-okay. Whether you remain in a relationship with a narcissist or leave, create boundaries that are also God's boundaries. Hebrews 12:11 reminds us that "no discipline seems pleasant at the time, but painful. Later on, however, it produces a harvest of righteousness and peace for those who have been trained by it."

When we have kind natures, we become easy prey for users to take advantage of us. Why do many Christians believe that letting others get away with things is being Christlike? Many Christians would cite the principle of forgiveness as the reason they allow people to get away with bad behavior. However, when does this principle become simply an excuse to avoid an uncomfortable confrontation? In Romans 8:29, Paul writes, "For those God foreknew he also predestined to be conformed to the image of his Son, that he might be the firstborn among many brothers and sisters." God's will is for us to look more and more like Christ. However, Jesus wasn't a doormat who kept himself available for abuse. Jesus set limits. He didn't heal everyone all the time. I am sure he wanted to heal everyone. However, he was one man with a mission to carry out. He carved out time away from his disciples to pray and to spend time with God. He also would go away from the masses with his disciples to train and minister to them. If Jesus had let his schedule be determined by what bullying people needed him to do rather than by what he was called to do and able to do, his ministry wouldn't have been effective. He needed time alone with God, and he took it. He also had a few things to say to the wicked and didn't back down before evil. He had self-esteem, self-respect, dignity, and courage, and so should you!

Boundaries limit destructive behaviors, and that is why both God and society have laws and consequences for those who overstep those laws (Romans 13:1–4). As described earlier, God's laws command you to be all the things that are true of a son or daughter of our Heavenly Father. Meeting God's demands will require you to move beyond being a narcissist's doormat to become a strong individual who knows their worth and isn't afraid to walk away to get what you are entitled to—respect. Author Brené Brown says, "Daring to set boundaries is about having the courage to love ourselves even when we risk disappointing others."

A healthy boundary might look like if-then statements. For example, if you insult my children, then I will leave the room. How many if-then statements do you have? Before you can set boundaries, you need take a long, hard look at all the unhealthy boundaries you already have. Do any of these apply to you?

Signs of Unhealthy Boundaries

1. Telling everyone about your private business and insecurities.
2. Talking about your problems when you first meet someone.
3. Being so preoccupied with someone that things such as church, friends, family, or hobbies come last.
4. Going against your personal values or rights to please someone else.
5. Allowing someone to treat you poorly without asserting yourself because you are afraid they will break up with you.
6. Accepting food, gifts, or gestures and behavior that you don't want because you don't want someone to dislike you.
7. Letting others direct your life.
8. Letting others describe your reality.
9. Letting others define your value.
10. Falling apart so someone will take care of you.
11. Having sex too early in the relationship to keep someone around.

Can you come up with more that apply to your life?

There are many reasons why people don't set boundaries or set unhealthy boundaries. Maybe you can relate to this list of reasons:

- Fear of what others think
- Assuming others will be mad
- Thinking it's not that important
- Not wanting the hassle
- Wanting to avoid conflict
- Preferring to go with the flow
- Fear of being seen as selfish or unforgiving
- Fear of being alone

Does any of the above strike a chord?

A person who doesn't have boundaries is a person who doesn't trust who they are. Do you agree? If you know you are a child of our Heavenly Father and God is looking out for your life, why would you allow so much disrespect from your narcissist or anyone else in this world? If you are unclear about who you are and what you will or will not accept, it becomes easy to second-guess and let others cross your boundaries. Maybe you're not clear on what is or is not okay in your life. Some of us have been conditioned to be compliant and accept how others treat us by role models who were also unclear about their boundaries, or who violated our boundaries. This caused us to believe that it was not okay to defend our rights and that the only way to be loved and accepted was to allow our boundaries to be violated. Or the opposite may be true: you were taught how to be treated, but your fear of leaving the relationship and searching for someone new made boundaries seem less important. Even if you know who you are, you're not applying it or you wouldn't be reading this book. You send a clear signal to your abuser that you are a pushover every time you let them cross your boundaries.

Author Brittney Moses said, "I learned soon enough that God called us to be people lovers not people pleasers. We can have the power to love people without becoming a slave to their opinions and behaviors. Boundaries are your responsibility. At some point us people pleasers must set the tone for how we should be treated and the direction in which we are called."

You are called to be an example of Christ. Therefore, setting boundaries requires keeping your boundaries consistent with what God wants of you. It requires knowledge of who you are, what your truth is, and what you will accept as this truth. Do you want love, peace, and respect? To receive these qualities in your life, you have to live your life by these qualities. And this means you need to stop associating with people who don't live by these qualities themselves. You are to model the life of someone who has them. In essence, you are taking back the script that the narcissist wrote for you and becoming the screenwriter of your own play.

A huge part of becoming a strong son or daughter of our Heavenly Father is knowing that you alone are responsible for setting the parameters of the truth, peace, kindness, and love you wish to have in your relationship. If your narcissist is not going to accept those glorious traits in you, then you will love yourself enough to walk away. After spending time in a narcissistic relationship, I lost sight of what my assertive rights were. Let me help you remember yours.

Your Assertive Rights

- You have the right to make mistakes.
- You have the right to be yourself.
- You have the right to be treated with respect.
- You have the right to have and express thoughts, emotions, or opinions.
- You have the right to say no and not feel guilty.
- You have the right to say I don't know.
- You have the right to feel and express anger.
- You have the right to have needs as important as others.
- You have the right to do things others don't approve of.
- You have the right to ask why or why not.
- You have the right to ask for help.
- You have the right to be responsible for your actions.
- You have the right to believe in what you want.
- You have the right to choose what makes you happy.

This is a starter list. I bet you could add your own rights. I encourage you to write them in your journal. You must understand that if you continue to allow disrespect and stay attached to it, then it will continue to happen. Don't relive the same pain 365 days a year and call it a life. We always get in life what we are prepared to accept. No more and no less. When we don't have deservedness and self-worth, we struggle to believe in and know that we deserve to live a happy, safe, and respectful life. We may unconsciously believe "this is all I am worth" and cling to the crumbs of hope for love and acceptance in the midst of being hurt and abused. You are worth more than the crumbs someone leaves for you. *You are worth fighting for!*

One of the main fears that might be holding you back from setting boundaries is the fear of being a powerful and creative source to yourself (becoming self-reliant), and instead you have given in to the neediness and reliance on others to be this source for you. You may be terrified of being left alone, of not winning approval, or of being rejected, abandoned, or punished. These fears can convince you that compliancy and handing over your power, despite it hurting you repeatedly and further diminishing your self-worth, is preferable to facing the fear of having to break up.

As survivors of abuse, we have two burning questions in our hearts: *Why did this happen to me?* and *What can I learn from it?* If you must know why you met this person or why all these bad things happened to you, then take a leap of faith in this theory: Maybe God let you get to this point so you would change by rebuilding the attributes of a son or daughter he knows you are capable of becoming. Maybe through this pain, you have finally come to a place in your life where you are pushed to draw a line in the sand where evil will not follow. Maybe it is time you prove who you love—God or an abusive man or woman who hurts you.

It is safe to say that your boundaries were not strong before you met your narcissist. After all, you were in love and you wanted to make your relationship work. Unfortunately, it is easier to have few boundaries because we can have more friends, more dating options, and less time alone. However, the easiness we equate as peace is a false peace. The fewer boundaries you have, the more Satan is able to get to your very spirit and whittle away at its Christlike light. Boundaries are not selfish when we use our freedom to serve and love one another, because we are keeping our own flesh under control (Galatians 5:13).

Boundaries can be difficult to establish because saying "no" may have been off limits or mistakenly taught as being ungodly. There is nothing ungodly about asking your loved one to hand over his or her cell phone so you can see whom they are calling. If trust is not in your relationship, then you are using the common sense God gave you by safeguarding your relationship from the temptations your narcissistic partner might have from the outside world. You do not have to maintain your boundaries in a hostile manner. You can enforce it instead with firm words, practice, patience, and restraint. You can even do it courteously and kindly. Sometimes it is as simple as saying that you are not going to listen further to an unpleasant exchange, walking away from them, or turning off your cell phone. You can close the door, drive away, and use other such tactics to enforce your limits.

Key Tips to Making Boundaries Successful

The key to setting boundaries with a narcissist is to stick to them. You will want to communicate clearly and directly each time. If you make a mistake and find that you "lose it" or say something wrong, just keep practicing and be accountable for your behavior.

Know where to draw the line. Decide which behaviors you are willing to accept and which you are not. For example, if you are not willing to tolerate rudeness, bullying, or name-calling, say so. Narcissists may call you more names, argue with you, or try to convince you that you are overreacting or treating them unfairly. They will likely cycle through games I have mentioned in this book to see if they can induce guilt or intimidate and confuse you. While their pressure or wheedling may be unpleasant, your boundaries are not up for discussion or a vote.

Having an exit plan is crucial: You don't need permission to leave a situation where your narcissist is throwing a tantrum or giving you the silent treatment. You leave. Therefore, if this means you pack up and go sleep on your mom's couch until they get over it, then that is what you do. If it means you jump in the car and go to the mall until the drama is over, then you do it. You will have a lot of drama when you start to institute boundaries. Like a child, they will test if you are serious or not. So don't stand there and listen to the same song and dance they are going to give you. Leave the conversation. For example, you can glance at your watch and say, "Gosh, look at the time. I'm late!" Then leave. Late for what? It doesn't matter. Every moment you spend indulging in their drama is another moment wasted, because it could have been spent in self-care or on your life mission.

Setting a boundary isn't hard. The only things that make it hard are our insecurities and fears. If you fear you will lose someone by setting a boundary, then you have the problem, not the narcissist for breaking it. A loving partner should have boundaries. You would want them in your kids, so why not yourself? If you choose not to set them, then you are stating to yourself that you are not worth it. If you are not going to see your value, then your narcissist won't see it either.

When setting up boundaries with narcissists, you have to know one thing: *They will test them!* As I mentioned before, they are like children and will test to see if Mom or Dad is serious. You have to accept that they might not stop testing you. They might keep at it to wear you down. Prepare for the worst before it gets better. Change bothers abusers. They want attention. They want their way. They want you to take it. They want your reaction. You will want to memorize the section about their games before your boundaries are finalized. Every time you get in a fight with your narcissist, I want you to stop and pause. Then silently identify the game they are playing. This will help you not react during the testing of your boundaries. It will remind you that it is a game played by a mentally ill person, rather than an opportunity to prepare for a counterattack.

Here are key things to consider when creating your boundaries:

- **Set your agenda.**
  This means you choose which battles to fight over your boundaries. Let's say you have a boundary that says you refuse to have someone put down your looks. Your narcissist might say, "How is your diet going?" when he sees you eating a brownie. You could start a fight, which is what he would love, or you could not fall into the trap of being offended. You can say, "Great," and change the subject. Or shift the conversation to something you know the narcissist loves to talk about—himself or herself. The point is to avoid fights or topics you don't want to discuss by evading their questions. When your narcissist makes a comment that leaves you uncomfortable, you don't have to stay on topic. Change the subject. You have to pick and choose your battles. Not every boundary has to be a battle!

- **Don't justify, explain, or overshare.**
  I don't advise you to march into the room where your narcissist is standing and tell them you have a list of boundaries they have to follow. That will put them on the defensive. Simply institute them silently. Stop trying to explain yourself and instead make short statements about what you will and won't do if backed into a corner by your narcissist. You do not deserve interrogation because you decided to stand up for yourself. If they criticize

something you are doing, you can simply say, "I feel confident about my actions" or "I hear your opinion, and I will keep that in mind."

- **Name what is happening.**
  The narcissist's goals are to create drama so they can get attention and feel above the other person. You might find it difficult when instituting boundaries to ignore their bad behavior. If you can't bite your tongue, you might try to defuse the situation by stating what they are doing. Say, "That sounded like a put-down," or "I notice that each time I start to talk about myself, you interrupt to talk about yourself." Don't state these observations in a condescending tone. Their response is irrelevant. You have set a placeholder in the conversation in which you spoke truth about what they did. This gives them something to think about and points out their bad behavior.

- **Realize that setting boundaries with narcissists is not a one-time event.**
  Setting boundaries with narcissists is a continuous process. Knowing this can help you adjust your expectations. If you are not getting anywhere with a boundary, then you might need to reach out to your therapist for suggestions. Bounce off them what you have tried and what their reaction was. Two heads are better than one when you're dealing with a mentally and spiritually ill person.

  Expect the narcissist to continue testing your boundaries, even ones they previously respected. Sometimes narcissists will out of the blue cross a boundary that you thought you had gotten past. Don't get relaxed with your boundaries just because they haven't been crossed in a long time.

- **Focus on being a son or daughter of our Heavenly Father.**
  Narcissists want you to act in ways that make them feel good about themselves, often at your expense. Every time they draw you into their drama, ask yourself these questions: What do I need to do to respect myself in this situation? What do I want to stand for?

  In the last section, I asked you to tell me why you are worth not being treated this way. Post this list in a place where you will be reminded of your worth every day.

Some of us are great at setting boundaries but poor at communication when it comes to them being crossed. This is when practicing in advance for what you expect your narcissist to say comes in handy. Let's look at practice dialogues to use when you are setting boundaries:

Your ex says, "I left some things at the house and I am stopping by later to get them."

You say calmly, "It is not all right with me for you to stop by my house at any time. You will have to schedule a time to do this when it works with my schedule. You must respect my property and schedule or I will contact law enforcement about your trespassing."

Your ex says, "I know I was supposed to be there at 5:30 p.m. to get the kids, but I am coming by after school instead."

You say calmly, "We are going to follow the court orders exactly, and you cannot change the times at your whim. The children will not be home after school because we have other plans. We will see you at six p.m. tonight, as planned."

Your ex or partner swears at you on the phone and is verbally abusive.

You calmly say, "I will not allow you to speak to me that way any longer. Just so you know, each time you do this, I will walk out of the room or leave the house if you follow me." (You leave the situation and follow through with your boundary.)

Your ex or partner disparages you in front of the children and you hear it.

You calmly say, "This is not okay for the children to hear. I will remove them from this situation and I will speak with them about why you shouldn't do this to me. They will be told this each time you are determined to put me down in front of them. I won't disparage you, but I will let them know that this behavior is not acceptable."

These are just a few common examples to get you thinking about what you plan to say in similar situations. When you think through what is consistently being done by your narcissist, then you can come up with your own responses. The key is to keep the responses short, to the point, mature, and without emotion. Picture yourself as the parent talking to a wayward child if it helps you disconnect from feeling upset or annoyed by your narcissist.

It does take a bit of the warrior spirit to stay firm. However, if you envision yourself pleasing your Heavenly Father every time you stand firm, then it makes it a lot easier.

To-Do List

1. Write down a declaration of who you are. I already gave you characteristics at the beginning of this section for what a son or daughter of our Heavenly Father looks like. You are going to take this a step further by writing a boundary for each of those virtues. For example, one of the characteristics is speaking the truth. Your boundary might be that you will never be in a situation in which you won't tell someone what is wrong with how they treated you. You will speak the truth and be assertive about how you are to be treated. Try to set up all the boundaries that a son or daughter of our Heavenly Father should have. God has already done much of the work for you in the Bible. The Ten Commandments themselves are a list of boundaries you shouldn't break.

2. Write a list of deal breakers that will end the relationship. This is an important list that your partner should know about, so share it. Make sure you are certain about the outcome if they break the rule on the list. For example, if they fight with you in front of the children, then you will leave to stay with your parents until they can be more appropriate. Or if they cheat on you, then you will get separated. The key to not getting your narcissist to cross boundaries is for you to remain consistent with the consequences if he or she does.

3. Write a list of the things you will say to avoid being pulled into a fight. I already listed some ideas above. Go beyond that list and come up with your own. Not sure what to say? There is an excellent book by Barrie Davenport called *Emotional Abuse Breakthrough Scripts: 107 Empowering Responses and Boundaries to Use with Your Abuser*. The work is already done for you in his book. Check it out on Amazon.com.

4. Make a list of boundaries that your narcissist is not to cross—for example, "There will be no infidelity"—and then indicate specifically what that means, such as no texting other women, no looking other women up online, or no using family members to help them communicate with an ex-partner or other person. Then follow up that boundary with a consequence. If they are caught doing it, you will do _____. This could be a separation or divorce or anything else you

want. However, be prepared to follow through instead of throwing out empty threats. The people who are stepped on by abusers are the ones who don't hold to their guns over their boundaries.

5. The last to-do on your way to setting boundaries is the ceremony. It is strictly optional. I made my lists just as you have, but I felt something was missing because this list of boundaries wasn't just a relationship rule guide; it was a way of life. I was starting over. I was taking back my right as a daughter of my Heavenly Father. My friend created a ritual to celebrate the birth of the "new me." We had pictures of both of the narcissists I had encountered in my lifetime and a picture of how I looked at my worst when the stress destroyed my health. We threw the pictures in a firepit she had in her backyard and set them ablaze. Then we knelt in prayer. The prayer was about thanking God for the new me and moving beyond the one who had forgotten who she was. The ceremony was simple, but it was symbolic and helped me to feel that the words I had written with my therapist were not just words but a code I would live by.

If you decide to stay in your relationship, throwing the person's picture into the fire might not be a wise move. Instead, throw your own picture in it. Let it symbolize the old you. Trust me when I say that I felt renewed after this simple declaration of the stronger version of me.

Should I Stay or Go?

If you have read up to this section, then you should know what will happen if you stay in a relationship with a narcissist, but let me recap. They will continue their way of manipulation because they don't believe any other way works better for them. Of course, they know what decency is and what forgiving is. However, these things don't give them what they are addicted to: control and the need for attention. Getting a narcissist to let go of these destructive techniques will be difficult. As I mentioned, both my narcissists are churchgoing Christians and no amount of religious guilt changed their ways. During the publication of this book, my narcissist hacker's wife was still posting sad quotes on her social media because she stepped into the role of enabler rather than trust God to bring her someone who wouldn't abuse her.

This may or may not be your fate if you stay with your narcissist. Maybe through consistent therapy and spiritual living, they will soften their heart. Who knows? Maybe change can happen. Don't give up until you have tried everything in this book. If you have, then you have done all you can, and God will go ahead and prepare your future. You have permission to leave. God will still love you and bring you blessings.

Remember that you have a difficult mountain to climb if you choose to stay in the relationship with him or her, and only you can make that decision. Nevertheless, whatever you do, don't play games to test their love for you (for example, getting separated just to scare them into being better when you never had any intention of following through with filing divorce papers). They are smarter than you think, because they have spent a lifetime manipulating people. If you get separated, be prepared to follow through if they cross the line. You don't walk away to prove your worth to them, in hopes they will say, "Wait a minute. I guess she has value because she is standing up for herself." Seriously? Do you really believe that nonsense? They should know your value without such drastic measures. *You walk away because you allowed someone to dictate your value and you found yourself believing it.* Let that be your real reasoning. When you see your self-esteem lowering and your faith dwindling, then they are no longer fighting for your eternal salvation.

When you drift away from the attributes of a son or daughter of our Heavenly Father, then you have had enough!

But you might be thinking, "God gives us second chances. Shouldn't I be the same?" There is nothing wrong with giving second chances. However, how many will be enough for you? Even God got tired of it all and cast Satan from his kingdom. Remember the War in Heaven? That was a bunch of good people tired of a lot of bad people. The more chances you give someone, the less respect they'll have for you. They'll begin to ignore the standards that you've set because they know another chance will always be given. They're not afraid to lose you because they know no matter what, you won't walk away. They get comfortable with depending on your forgiveness. Never let a person get comfortable disrespecting you. Please don't be gullible by believing that he or she loves you because they keep coming back. An abuser loves the power they have over you. They know you will take them back. Don't give part-time people a full-time position in your life.

One of the hardest things we must do in this life is to give up our attachment for something because God asks us to dwell with him. It's crazy to love someone who hurts you, but do you know what is crazier? Thinking that someone who hurts you loves you. Don't settle for someone who can't or won't fight for the attributes of a child of God. Don't fight for something that won't help you improve spiritually as a person. Let me recap what you shouldn't settle for:

- Do not settle for someone who is not willing to fight for you.
- Do not settle for someone who has messed up in the past and doesn't have the decency to make things right in the future.
- Do not settle for someone who only tries when it is convenient.
- Do not settle for someone who shows no progress when progress needs to be shown.
- Do not settle for lies and manipulation.
- Do not settle for lack of loyalty.
- Do not settle for disrespect, betrayal, and abuse.
- Do not settle for someone who doesn't care about your spiritual growth or can't grow with you.

Making the choice to stay or leave will be difficult either way. If I am leaning in the direction of you leaving, it is because most narcissists don't get better. However, that is not to say miracles don't occur and that effort on your narcissist's part can't pay off. Maybe your choice is to stay and apply all the suggestions I have offered you. If this is your choice, my blessings go with you. It comes down to your choice and your happiness. Just remember that it is okay to fight for someone *who loves you*. It's not okay to fight for someone *TO love you*. There is a huge difference!

If you are going to stay, be prepared for a difficult road ahead. Remember that if an addict is happy with you, you're probably enabling them. If an addict is mad at you, you're probably trying to save their life. Narcissists are addicts—addicted to attention. By staying, you have elected to reparent your loved one.

To-Do List

1. Start by seeing your doctor to get your lab values checked. Get on vitamins, if needed. I recommend B_{12} shots if you are under a lot of stress. You can ask your primary care physician or a psychiatrist for

an antidepressant or antianxiety medication to help alleviate symptoms that accompany narcissistic abuse.

2. Make an appointment with a psychologist or counselor. You will want to see them weekly until you are at a point that you can stick to your guns and employ tough love, if needed, when your narcissist crosses your boundaries. The goal of therapy is to help you know how to deal with the way your partner treats you. In addition, it is to help you sidestep potential drama or fights your partner will want to start with you. You should be going to your therapist with a problem and getting it fixed. If your therapist isn't giving you homework to practice, then they are just listening to you. You need a therapist who gives you homework. I went through three different therapists before I decided to say, "Look, I want to make progress. Let's break it down to what my problem is and let's set weekly goals that I will report back to you about. Plus, you give me homework." My therapist began having me journal and started recommending books based on things I needed to work on. She gave me homework, much as I do for you in this book. Don't be afraid to call your psychologist and ask for a different one. You're not supposed to be paying a person to be your friend and validate your experience. You need to pay someone to help you get out of the victim mode!

3. Make a list of the reasons why this partner is worth taking back one more time. I want you to write a list of pros and a list of cons. I have started the cons list for you. What would be the cost of having him or her back?

    •   Low self-esteem
    •   Increased anxiety
    •   Unpleasant toxic energy and feelings
    •   More struggles and pain
    •   Smaller social circle
    •   Uncertainty and wondering
    •   Instability and confusion
    •   Disappointment and heartbreak
    •   Feeling that you have taken a huge step backward
    •   Feeling that you missed out on being with someone right
    •   Never feeling you can trust him or her

These are a few off the top of my head. Make your list of pros convincing so you will be motivated to charge forward to make them happen.

4. Start building a healthy network of people to support you. Say good-bye to relationships with friends who are negative and want to pull you down with their problems. Visit them occasionally, but don't let them be your inner circle. You need healthy and happy people around you. Your mindset should be that you are in a healing cycle. So if you are that loving person who has to be the fixer of all your friends' problems, then hang up the job for now. You are spread too thin with your emotions and need to be focused on you. That is not being selfish; it is called being real about your health.

5. You are to stop hanging out on narcissistic abuse recovery forums or Facebook pages. Stop looking up information about narcissism. You learned everything you need to know about narcissism from this book. You are also to stop sharing private and personal information about your relationship with other men or women. Your relationship is between you and your narcissist. Respect your relationship enough not to air your dirty laundry to others. So tell Mom or your best friend that you are going to share those details with a trained professional. Then start having conversations with friends and family that aren't about your problems. Trust me, they will actually be relieved that you aren't bringing it up anymore. Besides, there is a whole world of things that can be discussed that don't deal with your pain or the pain of other people. Be positive, because you're changing your life.

6. Start attending a church if you are not already, and drag your narcissist along with you. If he doesn't want to attend, then bring the lesson to him. Tell him that you are having family night every Monday evening. During this time, you will be giving a lesson and discussing it with the family. If you are unsure what lessons to give, you can easily google "family home evening lessons" or "family night" and find several books or ideas. If you have kids, you can purchase my book *350 Questions Parents Should Ask During Family Night*. However, I suggest you start with lessons that apply to the problems you are having with your narcissist (for example, lessons about lying, manipulation, worldliness, and respect). Remember that you are trying to rehabilitate a spiritually ill person. This requires weekly work, not just the occasional trip to church on Sunday.

7. Enroll in a Bible class or other spiritual class offered at your church. You need to be around people with the same values. You also need to be getting a spiritual lift to remind you of who you are: a beloved son or daughter of our Heavenly Father. This will give you strength so you can institute boundaries.

8. If you are not doing so now, have morning and evening prayers with your family. If you are new to praying aloud with your family, you might feel awkward. However, it doesn't need to be. Just speak from your heart. Tell God what you need to spiritually grow and what you are thankful for, followed by "amen." This doesn't have to be a long, drawn-out process, but it keeps our Heavenly Father front and center in your relationship. Sooner or later, you can invite your narcissist to say the prayer if they are willing.

9. Read scriptures as a couple or a family. Dust off the Bible. Start with Genesis and read a chapter a night with your family. This is the best way to open a dialogue with your narcissist about God's will for your relationship. If your narcissist refuses, then incorporate it into your weekly family nights. When you invite Christ into your home, it changes the spirit of your home. Maybe you want to leave reminders around the house about God, such as a scripture quote or a picture of Christ on the wall. If your narcissist is not active in church, he might not like your revival in a religion. He might rebel. Just keep to your guns and remain faithful that your goodness will wear off on him or her.

10. Get involved in a service project with your partner. Narcissists have a serious lack of empathy. This is evident in the games they play. Getting them active in helping others with you can help them grow to think beyond themselves. Look to your church for activities to attend. It could be a night at a soup kitchen for the homeless or the bake sale at the church. Whatever it is, make sure he or she is actively doing something. Translation: They are not there only to socialize with other people and not get anything out of the service project. Put them to work. Also, make sure that he or she doesn't post a picture of them doing it on social media. It is not about them looking good, but doing good. Humility is what you are trying to foster in them.

11. Get involved in a marriage counseling class if you are married. These are offered at some larger nondenominational churches. If you are not nondenominational, still go. I wasn't nondenominational, but I still attended the marriage classes there because over two hundred people were in attendance. It was such a large turnout that I was lost in the crowd. This was a relief because I wanted to blend in and not be pounced on by members to convert to their religion. Therefore, a large church gathering might be your answer if you are having trouble finding a marriage class offered by your religion.

12. Sometimes, getting a narcissist to participate in these things is not easy, because they are public events and they have an image to uphold. If getting them there is a problem, then consider counseling with the pastor in a private setting. The reason is that you need a spiritual person to help mediate in your relationship. A psychologist is not going to whip out the Bible and tell your partner why they need to be acting in a different way.

13. Have your partner attend psychologist appointments with you. Go first to lay the groundwork with the therapist by yourself. Tell the therapist that you suspect your partner has undiagnosed narcissistic personality disorder. Tell the therapist that you want to establish boundaries with your partner and need help in getting that across to your partner. In addition, you need help with better communication between the two of you. Through her interviewing you, she might find other goals to work on, such as redefining in your mind what healthy love is or building your self-esteem so you can be stronger with your boundaries. Finally, you will want the therapist to make a referral to a psychiatrist to get your partner medication that could resolve mood swings, if your partner is willing to go that extra step.

14. Institute tactics and the boundaries I mentioned earlier when dealing with their games. In addition, follow through with your actions if they cross your boundaries. By now, you should know that narcissists are like adolescents. They throw fits when they have to abide by rules. If it takes moving out of the house and filing for separation to get them to wake up to treating you better, then you must do it. You are trying to help them change their ways. Your job as a son or daughter of our Heavenly Father is not to let them live an evil, sinful life and have you overlook it. You didn't sign up to ignore non-Christlike behavior. You were meant to be a light for what is right and true!

Your choice is not an easy one if you remain in the relationship, but people have done it. However, the healthy ones who did it were the ones who rewrote their blueprint and had to wake up to the fact that their narcissist's behavior wasn't going to change drastically. It would be a long battle of managing a disorder.

You might be wrestling with that vow that said, "For better or worse." Maybe you are wrapped up in scriptures about forgiveness and stories of the prodigal son. On the other hand, maybe you have taken your thoughts further and decided to stay, because you wouldn't abandon your child if he or she had narcissism. Let me step in and help you out of the religious martyrdom you have created for yourself. God wants you to try everything to help your partner, but not at the cost of your dignity, life purpose, happiness, and ability to serve him with your best self. Even God has consequences for his children. His rules are to help us grow. Your boundaries are your rules so people know to treat you with respect. Satan was once an angel in heaven. Even God had to let Satan go in the War in Heaven. Some people don't want to be saved. May heaven bless you for being one of those people who wants to rescue the brokenhearted. However, even God knew enough not to dwell with the wicked. Teach them and pray for them—yes. Stay and be affected by them while your testimony and goodness leave you—NO!

God loves you and knows how much you have loved this person who has been so abusive to you. If you haven't already drawn a line in the sand that states how much abuse is enough, then you need to. If you can't, then you need to put your faith in God. He has already drawn the line in the sand for you. His boundary over your life is to be nothing less than a son or daughter of dignity.

Act III

Exorcising the Narcissist from Your Life

"This above all: to thine own self be true,
And it must follow, as the night the day, Thou
canst not then be false to any man."

—William Shakespeare, *Hamlet*

Sadly, by now you have learned that the narcissist's behavior is by choice. The last act in your narcissist's play has led us to the finale—exorcising the narcissist from your life and heart. If you decided to stay in the relationship, then look at this section as simply purging yourself of fear, anxiety, anger, and low self-esteem. By reclaiming your dignity, you are leaving the old person behind and taking back the control that your narcissist took from you. If you are no longer in the relationship, let me guide you through the emotional land mines you might be trying to dodge.

In this section, we will deal with the aftermath of being in a relationship with a narcissist. These are the feelings one has when he or she experiences loss. Regardless of whether you are in the relationship, were discarded, or were the other man or woman who was used for narcissistic supply, you will go through the five stages of grief: denial, anger, bargaining, depression, and acceptance. Maybe you disagree and are wondering, "What is there to grieve? I hate this person!" Trust me, you will go through the stages! At one point in your relationship, you had a dream or blueprint for your life that included your partner, and it didn't go as planned. You will grieve the loss of the dream more than the loss of the person, because the person you wanted them to be isn't real. It was something you projected onto them. Painful emotions happen when you finally accept that your partner or ex is mentally and spiritually ill.

The realization that the narcissist will never give you what you want is heartbreaking. If you stay in the relationship, you will be their caretaker, parent, psychologist, and whatever other role you are to play to keep your narcissist happy. If you leave, you will be cast as the insecure, paranoid, or cruel person who victimized them. If you weren't in a relationship with the narcissist but were targeted for narcissistic supply, you will be portrayed as a stalker or unstable person who won't leave them alone. Any of these situations are bound to cause negative emotions.

I grieved over both my narcissists. I couldn't reconcile the difference between the person I thought they were and the person I had to accept they were. I remember nights crying myself to sleep and wondering if my narcissist hacker overheard any of my tears when he listened in to my room through my cell phone's speaker. How could he have missed so many tears? I cried so often over what he was doing to me. He knew I was upset over the hacking. He wanted me to hurt deeply. He enjoyed playing mind games with me and his wife. He liked using me to create drama to get attention from others. He felt justified in what he did and didn't believe I had the right to feel hurt because of it. He liked knowing I was suffering, and he didn't care because he was just a fan of Jesus, not a follower.

Maybe you are feeling the effects as I did. You feel yourself walking out of a dream or fog. For the first time in a long time, you are starting to see clearly who your narcissist really is: a cruel person. When you look at what they have done and what you have allowed, you might feel mad at yourself because you dismissed every ounce of intuition that was saying, "This isn't right! This isn't normal behavior!"

Embarrassment should be one of the stages of grief, but it isn't. I felt enormous embarrassment over what I put up with from both of my narcissists. I truly couldn't see them for who they were during that time. I overlooked their bad behavior because I liked the superficial things about them. Also, I had projected my own good characteristics onto them. "They had to be good people," I thought. "After all, they were active in their Christian faith." Boy was I naive! Inside of both of them was nothing spiritually good or worth liking. Important qualities like kindness, honesty, integrity, compassion, and empathy were so small that it was hard to say any were strong characteristics. If they were there in abundance, then I wouldn't have been treated so poorly, and neither would the women in my narcissist hacker's life.

When I look back, I see a woman who was truly lost, not the strong daughter of our Heavenly Father I am today. However, it took me a while to get to this place of strength—roughly two years, in fact, after my narcissist hacker's abuse. Recovery wasn't easy. I had to work on setting boundaries and rebuilding my dignity through recommitting myself to the standards God wanted of me. This was not an overnight thing. It takes time to heal, because you are repairing not only your heart, but also your mind and spirit.

Nothing ever goes away until it teaches us what we need to know. In my case, I learned several life lessons because of the abuse I experienced from these two individuals. One of the most important lessons I learned is this: You can't force someone to respect you, but you can refuse to be disrespected.

Unfortunately, it can be hard to know when to give up on a person when your narcissist is so good at pulling you back in with their charm or promises. Often, victims don't wake up from their dream until they are discarded or cheated on. That is when the real battle begins. The devil you cared for finally shows his or her true colors. They no longer hide their games. Instead, they come at you full force, ready to annihilate your heart. Regardless of whether you stay in the relationship or have already left, you will need to put on your spiritual armor to survive. Ephesians 6:10–13 talks about this armor that God wants you to wear:

> Finally, my brethren, be strong in the Lord, and in the power of his might. Put on the whole armour of God, that ye may be able to stand against the wiles of the devil. For we wrestle not against the flesh and blood, but against principalities, against powers, against rules of the darkness of this world, against the wickedness in high places. Wherefore take unto you the whole armour of God, that ye may be able to withstand in the evil day, and having done all, to stand.

This includes against the narcissists, sociopaths, and toxic individuals who wish to steal our happiness. God wants you to fight evil, not peacefully coexist with it. He clearly tells us to come away from the unrighteous and be separate (Isaiah 52:11; 2 Corinthians 6:17).

Jesus never ignored wrongdoings or settled for sin in people. From overturning the moneychanger's tables in the temple to the Seven

Woes of the Scribes and Pharisees, he bravely spoke the truth, publicly rebuked wrongdoing, and stood up to evil games. He did not ask us to honor people who were unrighteous and hurtful. If you believe that he was a spineless person who let others walk all over him because he was a forgiving and nice guy, then you don't know your savior at all. He was a confident being who made it known that he didn't tolerate evil. He stood up for what was right. He didn't settle for anything less. Neither should you!

So what is this spiritual armor you should wear? Ephesians 6:14–19 tells us, "Stand therefore, having your loins girt about with truth, and having on a breastplate of righteousness; and your feet shod with the preparation of the gospel of peace; above all, taking the shield of faith, wherewith ye shall be able to quench all the fiery darts of the wicked. And take the helmet of salvation, and the sword of the Spirit, which is the word of God. Praying always with all prayer and supplication in the Spirit, and watching thereunto with all perseverance and supplication for all saints."

If you decide to stay or choose to leave, you have chosen to fight a battle between goodness and evil. Even if you are no longer in the relationship, you will need to suit up for battle should your narcissist still have one foot in your life. You might be up against a Goliath who doesn't like your boundaries or a devil who is putting you down in a well-orchestrated smear campaign. Regardless, God is asking you to put on his armor. So what does spiritual armor look like in your life? Let's review:

- **Belt of Truth**: This is God's message over your life and what he represents. To wear the belt of truth means that you are making decisions in your life that center on God's word. Living and seeking the truth is your protection in life. It provides a strong foundation when you find yourself going through tough times. It is the religious beliefs you cling to. This means you're involved in a religion and reading the scriptures. You are doing all things spiritual to keep you on track and close to God.

- **Breastplate of Righteousness**: This is you maintaining your integrity and obedience by following God's commandments. You're not ignoring the bad behavior or sins of your narcissist just to have someone in your life. You're not staying stuck out of fear. You are not settling for unrighteousness in your narcissist. You are standing strong in your beliefs. You are trusting God to see you through this darkness.

- **Shoes of Readiness**: This is you always being ready to be that example for Christ and share his message to others by living a life of virtue. Therefore, you are the example for the narcissist. You set the tone for the relationship and keep your standards high. You won't live anything less than what God expects of you. That means the person who lives with you also lives by the same standards. If not, you trust God will find you someone who can.

- **Shield of Faith**: You believe that God is your refuge and strength. You know that God will conquer and prevail. He already won the battle in heaven. Satan is not stronger than he is. Therefore, you are not going to give into your insecurities or be gaslighted by your narcissist. You are not the problem. They are! You have faith not only in God, but also in yourself. You are strong and know that God is leading your footsteps, even when you can't see the future.

- **Helmet of Salvation**: The cost has been paid and our salvation is in Jesus. Nothing can separate us from his love. Forgiveness is granted to us if we only come to God with a humble heart and confess our sins. Through repentance, we can be washed cleaned and begin again. Therefore, if you made mistakes, you don't give up. God still has a life purpose for you and a plan for your life, with or without your narcissist in it.

- **Sword of the Spirit**: The word of God is your standard of truth and it will slay any attempt of deceit. It will expose it for what it is. You only need to pray and be aware of the promptings you get from the Holy Spirit. Pay close attention to your intuition. Look for the breadcrumbs that God is leaving you for clues. *You are not sitting in your relationship waiting for God to fix it.* Neither are you remaining a victim because someone discarded you. You are prepared for a spiritual battle against the narcissist's games. You are seeking the path God wants you on, which is not hard to find because it will always be one that maintains your dignity.

The road through grief is a battleground. Your battle will be with your emotions, your reaction to what your narcissist has done to you, and the meaning you give events. Don't sit around dwelling in unchallenged emotions and not take action to recover. Let your worship be your weapon and way out of inaction. Put on the armor of God, because your Savior won't leave your side! He is preparing a future filled with peace. However, you are going to have to walk through hell first to get to the other side, where the promised land is waiting. Don't settle. Trust him!

How Do You Break Up with a Narcissist?

Did you put on your armor? I hope so, because we have work to do! We talked about what it would take to stay with the narcissist; now let's talk about what it takes to leave the situation. This can be difficult because of the dream you have about your narcissistic partner. Who doesn't want a fairy-tale ending? For that reason alone, you will hang on until the bitter end. You are going to go through several stages that keep you from breaking up, so let's work through them together before you take the steps to end the relationship. Many of us struggle for years or our entire lifetime trying every possible alternative to make leaving unnecessary. Some of you are living in fear that you will be sinning if you walk away from your spouse, even if it's to restore your health. Others have a guilty conscience and think that their needs are selfish. Maybe you are turning to your pastors and bishops for a final consent that leaving this person is okay. Feel relief if you are one of those people who just wants to do the morally right thing. The Bible is full of scriptures instructing us, and in some cases demanding us, to leave, but these passages don't seem to be very well known. Here are a few of them:

> *"Do not be unequally yoked together with unbelievers. For what fellowship has righteousness with lawlessness? And what communion has light with darkness? And what accord has Christ with Belial? Or what part has a believer with an unbeliever?" (2 Corinthians 6:14–15)*

> *"But now I have written to you not to keep company with anyone, name a brother, who is sexually immoral, or covetous, or an idolater, or a reviler, or a drunkard, or an extortioner—not even to eat with such a person." (1 Corinthians 5:11)*

> *"A man that is a heretick after the first and second admonition reject; knowing that the that is such is subverted, and sinneth, being condemned of himself." (Titus 3:10–11)*

"Make no friendship with an angry man; and with a furious man thou shalt not go; lest thou learn his ways, and get a snare to thy soul." (Proverbs 22:34–35)

"But them that are without God judgeth. Therefore put away from among yourselves that wicked person." (1 Corinthians 5:13)

"Do not be misled: Bad company corrupts good character." (1 Corinthians 15:33)

"A hot-tempered person must pay the penalty; rescue them, and you will have to do it again." (Proverbs 19:19)

As you can see from the above scriptures, God is direct with us. He doesn't feel your spirituality can sufficiently grow in an abusive relationship. If you want to live in peace, then you are the one who needs to make the changes to have peace. However, Satan knows this and will do everything he can to keep you in an abusive relationship or thinking about your abuser long after you have been discarded.

We give ourselves excuses when it comes to avoiding change in our life. It's natural. However, this fear then allows us to lower our standards, which then causes us to have pain and anxiety because life doesn't measure up to our blueprint. I want you to pull out your blueprint for your life and look at it again. The things you wrote on your list are possible. However, they are extremely hard to obtain in a relationship with someone who is abusive and refuses to change, unless you cut off your emotions and become a robot in the relationship. Isn't it time you stop making excuses and start living in faith? God is waiting for you to take his hand.

It's difficult sometimes to trust God. We don't have the vision that he does. He can see far in advance the things he has in store for us. However, he doesn't tell us the route to get to that destination or how long it is going to take, where the funds are going to come from, or who we are going to meet. He leads us one step at a time. If you trust him and take that step into the unknown, then he will show you the next step. Step by step, he will lead you into your destiny. The problem with our faith is that we like details. However, if you had all the facts, then you wouldn't need any faith. If you are waiting for all the details, then you are going to be waiting your entire life. God wants us to pray and put our trust in him. That is how we grow spiritually. God isn't just interested in your destination; he wants to teach you along the way. He is getting you prepared and helping you grow up.

God will put us in situations in which our friends can't help us or we don't have the experience. Too often, we shrink back and give in to our fear about the things we haven't experienced before. We might say to ourselves, "What if I do this and it doesn't work out?" or "What if I leave and I am not any better off?" God knows you feel this way. These things are tests. He wants to see if you are going to let the fear of what you can't see hold you back or if you are going to trust him and step into the unknown. Did you know that in the unknown places of our lives dwell the miracles we are seeking? This is where you discover who you are, what you are capable of, and abilities you never thought you had. The unknown is where you will accomplish more than you ever dreamed. Just because you don't have the details doesn't mean God doesn't have the details. He knows what lies ahead of you. He wouldn't be leading you out of abuse if he didn't have the future mapped out for you and all that you would need to go through to get to the next level of your life.

God wants you to take the next step even when you don't know the destination or details of your future. This is what Abraham did. God asked him to leave the place he was living. He was to pack up his belongings and family and head out to the place that God was going to give him. The only problem was that God didn't give him any details. The scriptures tell us that Abraham went out not knowing where he was going. I can imagine that he told his wife Sarah that God was taking him to a better land. If my husband said that to me, I would be asking for details and saying, "Where are we going? Are you sure God told you this? How are we going to provide for the family?" Of course, Abraham didn't know the details to tell his wife. *What we can learn from trusting God is that some things are leaps of faith.* Sometimes things don't make sense, but they will later. So don't give in to the fear of playing it safe. Abraham understood that just because he didn't have the answers and just because he was nervous didn't mean he wasn't supposed to do what God asked of him.

The scriptures say, "The steps of a good man are ordered by the Lord; and he delighteth in his way" (Psalm 37:23). If you take the first step not knowing all the details, trusting that God knows what he is doing, then every step of the way there will be provision, favor, and wisdom. It is uncomfortable not knowing. You have to stretch yourself, pray, and believe. However, with each step, you will reap God's blessing and grow stronger.

Staying in the familiar even though it is comforting can stop being a blessing and instead become a curse. Familiarity can keep you from your destiny. Don't let your comfort keep you from being all that God created you to be. If Abraham had put his comfort above fulfilling his purpose, I wouldn't be talking about him, because there would be nothing great to remember. You cannot play it safe your entire life and reach the fullness of your destiny. Don't let the what-ifs talk you out of a better life. You might be saying, "What if I never meet anyone? What if I don't have the funds to make it on my own? What if I am worse off than where I was?" Here is the thing about those what-ifs. You won't know unless you try. Instead of those questions, ask yourself this one: "When you come to the end of your life, will you have more regrets because of the risk you didn't take or the risks you took?"

I didn't know the future after my narcissistic abuse. I started to unravel and lose faith in God and people because of what I went through. I looked at my future and couldn't see what God had in store for me. If I had walked away from God, you wouldn't be reading these pages. My story wouldn't have helped thousands of people. If God showed us the future, we might shy away from it. This is true in my own life. If God told me years ago that I would be writing a book about narcissism, I would have said, "This is nuts. No way do I want this future." However, I went through the abuse, took the lessons from it, and grew spiritually. Those lessons became part of my life purpose and have enabled me to help people who were hurt like I was. Benjamin Franklin once said, "Justice will not be served until those who are unaffected are as outraged as those who are." I hope that through my story of pain I am inspiring you to be so outraged that you will never again let someone hurt you. What I have learned through my faith is that God wants to groom us into the people we are meant to be. He has things in store for you that are going to boggle your mind. He has places he is going to take you, people you are going to influence, and things you are going to do because of the hell you walked through. However, you will never get there if you think abuse is all he had in store for you. Your blessings will always be found in the unknown, but it will take you stepping into those attributes of a son or daughter of our Heavenly Father to meet that destiny.

When Joshua and the Israelites came to the Jordan River, there was no way to get across. They had heard that Moses held up his rod and the Red Sea parted. I am sure Joshua felt that same thing might happen for him. However, God had a different plan. God told Joshua to tell the priests to walk into the river and then the waters would part. I am sure the priests thought that didn't make sense, because walking into the water would cause them to drown. The priests did as Joshua said and walked into the water. I am sure they had feelings of doubt and some felt they would perish. I suppose they could have talked themselves out of it. Instead, they dared to step into the unknown. The scriptures tell us that the moment their feet touched the water's edge, the waters upstream began to pile up, and before long the whole river bed was empty. They were able to walk over to the other side. However, realize that the miracle happened along the way. In life, some of us want God to part the river before we go across. However, that is not how he works. He wants you to go, and then he will part the river. He wants to see your faith. Stepping into the unknown is where you will see miracles. However, you won't get there unless you have faith.

God sometimes puts us in situations where he knows we can't make it on our own. That again is a test of our faith. Sometimes God uses the journey to prepare us for where we are going. Remember that the journey is more important than the destination. Look for the lessons in your abuse. Maybe you didn't have boundaries. Maybe you lowered your values. Whatever you did to let it continue is an important part in your story that you don't want to gloss over and forget. Those are the lessons you should learn to prepare yourself for the next part of your future.

So where are you going? Maybe you have come to a place in your relationship that you have reconciled a dozen times with no success, or maybe you are no longer in the relationship and wishing you had one more chance. A narcissist's lies and games eventually run out like money in Vegas or the coins of a child at a glass case trying to win a stuffed animal. This is when God wants you to let go and finally live.

So how do you tell the narcissist that it is over? The answer is very carefully. If you choose to make an exit, don't expect life to suddenly get better. Narcissists love drama and will make this their finest performance. No matter how careful you are, if you reject a narcissist, they will feel humiliated. It makes sense, doesn't it? They think they are "all that." It is most certainly a blow to their ego that you don't see that anymore. In an effort to assert their superiority, they may try to dominate the conversation and draw you into a debate. There are two responses when you dump the narcissist. They will show you how evil they can be, or they will try to win you back. When they take the hostile approach, they will do everything to destroy you. They might jump into a relationship with the first thing to come along to provoke jealousy, or they might take you off their medical insurance so you have to fight in court to win it back. Regardless of what they do, all narcissists like to start their smear campaign by telling your family and friends that you have insecurity issues. What once was private about you becomes everyone's business.

The opposite of all of this is trying to win you back. Don't get excited if they choose this option. It isn't because they are madly in love and all of a sudden respect you. They simply haven't been presented with an available option, such as another single man or woman to replace you. When trying to win you back, they will do things that are out of character with who they were the week before you told them you were leaving:

- They will claim to change into a different person.
- They will beg forgiveness and will tell you they are sorry for what they have put you through.
- They will shower you with gifts.
- They will start saying all the stuff you wanted them to say when you were with each other.
- They will go over all the good times you had together.
- They will show you love and be supportive for the first time in ages.
- They will cry in front of you and make it look sincere.
- They will tell you the other man or woman is not as good as you are.

Narcissistic abuse victims tend to report that they have given their partners more than one second chance, because they didn't want to believe that their change in behavior was simply a stage they were putting them through—idolization. They hoped that their narcissist wasn't like other narcissists and that this time they were sincere, but they are what they are. They use the same tactics to get what they want no matter where they are on the spectrum with narcissistic personality disorder. Your narcissist is not less of a narcissist than others with the same disorder. That is as silly as saying she or he is less a schizophrenic than others because they don't always hear voices. The fact is that they hear voices. No matter where your narcissist is on the narcissism scale, all narcissists use the phases of idolization, devaluation, and discard. It is the heart of their disorder.

Narcissists know what you want to hear. They are master manipulators. However, it doesn't last. Their seesaw of emotions will resurface, possibly with rage followed by insincere apologies and promises to never to do that to you again. Then will come the controlling actions, like telling you not to say certain things or the sly passive-aggressive comments to whittle away at your self-confidence. It always goes back to the same games and bad behavior. Many call this the boomerang effect. A normal person might see a breakup as a sad situation. However, narcissists get a sick dopamine rush off the drama, because it is giving them a temporary rush of attention. These boomerang cycles and the conquests make them feel alive and give them a thrill. This is why the narcissist will use every known lure, going to great lengths to reel you back in. It is a game of conquest and control—the ultimate rush. Therefore, it is imperative that you wake up to their romancing during this breakup phase. Sorry, it is just a phase like all the other times.

So what do you say to tell them it is over? The best way to leave a narcissist is to cut ties and say as little as possible. You might say something like, "I tried to make this relationship work, but nothing has changed since our last breakup. It's not healthy for me to stay with you. I wish you well." Then leave the room. If you can leave the building, even better, because they are going to follow you and try to trivialize everything you have experienced either to win you back by making you second-guess yourself or to beat you down with their rage. If you are lucky, they will give you the silent treatment. Therefore, you have to be okay with not making a big production out of ending it. By the time you have come to the decision that you need to leave, there isn't anything that needs to be said.

If you are ready to walk away, then let it be clean without a fight. Doing this in a public place can make it easier for you, unless your partner likes making a public scene. Most don't, because they care about what other people think and don't want to look out of control to a watching crowd. You could even do this in a letter if you're scared of how they will react. In addition, you might also do this with a family member present if you need someone to protect you from their reaction.

Whatever way you choose to tell a narcissist, make sure you are prepared for the outcome. If your name is on all the credit cards, make sure you change that or they might go on a spending spree to put you in your place. If you have to leave the house, make sure you have a place to stay for a few days. If you need to get your things from your old apartment and you don't want a confrontation with your ex, then call the police or a friend and have them present when you grab a few things to take to your new place. Don't be naive! Narcissists' emotions are extreme. Prepare for the worst or regret it later.

When you have a kind heart, being unpleasant to someone is never easy. Breaking up with a narcissist is a lot like standing in front of Goliath. Take counsel from the story of David. David was a shepherd, the youngest of eight sons. King Saul and his men were battling the Philistines, one of whom was a nine-foot giant named Goliath. The men of Saul's army were afraid of Goliath, and there was no one to stand up to him. However, David, filled with faith and a passion for God's name, which was being blasphemed by Goliath, slew Goliath with a stone and a sling. Then he cut off Goliath's head with the giant's own sword. When the Philistines saw that their champion was dead, they fled before the Israelites, who had a great victory over them. I am most certainly not suggesting that you cut off the head of your narcissist, but there is a parallel to be found in this story, because he or she has been a giant presence in your life.

An important point in this story is that Goliath was taunting God, not unlike the way the narcissist plays games with you. Until David came into the Israelite camp, no one was willing to step out in faith and face the giant. However, David's faith was so strong that he was willing to believe that the Lord would go with him and enable him to defeat Goliath (1 Samuel 17:36–37). That is how your faith should be if you choose to walk away or even if you stay. You are to defeat this giant with God's help, which is to be found in prayer, scripture, spiritual leaders, books, sermons, service projects, and counselors.

Here is more you can learn from David:

- Trust God no matter the circumstances. David completely trusted his Lord to bring him victory. You should trust that God is going to help you close this chapter in your life.

- Rely on God instead of on yourself or "things." David was small, but he had a strong faith in God, and because of that he triumphed. God will help you with your finances by opening doors of opportunity, but you have to do your part. Look for a job, get that certification in a trade, or get out there and network with people. God is going to open doors, but you need to take action to walk through them.

- When we prove that we're faithful with a few things, God will trust us with greater things (Matthew 25:21). David learned to trust God by killing a lion and a bear (1 Samuel 17:32–37) before he stood up to Goliath. He later became the king of Israel. As our faith grows, so do God's blessings for us. They start out small and then they grow over time. So plant your seed of faith and watch it blossom.

- When the enemy laughs at what God's people are doing, it is usually a sign that God is going to bless his people in a wonderful way. Goliath ridiculed David when the shepherd boy met the giant with only a sling. Jesus was mocked by the soldiers during his trial and while he was hanging on the cross. If your narcissist is cutting you down for wanting to leave, then they are no different from the unrighteous in the Bible. You are dancing with the devil and he doesn't want you to go off and be happy without him. Remember, when the enemy rages on earth, God laughs in heaven (Psalm 2:4).

- David had self-confidence because he believed in God and he believed in himself. When you have low self-esteem, you might rely only on God. Like any good parent, God wants you to rely on yourself too.

- Seek to honor God rather than yourself. Sons and daughters of our Heavenly Father are humble and speak the truth, as God would have us do. David said to Goliath, "You come at me with sword and spear and javelin, but I come against you in the name of the Lord Almighty, the God of the armies of Israel, who you have defied. . . . All those gathered here will know that it is not by sword or spear that the Lord saves; for the battle is the Lord's, and he will give all of you into our hands" (1 Samuel 17:45, 47).

Remember that you are standing as a strong son or daughter of our Heavenly Father in front of a spiritually and mentally ill child of God who has lost their way. You are not to back down because of them. You are to stand as a light and show them the way. If they love God, they will make the changes you need so you can live in peace and righteousness. If not, they must go.

Battling through the Stages of Grief

Fighting your way to the last stage of grief, acceptance, will be the greatest triumph in your recovery. However, it is the hardest place on the battlefield to get to because you must give up your dream about the narcissist and trust God will provide you with something better. Moses freed the slaves in Egypt, but even when they were free, many of them felt like God had abandoned them. "And wherefore hath the Lord brought us unto this land, to fall by the sword, that our wives and our children should be prey? Were it not better for us to return to Egypt?" (Numbers 14:3). Many of them wanted to leave Moses and the wilderness to return to slavery in Egypt because times were hard and they couldn't trust the Lord. Maybe you feel this way. Maybe you feel it is better to put up with intermittent abuse because there is nothing better out there for you. Maybe you are saying to yourself, "At least I have a roof over my head, a few good times, and someone to be with." And you think this isn't settling? Let me snap you out of that comfortable position. Yes, it is settling! Do you really think God has brought you all this way only to abandon you? The answer to that lies in our fears and insecurities. These are the battles that will help build you up as a son or daughter of God, not constantly being devalued by your narcissist.

Hold tight to your faith as you go through the stages I mention in the following text. Satan will test your boundaries and whittle away at your confidence. The Lord says, "Come unto me, all ye that labour and are heavy laden, and I will give you rest" (Matthew 11:28). God wants you to know he is not done with you yet. "The Lord is close to the brokenhearted and saves those who are crushed in spirit" (Psalm 34:18). He has plans to bring you a better future, but first you have to do the work to heal. Notice how I said "work." Yes! The cycle of grief shouldn't be a yearlong depression where you do nothing and let time do the work. You have to fight through this battlefield of emotions.

In her book *On Death and Dying*, Swiss-born psychiatrist Elisabeth Kübler-Ross popularized a five-stage model of grieving based on her research into how people respond to news of terminal illness. Her five stages have since been used worldwide to describe all grief responses.

Below is her model of the grief process with my examples of what you might be experiencing in them and what you can do to overcome them. Remember that you can bounce around from one stage to the next. You could have depression throughout the stages and then one day feel like bargaining, only to go back to denial the next.

- **Denial**
  This is the shock reaction. *"It can't be true." "No, not me."* You refuse to believe what happened. Maybe your narcissist left you, or maybe you found out they were unfaithful. Regardless, you just had your dream blown apart by what they did, and you do not want to believe it is true because it is too painful. You are not ready to give up on your dream.

  Some narcissistic abuse victims stay in this stage because of their strong desire for the fairy-tale ending, or they hang on to hope that the idolization phase will return. They don't want to accept that the idolization phase is just that—a phase. It too shall pass.

- **Anger**
  Resentment grows. *"Why me?" "This isn't fair!"* We direct blame at God, others, and ourselves. We feel agitated, irritated, moody, and on edge. This stage can last a long time, and that is why I asked you to stay off the narcissistic abuse recovery forums. I believe the posts stir the pot of anger in your mind. You rehash events and then relive the emotions. With prolonged anger, you can become irrational. You can even forget who you are and stoop to playing the same games as the narcissist. Engaging in war with a narcissist is not wise. I will talk more about that later in this section.

- **Bargaining**
  We try to make a deal, insisting that things be the way they used to be. *"God, if you heal my husband's abuse, then I won't miss a day*

of church." We call a temporary truce with God. However, there is no point in bargaining with God. There is nothing he needs that you are not already expected to do.

- ***Depression***

  This is when you say, "Poor me. Nobody loves me," to all your friends. You have taken on the role of victim and settled in for the winter. This stage can happen with all the others or after bargaining. It is when you are close to acceptance, but not quite there. You might be able to admit to loss and have sadness about it or you might feel hopeless and are one step away from driving past your narcissist's house to try to win them back. You haven't quite gotten to the part where you sort out the lessons in all this grief. You haven't planned your future without this person.

- ***Acceptance***

  In this stage, you are calmer. You are past the tears and rages over what happened to you. It is a time of silent reflection and regrouping. You now say, "Life has to go on. What do I do now?" You are willing to admit your ex-partner has an undiagnosed mental disorder, which was the unexpected plot twist in your relationship, and everything is making sense. You are starting to learn life lessons in all this pain. You are maintaining your boundaries and not engaging the narcissist in their games. You have given up on the idea that narcissism can be cured. You have accepted that it can only be managed and you are a caretaker if you choose to remain in the relationship. If you are no longer in the relationship, you have no contact with them because you know they won't change, and any attempts by them to lure you back into a relationship is a game. You understand that if they really wanted you they would have treated you better or wouldn't have consistently crossed boundaries in your relationship. You are in a confident place and you trust God is going to provide for you. You are striving to have the attributes God wants for you. You are rebuilding your confidence, authentic self, and identity. You are rewriting your life's resume and blueprint. You are establishing boundaries that you will never let anyone cross again. Remember that you will never accept gratitude as a solution to your problems until you have reached the last stage of acceptance.

I would love to tell you that you can move through these stages quickly, but that would be a lie. Your level of attachment to the dream of the person you wanted in your life can be so strong that you will go back to the bargaining stage several times to see if you can try a different approach to fix them. It is not uncommon for narcissistic abuse victims to give their narcissists dozens of second chances. Your ability to navigate each stage will depend on you overcoming your fears and rebuilding your faith in God.

My therapist told me my abuse would take me through these stages of grief. However, I found them to be like waiting rooms rather than doors I could walk through. However, I had to wait for "time" to call my number. What I found lacking was God. Don't get me wrong! You need to change either your perspective or your behavior if you want to overcome a stage. But without the answer to why you should change your approach beyond a therapist telling you that you will feel better if you do, some things in therapy don't stick. There needs to be something greater for us to believe in, and this raises questions such as, *Why am I here? Why should I be good? Why should I let go? Why should I choose a spiritual life? Why should I strive after the attributes of a son or daughter of our Heavenly Father?*

Your therapist is not going to give you those theological discussions during therapy. The stages in the grief process track typical grief responses. However, they do not attempt to assess if this is what is best to occur. Nor could they assess, simply through scientific research, whether these responses correspond to God's process for grieving and growing. Believing in the sufficiency of scripture, we can focus on a revelation-based model of grief. We can address and assess the typical five stages of grieving; however, we can move beyond them faster.

I have come up with my own model for grief that includes God. I call it PEACE. Let's look at the stages of grief again but change our perspective. If God were to create a model of grief to outrank Elisabeth Kübler-Ross's model, I think it would look like this:

Instead of . . .	Would be . . .
Denial	**P**roactive—Honesty with Yourself
Anger	**E**xpression—Honesty with God
Bargaining	**A**ssistance—Asking God for Help

| Depression | **C**omfort—Receiving God's Help |
| Acceptance | **E**ducation—Remembering You're a Daughter or Son of our Heavenly Father |

Can you see that I have gone from a hopeless list of stages in grief to one of hope with my list of peace? More than anything else, Elisabeth Kübler-Ross's model of the stages of grief keeps people a victim. Being told you're in a stage of grief gives a person excuses to stay there. That is not God's plan for you. Instead, picture yourself in counsel with God and formulating a plan that is in line with being a strong son or daughter of our Heavenly Father. Let's look at my new model of grief closer:

- **Proactive**
  Instead of denial, this stage is replaced with opening yourself up to everything you have denied. You are seeing the relationship through God's eyes. His eyes are truth. When you want to give in to refusing all of it to be true, you are in counsel with the Lord, feeling his spirit and being strong enough to face the worst because you know your worth.

To-Do List

1. If you are stuck in this stage, ask yourself what you are in denial about. This is when you go back through the first section and list all the things you see that support the idea that your partner has narcissistic personality disorder. Maybe you are not sure. Do you really need to have a diagnosis from a psychiatrist to be certain? Isn't it certain enough that you are being abused?
2. Step back and try to see your narcissist's actions, not the breadcrumbs they are leaving for you. You don't want to live in a state of hope about your narcissist's feelings, rather a place of certainty. If they wanted to be with you, they would be chasing after you. If they are giving you excuses, saying things like "If it was meant to be, it will be," then they are playing games with you. People who love you don't play games. They are straightforward with you. If you have to guess if someone loves you, then they don't. If you have to convince them of your worth, then they don't value you.

- **Expression**
Instead of anger, this stage is replaced with being honest with God about what has transpired and how you feel about it. You are not blaming him but working with him through the scriptures or through church leaders to come to terms with what happened. You are humble in spirit and in control of your emotions.

To-Do List

1. Read the next section, where we talk about how to deal with anger and get to the truth behind why you are feeling this emotion intensely. For now, dig deeper to see why you are mad. For example, let's say you are mad that they broke up with you. Go deeper. What does that mean to you? Does it mean that you believe that you won't find someone better than him or her? Does it mean you feel like you're not good enough for someone? Do you really believe that? If you do, you must concede that you have a self-esteem problem and don't trust that God can help you find better. Instead of focusing on anger, you need to work on confidence instead.

- **Assistance**
Instead of bargaining, you are crying out for God's help. You are praying and seeking spiritual guidance, not trying to get healing from the person who broke you. You are not making God promises if he gives you this person back. You are humbling yourself to be teachable and listening to God's plan for your life, which is one of dignity.

To-Do List

1. Write a list of all the things you are bargaining with God about. Also, write a list of all the things you are bargaining with this narcissist about. Now write a list of why God doesn't feel you need to bargain at all. In this stage, you might be saying to yourself, *"Maybe if I weren't so insecure about the exes he had or the trust I didn't have with him, things would have turned out differently."* Stop saying these things to yourself and look deeper. Ask why you are rationalizing the behavior of an abusive person. Then go even deeper and ask why your insecurity is allowing you to bargain for someone who is not God's best.

2. Start looking for God's messages in your life. You should be picking apart the sermons and lessons you heard in church to see what message God has for you. You might find answers in a Bible-study class, books, or videos to help you recover. During this stage, you should also be reading your scriptures. The point is to search for God's guiding hand. He hasn't abandoned you.

- **Comfort**

  Instead of depression, you are lifting your heart up to God in gratitude for what you still have, and you are embracing a renewed chance to create a better version of yourself. You have put your total trust in God's word.

To-Do List

1. Depression needs to be managed, because it will eat away at your health. It most certainly did mine. I had all sorts of lab values that were off. Talk to your health provider about getting you started on antidepressants. If you prefer something natural, then look into alternatives. Valerian is one way to combat stress, as well as getting B_{12} shots. Friends are great to discuss your problems with, but they are not trained professionals. This book helps you spiritually. However, a counselor or psychologist can help you mentally. You should be making an appointment so they can help you through this process.
2. Join my Staying Positive University community on Facebook or any positive community so you can have daily positive quotes or affirmations to keep your outlook up. Stay off the narcissistic abuse recovery Facebook pages and forums.
3. Plan a trip or an adventure to get your mind on the fun God has in store for you. If you are still in the relationship, escape to your favorite place alone or with friends to get your mind straight about what happened. You need to come out of the fog and see life as a daring adventure full of happiness to come. It is a beginning, not an end.
4. Stop dwelling in the ridiculous notion that you were not good enough for this person. Actually, you are better than him or her! They will live their life always trying to get attention from others. What kind of life is that? A terrible one. You, on the other hand, have talents and character that surpass the games of the narcissist. If they discarded you, it is because that is their disorder. It has nothing to do with you. If you

looked like a supermodel and were a millionaire, they still would have treated you poorly and discarded you. They are just unhappy and bored individuals. Pull out your journal and write all the qualities you like about yourself and all the qualities you want to have. Then set a goal each week to strive to have that quality. It is that simple and much better than feeling sorry for yourself.

5. You are showing God your gratitude for the things you have by helping others. You are giving back to have his blessings in your life. You're putting yourself in situations where you might meet people who will lift your spirit and help you learn the lessons from this tragedy.

- **Education**
  Instead of acceptance, you are in your cocoon state, transforming into a stronger and more improved version of a son or daughter of our Heavenly Father. You are looking for the lesson in all the pain. You are letting God teach you about a better life. You are also preparing your heart so you can forgive.

To-Do List

1. You are now in a place that might feel bittersweet. You have moments of sadness when you think back on the situation, but you trust God is planning your footsteps. Therefore, you are making plans for the future. This means you are now in a place where you can make five-year plans. Take out your journal and write a goal for your finances, career, home, love life, friendships, spiritual life, and health.

2. I want you to dissect the dream you had about your narcissist. Write a letter to God asking why the dream you had of them doesn't fit who they are. It is important that you acknowledge that it was a dream based on unhealthy love and desperation.

3. Journal why you are worthy of someone who can share your life's blueprint. What do you have to offer? I know you have a lot, because narcissists always try to find someone with a good heart to make others believe they have one too. So boast while you write. Then write a letter to God telling him who you are going to become so you can attract the right type of person into your life. Use the attributes I have listed in this book as a reference. What attributes are you missing?

4. Create a list of boundaries to teach people how to treat you, so you will always have respect and dignity.

These are the stages of grief that God expects us to be in, and they are stages of peace because we have faith that he will see us through them. Grief is an emotion common to the human experience, and we witness the process of grief throughout the Bible. So don't feel like you are alone. God wants you to know that you are not. Multiple people in the Bible experienced deep loss and sadness, including Job, Naomi, Hannah, and David. Even Jesus mourned (John 11:35; Matthew 23:37–39). After Lazarus died, Jesus went to the village of Bethany, where Lazarus was buried. When Jesus saw Martha and the other mourners weeping, he also wept. He was moved by their grief and also by the fact of Lazarus's death. The astounding thing is that, even though Jesus knew he was going to raise Lazarus from the dead, he chose to partake of the grief of the situation. Jesus truly is a high priest who can "empathize with our weaknesses" (Hebrews 4:15). I am sure he has wept with you. Therefore, it is okay to grieve for a while. However, notice that Jesus didn't wallow in his grief for a prolonged period of time. He had things to do. He took action and raised Lazarus. Your job is to rise up with God's help.

One step in overcoming grief is having the right perspective. First, we recognize that grief is a natural response to pain and loss. There is nothing wrong with grieving because your relationship didn't work out or grieving because your narcissist used you in a game of triangulation with no real motives to pursue you. There is no shame in grieving even if you weren't in the relationship. Being used by someone is hurtful.

Second, we know that times of grief serve a purpose. Ecclesiastes 7:2 says, "It is better to go to the house of mourning than to go to the house of feasting, for this is the end of all man, and the living will lay it to his heart." This verse implies that grief can be good, because it can refresh our perspective on life. This a place for you to look for the lessons in your pain. What did you learn? How were you supposed to change?

When you start to change your perspective, two things happen. You change your actions or feelings—and sometimes both. This shift in thinking helps us to get unstuck in the process of grieving, because we have new information that helps us satiate this need to know why this happened to us.

As I battled for the answer to why this abuse happened to me, I kept looking to myself as a reason. I believed I said or did something that warranted abuse from these two men. That was the wrong perspective. Once I changed my thinking, I became unstuck. I needed to accept that these two individuals had narcissistic personality disorder. They could have left me alone, but there would have been no fun in that for them. I wanted to see them as normal. But they weren't. Therefore, I was projecting normal traits and reasoning onto them. They had messed-up reasons for why they did things, but my rational mind was trying to see where they were coming from. *I was trying to understand crazy.* That was my problem. When I changed my perspective, I stopped giving excuses to my narcissist's behavior and began seeing all the symptoms of their illness. This realization helped bring me out of the denial and bargaining stage.

My beautiful friend, you will get through this pain! I did. Feelings are temporary. "Weeping may endure for a night, but joy cometh in the morning" (Psalm 30:5). Eventually, there is an end to mourning. Grief has its purpose, but it also has its limit. The scriptures also go on to say, "Cast thy burden upon the Lord, and he shall sustain thee: he shall never suffer the righteous to be moved." (Psalm 55:22). Therefore, I will say it again, "This pain you have experienced will pass!" There is hope on the horizon!

I finally got over what both of my narcissists had done to me. It was a slow process, but I never gave up. I had faith that the Lord would get me to this point, so I could share what I learned with you. Maybe healing won't happen immediately. However, if you put your trust in God, you will get there faster rather than waiting on time to pass. Remember that God closes doors for reasons we might not understand until later. Look for the lesson he wants you to learn. It is not one of punishment, but of love. He knows your eternal potential and, like any parent, loves you immeasurably.

How to Handle Your Emotions

Now that we've talked about the stages of grief, let's talk about the emotions you are dealing with because of the narcissistic abuse. The key to changing how you feel about something is to question what it means and gain a different perspective.

Every time you experience a negative emotion, I want you to see it as a call to action instead of as something to endure. You need to change your perspective about the negative emotions you are experiencing. Don't see them as your enemy, but rather as your best friend, because feeling them is pushing you to change by seeking your Heavenly Father's help. Notice that I didn't say they are pushing you to change your narcissist's behavior. As I mentioned before, this book is not so much about changing your partner as it is about changing you within your circumstances. Setting up camp in negative emotions, hoping they will go away, is a life waster. Let's tackle them and get rid of them once and for all. But first, let's look at how people handle their emotions recklessly. They do this in many ways.

- **They avoid them**. People avoid rejection so they don't have to feel the pain associated with it. Therefore, this choice might cause them to not have deep relationships, because it requires vulnerability and openness to take that relationship to the next level. The problem with this is they can't avoid emotions. Sometimes the very emotions we avoid create them for us. Doesn't it make sense that if you avoid the uncomfortable emotion of rejection, then you create more bitter emotions in its place?

- **Some downplay emotions**. People might be in an abusive relationship but rationalize that it isn't that bad, thus avoiding the intensity of emotions like anger or sadness. Therefore, they continue to endure emotions or pretend they are not there because they don't want to take action. Embracing emotions compels us to act. The problem with this is that the more you ignore your emotions, the more intense they get, until you erupt.

- **People use emotions for competition**. They gossip with their friends about who has the worst things happening in their life. They do it for the attention. Unfortunately, this approach gets them nowhere. It only allows people to know too much information about their private life and possibly provide information they can spread to others, which can create more problems down the road.

A healthy individual's approach is to learn from and use negative emotions. This is what I want from you. Whether you are in a relationship with a narcissist or have left that situation, you will want to strengthen this area of your life. You have been in a constant state of reaction to your narcissist's behavior. This has caused a surge of negative emotions. It is time to zero in on these emotions and eradicate them so you can move forward and live a happier future. By digging through your emotions to understand them, rather than just feel them, you can progress out of the various stages of grief.

Negative emotions are created when *we give meaning* to the experiences we encounter. Therefore, it is safe to say your narcissist didn't make you mad. You made yourself mad by giving meaning to what the narcissist said to you. For example, if your narcissistic partner is putting you down, you might interpret the meaning behind what they are saying as true or false. This choice will require you to call on experiences you had that support or reject their claim. This internal check-and-balance system is our self-esteem. Your self-esteem is all the supported claims about yourself that you use as a guideline for how people treat you.

All those negative feelings that you are having about your narcissist need to be seen not as emotions, but as calls to action. Every time you have a negative emotion, you need to ask yourself, "What do I have to believe to feel this way?" Behind every emotion is a belief that is driving it. For example, if you're angry because he quickly moved on to another person, instead of saying that is the source of your anger, you need to go beyond it. What is the belief you have about that situation? Question it. Do you believe that you are not attractive enough? Do you believe that you won't find someone who thinks you're as good as the new person in your narcissist's life? When you look beneath those negative emotions, you find beliefs about yourself or about fairness that you feel are being challenged.

What we feel is not based on our experience but on our interpretation of our experience. I want you to close your eyes and think about something that you hope will occur in the future. Now open your eyes and tell me whether you see two possibilities when you hope. You probably see two expectations: either it will happen or not. Now close your eyes and think about the same thing you hoped would happen, but this time expect it to happen. Open your eyes and tell me whether you feel a difference between the two. Some will say that hope felt passive and uncertain, while expecting made them feel better because it felt like real action. They were more alive with envisioning that wish happening. This exercise was meant to let you know that you can change your emotions. Notice that nothing changed about the expectation I had you think about. Only you did. You changed your feelings. Therefore, it is possible to change your emotions *if you are willing to change your perspective.*

I believe that when God designed us he gave us negative emotions because he wanted them to be a signal to us that something has to change. Positively used, they can become fuel for changing our lives. So in a positive way, negative emotions are needed. In my recovery, I wasn't changing my emotions; rather, I was reacting to them. Through spiritual wisdom, I learned that Satan is to be found in negative reactions. God is to be found in change. In essence, I wasn't doing God or myself any good by sitting around feeling angry all the time. God wanted me to transform into something better.

Below is a list of negative emotions and what they are calling you to fix. I want you to copy this list and put it somewhere visible for the next week. You can refer to this list for help understanding why you are feeling this way beyond the typical answer, "My narcissist hurt me." Much of the wisdom I gathered about changing my emotions can be further explained by author Tony Robbins's motivational DVDs *The Ultimate Edge*. His simplification of the process of getting over anger cut my therapy time in half. I was able to cut through my confusion with unmanaged emotions and recover with this wisdom-based formula. However, before we get to the "handling part" of our emotions, let's look at the hidden reasons behind them. Once you understand your own emotions, you can use this guide to understand others'. I have listed ten emotions. Of course, there are more than ten. However, the categories are broad enough that you can figure out where yours fall. For example, let's say you are experiencing boredom. That would fall under loneliness, because you are not finding anything to do because of a lack of interactions with people. You get the idea, right? Let's look at the table below:

Negative Emotions	What These Emotions Mean
Uncomfortable emotions (embarrassment, self-consciousness, awkwardness, or shame)	You are avoiding feeling because of fear.
Fear emotions (anxiety, worry, unease, or panic)	You must prepare. Something is coming that you need to deal with.
Hurt emotions (sadness, the blues, and sorrow)	There is an expectation that has not been met, and you feel a sense of loss.

Anger emotions (rage, disgust, or hatred)	You have a standard for your life that is not being met by another person or by yourself. Anger is usually an outgrowth of hurt, which is a feeling of loss. This is the buildup of frustration because of one too many hurts that haven't been expressed.
Frustration emotions (discontent, irritation, annoyance, or dissatisfaction)	You need to change your approach to reaching your goal. Whatever you're going after isn't happening because you haven't changed your approach.
Disappointment (regret or dismay)	You need to realize that an outcome you are going after isn't going to happen unless you change your expectations and make them appropriate for the situation at hand.
Guilt (self-condemnation or self-reproach)	This means you violated your own standards and you have to do something immediately to change yourself so it doesn't happen in the future. You can only change your present or future actions. You can't change the past.
Inadequacy (insecurity or low self-worth)	This means you need to do something right away to be better in this category.
Hopelessness (despair, giving up, or feeling lost)	This means you need to reevaluate what is most important to you in this situation.
Loneliness (ruin, desolation, or friendlessness)	This means that you need a connection with someone. It says you love people and need them in your life.

Now that you know what the emotions are telling you, how will you change them? This requires you to do the following seven steps. Again, you will want to make a copy of this list and put it in a place where you can see it daily. Downloading it to a notepad cell-phone app and listing it there is a great place to access it quickly. Throughout your recovery, you will need to do the following steps when an unpleasant emotion occurs. By doing so you can change your state and quicken your recovery.

1. **Identify your emotion.** Look at the above list and see which category your emotion falls under. For example, you might want to see where jealousy fits. Are you really jealous or are you feeling inadequate that you can't meet the standards your spouse wants in a relationship? On the other hand, is it really anger because he doesn't make you feel desired? You might have one emotion competing for both spots—anger and inadequacy. Regardless, identify where it falls on the list above, and remember that a big part of emotional maturity is being able to feel an emotion without having to act on it.

2. **Acknowledge the signal it is offering you.** Look at the list to see what that emotion really means. Don't be satisfied with stating you are mad. Know why you are mad! This goes beyond what the narcissist did to you. Dig deeper. For example, instead of saying your narcissist put you down as the reason you are mad, you should be saying what that *represents to you*. Let's say your narcissist is always busy. You may be feeling mad at them. But what does that represent to you? Maybe it means you feel worthless to them. The point is to zero in on what that emotion means to you, rather than just feeling it.

3. **Question your emotions.** Once you know what it means, you need to question it. Is this valid? What else could this situation mean? Is this anger justified? Do I really believe the things the narcissist is saying behind my back? Isn't he mentally ill and making up stuff for a reaction? Am I giving in to anger because I have self-esteem issues and the blame I have for others cutting me down should be directed to myself because I don't think highly of myself or haven't stood up for myself? Inner peace begins the moment you choose not to allow another person or event to control your emotions.

4. **Learn from this situation.** Step back and see the situation with a broader perspective. Maybe you have a history of picking the wrong people to be in your life. Maybe God wants you to be more in alignment with his attributes for a son or daughter of our Heavenly Father. Maybe you need to work on your self-esteem so you don't lose your dignity to anyone ever again. Or maybe God was trying to warn you, but your definition of love was not

healthy. Maybe this entire experience wasn't a waste of time, but an opportunity to grow and become stronger.

5. Not everything is supposed to become something long-lasting. Sometimes people come into your life to show you what is right and what is wrong, to show you who you can be, to teach you to love yourself, to make you feel better for a little while, or to just be someone to spill your life to. Not everyone is going to stay forever, and still we have to keep going on and thank God for the lessons he gives us.

6. **Reassure yourself.** What do you want to feel instead? Pull out the blueprint for your life. This is the time to focus hard on it. How is this emotion serving you and furthering your progress toward how you want your life to turn out? Maybe you have been through painful moments like this before and you need to reassure yourself you can get through it again. Or maybe you need to read your scriptures to remind yourself that other people have been through painful emotions but overcame them when they increased their faith by believing that God has a plan for you that doesn't involve this person.

7. **Take action to change your perception or change your procedure.** If you are feeling pain, then it is a message telling you one of three things:

   » Change the way you are looking at things and what the discomfort means to you.
   » Change the way you are communicating your desires or needs to someone.
   » Change the way you are behaving.

   Don't just sit in emotions and dwell there for weeks on end. Take action! For example, you might feel hurt that your narcissist put you down. First, you need to stop and ask, "Do I need to change my perception? Is this true or false?" Your answer might be "no." Therefore, your emotion is not valid, and you are falling into the trap of self-pity. If the answer was "yes," then you need to proceed to changing your procedure. Maybe you feel your narcissist's points are valid. Therefore, you need to proceed with changing your behavior or building your self-esteem so you don't feel that way anymore. If your narcissist's opinions of you are not valid, then maybe you need to stand up for yourself or set a boundary. Do not just sit around mired in this feeling. Do something about it!

8. **Get excited about the changes you are making!** If you can narrow down your negative emotions to not only what they really mean but also how to change them, then you are in the process of recovery. You are not stuck! You are working on it rather than wasting time in therapy rehashing events. Don't get me wrong; it is important to release your emotions to your therapist and to be heard. However, I have met one too many narcissistic abuse victims who told me that was all their therapist allowed them to do, which was get validation for what they felt. If you find your therapist is letting you do all the talking and only occasionally throwing in questions with no direction, such as "And how does that make you feel?" then find a different therapist. They need to be actively involved in helping you change your emotions rather than only scribbling things down in your medical chart. I went through several therapists before I found the right one. You should never come out of an hour-long therapy session wondering what you accomplished with your time.

Now let's go through each of the below emotions and come up with an action plan. I will give you some examples to get started.

Negative Emotions	What to Do When You Experience This
Uncomfortable Emotions	You need to work on your confidence. Make a list of the things you can do to become comfortable. For example, if you feel ashamed of how the abuse caused you to gain weight, then you should actively be attending a weight-loss program and doing exercise to reclaim what you lost, rather than complaining about it.
Fearful Emotions	You need to prepare for the worst instead of avoiding it. For example, if your narcissist breaks your boundary that states, "I will separate from my spouse if he or she cheats on me," then you are actively preparing for that to happen. This means you are taking college classes if you have to better your financial situation. You are thinking far in advance of what you would do to make that possible with the least amount of stress on you. So when you have to separate from them, you have a place to go and can financially support yourself.

Hurtful Emotions	You move yourself from a place of loss to a place of gratitude. You make a list of all the things that are going on in your life that you are grateful for. You uproot yourself from the past by planting yourself in the future. Dust off that blueprint and rewrite a new one. Immerse yourself in scriptures that talk about forgiveness.
Angry Emotions	This means you voice what your boundaries are when they are being violated. You might have to strengthen your boundaries or redefine them. You might also have to rebuild your confidence to restore them. It also means that you are not sitting around and stewing in anger because your fairy-tale ending didn't come true. You are redefining your life's blueprint and setting goals for a different life. You realize he or she is just one person out of millions you could be with. You are therefore making yourself available to meet someone else through friends, online dating sites, church activities, or other avenues.
Frustrating Emotions	Whatever you're going after isn't happening because you need to either change your expectations or change your approach. For example, if your narcissist is using the blame game on you, instead of trying to make your point, choose not to win. Walk out of the room rather than listen to mentally ill drivel. In reality, that is winning because you're not giving your narcissist a reaction.
Disappointing Emotions	This means that you need to change your expectations and make it appropriate for the situation at hand. For example, your narcissist cheated on you, but he doesn't make you feel that he has remorse about it. This is where you go back and reread the section in this book about narcissists not feeling remorse. Maybe you need to adjust your perspective to understand that this is their illness and not a reflection of your worth.

Guilty Emotions	This might require you changing how you deal with future problems so something doesn't happen in the future. For example, your narcissist cheated on you, so you took revenge and cheated on them right back. You might double your efforts in your faith to get back in alignment with the person you want to be. You might go through the steps of repentance to make it right with your Heavenly Father. If you feel guilty about leaving them, maybe you need to speak to a pastor or reread the sections in this book that talk about what God wants for you. I can guarantee it wasn't abuse.
Inadequacy Emotions	This means you need to do something to be better in this category right away. This could mean taking a class, exercising, or learning a skill. Comparing yourself to another man or woman in your narcissist's life won't help you heal. Remember that they would discard a supermodel, sooner or later. They get bored and don't have loyalty. It isn't about who you are. It is about their lack of morals.
Hopelessness Emotions	This means you need to reevaluate what is most important to you in this situation. Make a list of things to be grateful for. Get active at church so you can feel closer to God and develop a healthy support system.
Loneliness Emotions	This might mean you state your needs to your partner rather than think your needs are insignificant. On the other hand, it might simply mean you seek out new friends or reach out to family.

Above are examples to get you started. You need to come up with your own that are more pertinent to what you are feeling. The point of this deep review of your emotions is to break the victim cycle. You need to give *actions* to your emotions. Those emotions are calling you to do something about them. They are not calling you to feel them for months. Some people actually believe that love hurts and it's justified for your depression to carry on for years. Love doesn't hurt! Loneliness hurts, rejection hurts, losing someone hurts, envy hurts. Everyone gets these things confused with love, but in reality love is the only thing in this world that destroys pain and makes a person whole. Don't settle into negative emotions and make them your new home, because the length of your grief should be equal to the amount of love you had for someone. You are not a martyr for love! Let's change your emotions by making an action plan. It is your turn to come up with a way out of what you are feeling.

To-Do List

1. Look at the ten emotions above. Which are you feeling right now? Write them down in your journal.

2. Using the seven steps, narrow those emotions down to an action plan.

3. Put this action plan in a place where you can see it daily. Go through the list, and complete it by the end of the week. For example, if your fearful emotion means you are afraid to leave him because you have no money to afford an apartment on your own, then by the end of next week you should have looked for a roommate online, looked for an apartment you and a roommate can share, or started looking for a new job or college program you need to get a better job.

4. As mentioned before, when you experience a negative emotion, you either change your perspective or change your procedure. Let's say you need to change your perspective. Refer back to the list of qualities you want in a partner and what your narcissist has. One of the things that helped me through my anger was that I started applying the attributes of a daughter of our Heavenly Father that I mentioned in the last section. This reminded me of who I was and how I was to be treated. This wasn't a onetime event. I was mad for a long time! However, when a negative emotion came up, I would pause and go through the seven steps above to change my emotional state. Sure, I didn't eliminate my feelings. Occasionally something would trigger them and I had to go back through my journal and read some of the answers in my to-do lists. The point is that I was getting myself unstuck. I went from hopelessly rehashing the same events to healing my mind and challenging my faulty perceptions about what took place.

5. Take the list of emotions you just created to your therapist. Your therapist should know what your action plan is. Together, you should be creating more actions or changes in perception to add to your arsenal when unwanted emotions arise.

Even Jesus Got Mad:
Understanding Your Anger

I want to talk to you more about anger—the third stage of grief. When I spent time on narcissistic abuse recovery boards, I noticed that anger was the one emotion that people had the hardest time getting over. This need for validation and venting their frustrations kept a lot of them stuck on those boards for months and even for years. In essence, they were keeping alive their trauma, which kept them in the emotion of anger. They would not let what the narcissist had done to them go. A lot of anger comes about because of the unanswered question "Why?" that many victims need to have answered. However, few got that answer from their narcissist—or at least not in a way that makes logical sense to them. Therefore, anger lingers with no way of releasing itself. I am not saying that being mad is unjustified. It is a natural response to what happened to you. You have the right to be angry. You don't have to condone someone's actions to be a spiritual person. Narcissists play mind games, and they don't care about your feelings when they do it. However, when is anger enough? When does anger become destructive? And when does it keep you victimized? They caused the first wound, but are you causing the rest? I think they got it started, but you kept it going by staying stuck in negative emotions. Now here you are after all this time still giving them the reaction they want: your anger or sadness. That is the only thing that should make you mad: your own noble position of remaining a victim. You're making your narcissist happy with your misery. You're better than this! Don't let any person steal your joy.

We can learn a lot about keeping our anger under control if we look at Jesus's message about that emotion. He has a lot to teach us about dealing with hatred, injustice, and conflict in loving ways. When Jesus cleared the temple of the moneychangers and animal sellers, he showed great emotion and anger (Matthew 21:12–13; Mark 11:15–18; John 2:13–22). Jesus's emotion was described as "zeal" for God's house (John 2:17). His anger was pure and completely justified, because at its root was concern for God's holiness and worship. Because these were at stake, Jesus took quick and decisive action. Another time Jesus showed anger was in the synagogue of Capernaum. When the Pharisees refused to answer Jesus's questions, "And when he had looked about on them with anger, being grieved for the hardness of their hearts, he saith unto the man, stretch forth thine hand" (Mark 3:5).

Many times, we think of anger as a selfish, destructive emotion that we should eradicate from our lives altogether. However, the fact that Jesus sometimes became angry indicates that anger itself, as an emotion, is not amoral. However, it becomes a problem when we turn it from righteous disgust over a situation to acting with revenge. Ephesians 4:26 instructs us, "Be ye angry, and sin not: let not the sun go down upon your wrath." The command is not to "avoid anger" (or suppress it or ignore it) but to deal with it properly, in a timely manner.

Sigmund Freud tells us that all defense mechanisms exist to protect the personality from an intolerable attack of anxiety when the ego is under siege. Anger is an instantaneous, knee-jerk reaction to provocation, yet there's always some other feeling that gave rise to it. Moreover, this feeling is precisely what the anger has contrived to camouflage or control. If you are suffering with anger as your main symptom, then you need to do the seven steps to dig a little deeper. Usually, a secondary emotion is masking others.

Before I was in a relationship with my narcissist, my life resume, which is who you think you are, stated that I had self-worth and was worth respect. However, over time, the abuse made me change that part of my resume. When you are beaten down often enough by a master manipulator, that can happen. When the relationship was over with, I questioned my worth. I became angry but learned in therapy that another deep emotion I was feeling was embarrassment. I was truly embarrassed by not recognizing that this person was mentally ill and had played me. In addition, I was embarrassed by how public our relationship became because of his smear campaign. Therefore, I wasn't mad at this individual as much as I was mad at myself. I allowed this person out of hundreds of people I could have been with to dictate what my life resume should be. Because of this faulty thinking, I kept myself stuck in a place of blaming other people for how I felt. I also learned something about his cruelty. Author Thich Nhat Hanh once said, "When another person makes you suffer, it is because he suffers deeply within himself, and his suffering is spilling over. He does not need punishment; he needs help. That's the message he is sending."

I believe loss of control is at the heart of most narcissistic abuse victims' anger. Think about it for a moment. You are gaslighted, manipulated, lied to, and played games with. You feel helpless to change the narcissist and confused as to why they are doing this, because all you have offered them is your love. You are going crazy trying to make them see that they are hurting someone who cares. You can't wrap your mind around their illogical behavior, which then leaves you feeling helpless to change it. When you are finally discarded and the smear campaign begins, you feel even more loss of control. You want some-one to listen and hear your side of events. You need validation that you went through this, and you are hard-pressed to find it because your narcissist already has his or her versions out there for other people to believe. You are abused further because the narcissist is saying you are the abuser. The helplessness continues. You can't help but walk away from the situation feeling psychologically raped. However, the narcis-sist does one more thing to crush you: he tells you that you have no right to feel hurt.

Most narcissists' victims feel psychologically raped. Left uncon-trolled, anger results in stories that challenge our worth because these stories came from our narcissist. You might be forming false opinions based on all the negative things your partner made you believe. For example, if your narcissist told you during the gaslighting stage that you were being overly sensitive and paranoid, you might have changed your life resume from "I am a person in control of his or her emotions" to "I am a person who doesn't trust people and can't control my jeal-ousy or suspicions."

It can be hard to get beyond anger to resolve the emotions hiding behind it because anger is ego based. Some safeguard vulnerabilities because dealing with them makes us feel weak. Therefore, we throw up protections such as anger to shield us from getting to the heart of the matter. Often, beneath anger are statements like "I'm right" and "I want my way." What does it mean to be right? What are the implica-tions? Exploration of these "I"-focused beliefs can help you to untangle the knots blocking your happiness.

Maybe your anger was like mine. You were robbed of having any control in the relationship because the narcissist had to own the stage and write the drama. Let me be the first to validate your anger. What they did was hurtful. However, it is time to move beyond anger. To reach the last stage of acceptance, you have to let go of your stubborn position of trying to get them to recognize your pain and feel sorry for causing it. They won't! You have to accept that there are people in this world who don't fight fair; they don't care and they will never recognize that they did anything wrong. You're just lucky enough not to be one of those people.

Anger separates us from others and gives us unwanted attention. Anger pushes people away, scares them, and makes them fight back or shut down. While I was angry, I was pushing my friends and family away. I confined myself to the house and stopped living. I cut off friendships because I wasn't getting my friends to say what I needed to hear. I wanted them to be as mad as I for what these narcissists had done to me. However, after one too many conversations about the situation, I began alienating them, and they began distancing themselves from me, which made me madder. I had projected this terrible need to be right and get my frustrations out, which unfortunately took its toll on my friends. Rehashing the anger with them repeatedly was what drove me into therapy, especially for the abuse caused by my narcissist hacker. One day, my best friend said, "I've heard enough! You can't let it go!" And she was right! I let this person's cruelty consume my life. I became bitter.

The growing bitterness we have toward our narcissist can make us believe our emotions are genuine and valid. In reality, our anger is only rooted in the meaning we gave to the situation. If we are not careful, we can take the meaning of what they have done to us as truth, like I did when I was in the relationship with my narcissist and felt a loss of worth.

Bitterness is not a place you want to remain after narcissistic abuse. However, many people are stuck in this part of their recovery. We see how bitterness can prolong recovery in the story of Jonah. Jonah is one of the most striking examples of a heart in need of expansion. He was asked by God to preach to the Ninevites, but instead, he flees from God. Unfortunately, for his disobedience, he ends up in a fish and housed in its belly for three days. While in the fish, Jonah prays eloquently to the Lord, thanking him for his hand of safety. After the three days are up, the fish promptly vomits Jonah unscathed back onto dry land.

Then, Jonah *finally* does what the Lord asks: he travels to Nineveh, an enemy of the Israelites, to proclaim the Lord's judgment. The Ninevites almost immediately repent and are shown mercy by the

Lord. However, Jonah's heart turns to bitterness because he is angry with God for the grace he gave to the people Jonah so despises.

To truly understand Jonah's bitterness and fear, however, it's important we understand what Jonah is facing when God tells him to go to Nineveh. During this time period, the Ninevites were not only enemies of the Israelites but had violently oppressed the nation of Israel. God's command for Jonah, therefore, is not just unreasonable; it's terrifying—and seemingly impossible.

These cultural realities are most likely a huge part of why Jonah runs from God's will. He is naturally terrified of the enemy. Maybe he's also afraid of failure. Proclaiming God's judgment to an enemy nation is a daunting task. Perhaps Jonah figures the odds of the Ninevites heeding God's command are too small for him to risk his life and dignity.

At the core of Jonah's trepidation, though, is something even deeper: fear of triumph. Jonah knows that if he succeeds at winning over the Ninevites to the Lord, they will be shown mercy. That's just the kind of god Jonah serves: one who shows his abundant grace to undeserving people. Jonah, on the other hand, wants his enemies to suffer.

Like Jonah, we often have the appropriate religious words and the actions to match those words. However, our hearts can be hard, unwilling to extend God's love to others. Who wouldn't want their narcissist to experience what they have done to us? However, anger and resentment don't change the hearts of others; *they only change yours.* True recovery is not about hating the narcissist. It's about releasing ourselves from our demons (pain, fear, and trauma). Sometimes we are just collateral damage in someone else's war against themselves. The problem is them, not you.

Setting up camp as a victim of narcissistic abuse *doesn't* punish our narcissist. In God's infinite mercy and grace, the Lord can rescue any sinner, even one as wicked as the pagan king of a barbarian nation. Jonah recognized the magnitude of God's grace, which is why he initially ran in the opposite direction; he wanted nothing to do with divine pardon being extended to Israel's hostile enemies. Ironically, when Jonah himself was in trouble, he cried out for God's mercy and it was granted. God has mercy for us all.

In annoyed disbelief—angered that his prophetic mission had been so stunningly successful—Jonah set up camp on the outskirts of Nineveh to see if God would still judge the city, not unlike narcissistic abuse victims who set up camp hoping the narcissist will suffer when God intercedes on their behalf. This is how my narcissist hacker's wife felt about me. She had taken the self-righteous position that I was her enemy and God loved her more. She lacked humility and didn't realize God loved us both and also had blessings in store for me. I think God was as perplexed as I was with her online prayers that she would post. I am sure he was wondering, "Why does she expect me to bless her marriage when she is committing criminal activity toward another person?" Did she really think God was going to overlook that? So what about you? Has pride taken over in your abuse?

Jonah hoped that the people's repentance would prove to be hypocritical and superficial so that the Lord would still destroy them after forty days. The prophet hastily constructed a temporary shelter to shade him from the blazing sun and waited to see how it all played out.

As Jonah sat disgruntled in his lean-to shanty on the eastern edge of Nineveh, the Lord caused a large plant to grow up behind him, the shade providing the melancholy prophet relief from the beating sun. The text states that Jonah was thankful for the plant. But the next morning, when God sent a worm to eat the plant, the prophet's anger was again incited. The situation worsened when the Lord sent a scorching east wind, which overwhelmed Jonah's makeshift shelter and brought him to the point of extreme heat exposure. In the same way that God had hurled a great wind on the sea to affect Jonah, he prepared this hot desert wind for the same purpose—to humble his servant and teach him a vital spiritual lesson.

Jonah's perspective was completely backward and entirely self-centered. He was passionately concerned about a short-lived shade plant to protect himself from discomfort, but he had no compassion for the entire population of Nineveh. He had been operating in his own self-interest, but the Lord wanted him to put the eternally significant message of salvation above his own concerns and trivial comforts. How could he be concerned about a weed when hundreds of thousands of souls faced judgment and he had the opportunity to see them saved? Don't let your anger over your narcissist pull you away from God.

The Bible talks about the War in Heaven. It says that Satan was once an angel, but he wanted man to worship God, rather than letting them have freedom of choice. He also didn't want mankind to have the plan of salvation that Jesus offered us. Jonah's hardened heart is not unlike Satan's. He would rather see the ruin of wicked people, without any plan of salvation. Sadly, I have witnessed many hardened hearts on narcissistic abuse recovery boards—people unwilling to forgive and move on. Why is it that God extends us forgiveness, but it is difficult to offer forgiveness to a narcissist? I believe many victims stay in a state of anger because they know how merciful their God is and they are impatient for justice. The truth is that if God were not so patient, all of us would come under his immediate judgment. However, take heart! God has seen your suffering. Ecclesiastes 3:17 says, "I said in mine heart, God shall judge the righteous and the wicked: for there is a time there for every purpose and for every work." Sometimes judgment from God happens in this life and sometimes in the next. However, that is no reason to give up faith in God. He promises us that we will have our day in his spiritual court.

The soil of bitterness is a heart that harbors hostility and does not deal with hurt by the grace of God. Anger can become an addiction, because it makes one's ego feel righteous or justified. Pointing the finger at another is much easier than examining one's own faults. However, you don't get over an addiction by stopping to use. You recover by creating a new life where it is easier to not use. If you don't create a new life, then all the factors that brought you to your addiction will catch up with you again. Greek philosopher Epictetus once said, "Any person capable of angering you becomes your master; he can anger you only when you permit yourself to be disturbed by him." And what is anger other than sad's bodyguard? It is the protection of our ego. When I went through this, I often felt like I chose anger over deep sadness, because I felt more empowered and in control of my life. And I could only choose one or the other. Choosing anger prolonged hanging on to these people. You cannot be holy unless you follow peace with men. It is worth it when you forgive. But you say, "Look what they've done! I am not going to let them off the hook." Well, they are not on the hook—you are! When you forgive, you set two people free, and one of them is yourself.

How many of us have, like Jonah, refused to bring our thoughts into line with the mercy of our Heavenly Father? This is what God wants you to know. Romans 12:14,17,19 tells us, "Bless those who persecute you; bless and do not curse. . . . Live in harmony with one another. . . . Do not repay anyone evil for evil. . . . Do not take revenge, my dear friends, but leave room for God's wrath, for it is written: It is mine to avenge; I will repay, says the Lord." To overcome your anger, you must leave room for God to act. He alone is positioned to make the most thorough and accurate judgment. The Bible defines responses to anger and love as *choices* rather than emotions. Therefore, we are not slaves to something we can't control. We can choose to let it go.

Dwelling upon God's love is a powerful replacement to dwelling on anger. The life of Jesus testifies to this. Some of his closest friends abandoned him in his hour of need. Judas, whom he had known for years, betrayed him. Religious leaders rejected him for political gain. A fickle crowd that five days earlier had heralded his arrival as king turned on him. Any of these things would have stirred up an unrighteous anger. Yet notice where Jesus directed his thoughts. In John 17:23, we read Jesus's final prayer: "I in them, and thou in me, that they may be made perfect in one; and that the world may know that thou has sent me, and hast loved them, as thou has loved me." By dwelling on his Father's love, Jesus was able to graciously respond to the evil done to him. By focusing on loving others, he was able to avoid the temptation of being sinfully angry. Forgiveness made it possible to do this.

Do I Have to Forgive My Narcissist?

I never knew how strong I was until I had to forgive someone who wasn't sorry and accept an apology I never received. That was the case with both of my narcissists. They didn't care about my pain. They treated me as less than human and were devoid of all empathy. The only thing that mattered to them was them.

It wasn't easy to forgive someone who was still invading my privacy and lying to everyone that he was a righteous and faithful husband— not to mention all the other things he did to me that I am leaving out of this book (it would take a whole other book to record it all).

However, I finally did forgive him, but it is not what you think. My forgiveness didn't mean I had to give up my right to take him to court. It didn't mean I had to give up my disgust for what he did. It didn't mean I had to give up the viewpoint that he was an evil, abusive man. It didn't mean I had to acknowledge his presence if I ran into him. It didn't mean I wouldn't ever feel moments of anger when something triggers me to remember what he did. It simply meant I chose to let go of the daily hate I had for him and the anger over the situation. In addition, I chose to let go of the happiness I derived from knowing he was married to someone whom he wasn't in love with but had settled for instead. I went from hating his wife and ex to having pity for them. I realized that the reason they did the things they did to me was because both of them were insecure and had anxiety disorders. They'd rather hurt someone they were intimidated by than work on their self-esteem. What they needed to do was to stop blaming me for their pain and start blaming their narcissist for his disloyalty. They had the maturity of grade-school bullies fighting over one man—a stupid man—out of hundreds they could have been in a relationship with and who would have treated them better.

All of them were flawed, broken individuals who might have been fans of Jesus, but they weren't followers. When I realized this, I stepped back from my pain and stopped seeing them on equal footing with me. Each of them, in their own way, was living a lie. At least I could admit my shortcomings. On the other hand, they thought they were normal human beings and hacking was completely acceptable behavior becoming of a Christian. There was nothing normal about what they did to me! What kind of woman thinks it is okay to let their husband listen in to another woman's house that he was admittedly attracted to? Does it make sense to hack someone's cell phone if you wanted nothing to do with that person? Crazy, right? They didn't make sense. They were all mentally and spiritually ill. Therefore, they didn't deserve my hate. They needed my prayers so that God would soften their hearts and humble them. However, for a long time, I couldn't forgive them. It wasn't until I understood the act of forgiveness that I was able to bring myself to do so. Let me explain forgiveness to you, because maybe you were like me and felt that granting them forgiveness was allowing them to get away with what they did.

To understand what forgiveness means, it is sometimes easier to start with understanding what forgiveness is not:

- **Forgiveness is not a feeling.**
  If it were, we would rarely forgive others, because we would not "feel" like it. So don't think that you can't forgive your narcissist and still be angry. You can still be upset. Years after a breakup, you could be standing in your kitchen and have something trigger an upsetting situation you had with your narcissist. You might feel yourself getting mad. That doesn't mean you didn't forgive. It means you're human. Feeling an unwelcome emotion is different than wishing someone ill will and plotting revenge. If you can move past that state and go back to the things in your present, then you have done nothing wrong.

- **Forgiveness is not a weakness.**
  Many people feel that forgiveness is a weakness. This couldn't be further from the truth. It might feel that forgiving the person allows that person to get away with whatever was done. *The truth is that forgiveness is not for the other person, but for yourself.* When you hold on to a grudge or repeatedly run an incident through your head, you're only harming yourself. To forgive takes great strength, and it is empowering. It doesn't make what the other person did right, but it certainly releases you from reliving the situation. Why give someone the energy by thinking about what he or she did when you should move on? Being mad at them doesn't change them; it changes you. They could be on a vacation having the time of their life with someone at this very moment. How is your anger ruining their life? It is not. So giving them anger doesn't get you what you want. In fact, with a narcissist, they are probably enjoying that you are angry. It takes a strong person to move on and not let one person out of millions affect you. Jesus forgave many people for hurting him. Forgiving is a strength of character, not a flaw. In the shadow of your pain, forgiveness feels like a decision to reward your enemy. But in the shadow of the cross, forgiveness is merely a present from one undeserving soul to another.

- **Forgiveness does not mean pretending it didn't happen or hiding from it.**
  The narcissistic abuse happened, and the behavior shouldn't be minimized. It broke your heart, and there is nothing trivial about that. You are "accepting" that it happened, but you are not going to let it ruin your future. If Elisabeth Kübler-Ross's grief stages were geared toward cutting ties with a loved one because of abuse, forgiveness would definitely be the sixth stage.

- **Forgiveness does not mean forgetting.**
  The phrase "forgive and forget" is not reality. I will never forget what these men did to me. I wish I could, but the body and mind do not forget trauma. At the time of writing this book, I still have PTSD, and forgetting will be difficult until those symptoms subside. My job is to do the seven steps of dealing with negative emotions, just as you are to do. This can be a daily battle at first, but over time negative emotions lessen because it becomes a habit.

- **Forgiveness does not mean condoning or excusing a wrong or that it is justice.**
  This is where many people become confused. They think that if they forgive, there will be no justice because they gave that right away by forgiving. There is a difference between forgiveness and justice. Let me explain in a judicial way. If I forgive my narcissist hacker, does that mean I am not allowed to take him to court to be sentenced to a few years in jail for invasion of privacy? The answer would be no. I forgave, but justice is to be served. That is different from revenge. There are two sorts of retributory punishments. One is vengeance, the other, chastisement. Man has not the right to take vengeance, but the community has the right to punish the criminal, and this punishment is intended to warn and to prevent so that no other person will dare to commit a like crime. This punishment is for the protection of rights, but it is not vengeance; vengeance appeases the anger of the heart by opposing one evil with another. This is not allowable, for people have not the right to take vengeance. However, if criminals were entirely forgiven, the order of the world would be upset. Punishment is necessary for the safety of communities. The constitution of the communities depends upon justice, not upon forgiveness.

By forgiveness and pardon, Christ did not mean that you should be submissive in the presence of tyrannical foes and allow them to perform cruelties and oppressions. If one person assaults another, the injured one should forgive him. However, communities must protect people's rights. So if someone assaults, injures, oppresses, and wounds me, I will offer no retaliation and I will forgive him. The law will give me justice. The judges in that trial are your local courthouse and your Heavenly Father.

In the case of your narcissist, there is no earthly court to which you can take him (unless he committed a criminal act). Therefore, immoral sins that others have committed against you will be judged by our Heavenly Father—maybe not in this life, but in the next. If you forgive your narcissist, it doesn't mean you give up your trial in the next life. There will be a judgment from God, and the angels that have watched over you will be your witnesses. Your job as a son or daughter of our Heavenly Father is to have faith that God will prevail with justice. It won't be on your timetable, and it won't be you who does the judging.

- **Forgiveness is not based on the wrongdoer's actions**.
Your narcissist might never ask for your forgiveness. Even if you did receive an apology, it wouldn't be able to undo the hurt you experienced. My forgiveness isn't dependent on whether others are sorry or not. God still requires me to forgive. This is a commandment. "But if you forgive not men their trespasses, neither will your Father forgive your trespasses" (Matthew 6:15).

Even Jesus forgave. One of the last things Jesus did while alive was to make sure he forgave the people who murdered him: *"Father, forgive them; for they know not what they do"* (Luke 23:34). Your narcissist has no idea of your importance in this world: "they do not know what they do." You have a great purpose or God wouldn't have sent you down here to take up space. What good can you do if your thoughts are resentful? God can't use you. God can't bless you. Resentment sours your thoughts and your spirit. It makes you impure. *Pulling away from God is something we are completely responsible for, and it is not the fault of the person who has wronged you.* "Follow peace with all men, and holiness, without which no man shall see the Lord: Looking diligently lest any man fail of the grace of God; lest any root of bitterness springing up trouble you, and thereby many be defiled" (Hebrews 12:14–15).

We offer this forgiveness to others purely in *response* to the grace we have already received from the Lord. If we are not willing to forgive, it is an indication that we have not fully understood or experienced the grace of being forgiven (Luke 7:47). We can understand this further when Jesus comes across a woman being stoned for adultery. The multitude are about to stone her, but Jesus said, "He who is without sin among you, let him first cast a stone at her" (John 8:7). None of them killed her, because they were sinners also.

You must not resent or judge people who don't apologize to you, knowing that you also have things to apologize for. Jesus calls us to judge ourselves, to examine our motives and what is deep in our heart. When I do this, I can see how I need God's forgiveness and the forgiveness of others. I am not as blameless as I would like to think. I could have had stronger boundaries and attributes as a daughter of my Heavenly Father. I could have let God guide my footsteps, instead of my emotions regarding my narcissists.

Forgiveness is not about changing the other person, their actions, or their behavior. You don't give forgiveness when the person has been completely rehabilitated. Would it be fair if Jesus expected that of us? Therefore, if you are waiting for your narcissist to show Christlike behaviors or a repentant demeanor, then you have lost sight of what granting forgiveness means.

- **Forgiveness is not conditional.**
It's not *If you do this and this, then and only then will I forgive you.* If your narcissist cheated on you, then to forgive doesn't mean he has to call the police and get a restraining order against her to prove he is real about his feelings for you. In this situation, that would be revenge and far from granting forgiveness. *Forgiveness doesn't demand proof of love.* That is important to remember, because people tend to give forgiveness only if they can get revenge or retribution for what was done to them.

God commands us to grant it otherwise. We learn in Matthew 18:21–35 about the unmerciful servant. Jesus tells us that the kingdom of heaven is like a king who wanted to settle accounts with his servants. As he began the settlement, a man who owed him ten thousand bags of gold was brought to him. Since he was not able to pay, the master ordered that he, his wife, his children, and all that he had be sold to repay the debt. At this the servant fell on his knees before him. "Be patient with me," he begged, "and I will pay back everything." The servant's master took pity on him, canceled the debt, and let him go. But when that servant went out, he found one of his fellow servants who owed him a hundred silver coins. He grabbed him and began to choke him. "Pay back what you owe me!" he demanded. His fellow servant fell to his knees and begged him, "Be patient with me and I will pay it back." But he refused. Instead, he went off and had the man thrown into prison until he could pay the debt. When the other servants saw what had happened, they were outraged and told their master everything that had happened. Then the master called the servant in. "You wicked servant," he said, "I forgave all that debt of yours because you begged me to. Shouldn't you have had mercy on your fellow servant just as I had on you?" In anger, his master handed him over to the jailers to be tortured, until he should pay back all he owed. Jesus cautions us with this parable. He tells us that we are to forgive because we have been forgiven. He doesn't tell us that we must "get" first.

- **Forgiveness does not mean trust.**
  This is important if you remain in the relationship. Your narcissist, especially if religious, might demand you trust them because you forgave. *Forgiveness should be freely given. Trust must be earned.* You are not any less of a person for knowing when you need distance from people who have broken you. You are not spiteful, hateful, bad, or evil for taking time to heal and removing yourself from a toxic relationship.

  Forgiveness doesn't mean you're obligated to stay in a relationship or marriage with someone who has destroyed the foundation of everything you've built. Forgiveness doesn't mean you keep a close friendship with the person who betrayed you. Forgiveness doesn't mean you continue to engage with family members or enablers who have proven their disloyalty, time and time again. Forgiveness is one of the most powerful forces on the planet. However, it shouldn't be loosely given simply because the wrongdoer requests it. Forgiveness should come when the person who has been hurt has decided to heal. In addition, the forgiver can decide to forgive but then walk away rather than engage again.

- **Forgiveness is not about changing the past**.
  It's about changing the future. Forgiveness does not condone behavior but asks us to accept it happened and that there is nothing we can do about it. It looks toward a future of healing and hope. The truth is that you can't change words that have been said. They are already said. If they cheated on you, then it is already done. You can't undo actions. You can only move forward.

Now that you know what forgiveness is not, let's talk about what it is.

- Forgiveness is letting go of the intense emotions attached to the past. We still remember what the narcissist did to us, but we no longer feel hateful, bitter, resentful, or damaged because of it. We recognize that what happened to us in the past doesn't dictate our future.
- Forgiveness no longer wants to get even with the people who hurt us. If criminal activity took place, you might prosecute them so they can rehabilitate, but you don't suffer in hate until that day comes. It is the realization that you can't undo the past or become a good person through revenge.
- Forgiveness is letting go of the self-pity, victimization stage, grudges, and resentments. You don't need these emotions to define yourself. You don't need them as an excuse for getting less out of life.
- Forgiveness is accepting that revenge will not heal you. It is accepting that anger has served you no real purpose. It has only allowed the narcissist to hurt you more by remembering their cruel acts. In addition, if they know you are angry, they are rejoicing because it is giving them attention. Forgiveness gives them no attention because you are through with them in your heart and mind.
- Forgiveness is putting your energy to better use. It is letting the past be the past. This means you stop dwelling on it, stop talking about, stop keeping it alive, and stop living poorly because of it. Forgiveness has nothing whatsoever to do with how wrong someone else was—no matter how evil, cruel, narcissistic, or

unrepentant they are. When you forgive a person, you break the unhealthy bonds between you and your abuser, and you redefine yourself as a victor in your own life.

- Forgiveness is building your self-esteem. It is the realization that negative emotions are not who you are and you are more than just a victim or someone's ex. You are a strong son or daughter of our Heavenly Father and you refuse to let anyone's actions ruin your future, because you believe God has a great future in store for you.

- Forgiveness is moving on and being the better person. It is recognizing that you have better things to do with your life. It is striving to be a son or daughter of our Heavenly Father through taking the high road, rather than stooping to the evil level of your narcissist. It is aligning yourself with the principles Jesus has spoken about in the Bible.

Maybe you were like me. Maybe you have been in a relationship with someone who turned on you by starting a smear campaign. Maybe you are trying to let go of the pain you have suffered because of the meddling of their enablers or their gossip. Maybe you can't let go of your narcissist's disloyalty because they emotionally cheated or flirted with other people. Or maybe you can't let go of the belittling, mind games, or silent treatment you have been forced to endure. Whatever you can't get over will prolong your recovery. It may very well keep you in a constant state of victimization. What does that translate to? That means your narcissist wins. If you continue to hurt, react, and pursue your narcissist for closure, then you are abusing yourself. You are also making the unspoken choice not to trust that God has a better plan for you that doesn't involve ruminating on the past, sad Pinterest quotes, and being forever stuck in the bargaining stage of grief. Remember, the survival mode is supposed to be a phase that helps save your life. It is not meant to be how you live.

I understand your pain because I too have suffered greatly. I know what it is like to carry anger and not have either of my narcissists feel remorse for what they did to me. My narcissist hacker and his enabling family member psychologically raped me. I cried for months over their cruelty. I know what it is like to have my abuser trivialize my tears and believe that I am not allowed to feel hurt because I brought it on myself. I also know what it's like to play out unspoken conversations in my mind about what I would say if I ran into my narcissist hacker. Sadly, these conversations never brought me peace. Instead, my thoughts led me to the inevitable truth that talking to this person would only cause him to shrug off his actions and cast me as the abuser, rather than him being honest about his cruel behavior toward me. He would do what he always does and turn my encounter with him into drama. More than likely he would escalate the situation by calling the police. Therefore, I would be setting myself up to be abused again. He was a loser and a scoundrel. There is no way to win with a narcissist, except for this one thing. You are to move on and live a happy life without them and give them no attention. Your narcissist can't stand it when your happiness doesn't revolve around them. However, I don't know how you can successfully move on without forgiveness.

As I mentioned at the beginning of this book, I felt something lacking in my therapy sessions. There were no discussions with my therapist about forgiveness. This was an important part of healing my anger, but it was skipped because it was a church-based principle. Instead, she told me to seek out spiritual counsel regarding this matter, and I did. I began attending church regularly and prayed that each sermon I heard would offer a healing message or principle that would allow me to forgive. I spoke to several church leaders for guidance. I then enrolled in a Bible-study course so that the scripture reading would further my pursuit of forgiveness. In addition, I sought out books on Amazon.com about forgiveness. One of the books that helped me the most was *The Shack* by William Paul Young. The story is about a man whose daughter is kidnapped by a child molester and killed. He never finds her body and is filled with grief and guilt over what happened. He is unable to let go of the hatred he has for the sexual predator and is mad at God because he feels he allowed the predator to get away with it. What makes this story so wonderful is the transformation he makes when God, Jesus Christ, and the Holy Spirit appear to him at the shack, which is where the police found his daughter's bloody clothes. He spends several days at the shack with God, Jesus Christ, and the Holy Spirit, and through their counsel he finds the power to forgive and heal from the tragedy.

The Shack Revisited is a follow-up book written by C. Baxter Kruger. It is also well worth reading, in large part because it is in a workbook format to be used in your process of forgiveness. It also goes deeper into the core message of the original book. You might also consider renting the movie *The Shack*, which brought the message to life on the big screen. On bad days, when I ruminate about the past, I throw this movie in the DVD player. Watching it helps me to release my anger and get back to a place of forgiveness. Little things like this helped my recovery.

Embracing forgiveness is a process that takes all sorts of reinforcement. For me, it wasn't just a onetime event. It was a daily choice for a long time because I was full of anger. Some people are too quick to say they forgive, because they want to look like the better person, when in their heart they are not at a place that supports what forgiveness really means. God counsels us to forgive, but if it takes you time to do it, then that is okay. As long as you are working toward it in therapy and with church leaders, then do not let other people push you to a place you are not ready for. Forgiveness should be sincere and not for show.

Bringing myself to forgiveness wasn't easy. Trust me! There were days in my anger and grief that I wished all sorts of evil things to befall both my narcissists, especially my narcissist hacker. I was reluctant to grant forgiveness because I thought I had to give up my viewpoint that both of them were evil. However, not forgiving my narcissists was equivalent to staying trapped in a jail cell of bitterness, serving time for their crimes. I held on to hate because it was the only weapon I thought I had against them. However, I was taking poison instead. What forgiveness was asking me to do was to give up my hatred so I could be free to live. It wasn't asking me to give up the viewpoint that they were evildoers. There is no debate about that.

Letting go of pain was the lesson Jesus was trying to teach Peter. One day Peter approached Jesus and asked, "Lord, how many times is my brother to sin against me and I am to forgive him? Up to seven times?" Peter likely thought he was being generous. After all, the religious leaders of the day taught that one had to forgive only three times. Jesus replied, "Not seven times, but seventy-seven times" (Matthew 18:21–22). Was Jesus suggesting that Peter keep a running tally of his transgressor's actions? No, by turning Peter's seven into seventy-seven, he was saying that love does not allow us to set an arbitrary limit on forgiveness. God is making the same request to you as he did to Peter. Forgive always because he forgives you.

Forgiveness is for you, not so much them. So how does one forgive? Do I have to let them know I am forgiving them? How do I go about it? Let's look at these four steps:

1. **Let it go.**

   After my therapy sessions were over, the last stage of my recovery ultimately came down to forgiving in order to move on. I didn't go up to these people and tell them I forgave them. They didn't care, and what purpose would it serve anyway? Don't fool yourself into using your announcement of forgiveness as a way to get closure. You won't get it. Instead, let your announcement about forgiveness be done in prayer to your Heavenly Father. That is what I did. If that doesn't seem profound enough for you, then tell your closest friends or family. Let them support you.

   Remember that just because you have agreed to forgive doesn't mean you can't be pulled back into depression. Forgiveness is a daily event followed by a lot of distractions before finally getting to the point that things don't bug you anymore. During this time of forgiveness, you should be clearing the present of clutter from the past. Remove things that trigger the anger:

   » Get off narcissistic abuse recovery forums.
   » Stop looking up narcissist information on the internet.
   » Stop looking them up or their other narcissistic supply on the internet.
   » Stop texting them.
   » Don't take phone calls from them. If you have a child together, communicate through a third party.
   » Remove pictures or items of theirs from your life so there is no trigger of emotions when you see them.
   » Distance yourself from people who associate with them so you have no desire to find out information about them or have to worry about those people running to your narcissist to share information about you.
   » Don't respond to any drama they create.
   » Stop talking about them to family and friends.
   » Block him or her from seeing your social media.
   » Unfriend them from your Facebook account. You can forgive them, but that doesn't mean you have to associate with them.
   » Stop looking for occasions to be offended by this person.

2. **Learn the lesson.**

   Life is one big lesson. You can find a lesson in your narcissistic abuse. I know I did. I learned that outward appearances are not worth chasing after. Spiritual qualities are the only thing worth loving in a man, because those attributes are the things that will help me grow as a person. I also learned I didn't have strong boundaries. Further, I learned that my happiness would never be found in another person. It would be found in me doing things that make me happy and in gratitude for what I have. As part of your process of forgiveness, you need to also forgive yourself. This tragedy has learning experiences that can make you stronger and wiser. Praise God for the wake-up call.

3. **Pardon.**

   Pardon your narcissist by forgiving them; let go of your right to punish them for the offense in the future (unless your decisions demand legal action). You are *not bringing this incident up again and using it against them.* In so doing, you are choosing to hold on to the person, not the offense. That doesn't mean you give up the opinion that they are immoral. They may be, but you won't keep reminding them because I am pretty sure your narcissist knows that already. It also means you don't have to associate with them. This can be hard to do when your narcissist keeps doing evil things and is still in your life. If that is the case, then you need to ask yourself this: Why am I letting a person do evil to me continuously? Why am I still in a relationship with someone who doesn't feel remorse? How can I lessen contact if we have kids together?

   If you keep contact with someone who consistently does evil to you, you will never develop forgiveness for him or her because it will always be another offense to get over. Does that mean you keep forgiving? I think it means you stop seeing them as a normal human being on equal footing with you and you start seeing them for what they are: crazy and unevolved. You distance yourself so they are not repeatedly doing things to you, and this gives you the chance to develop forgiveness. This requires no contact, which we will talk about later.

4. **Reconnect to the spirit.**

   Get yourself back in the spirit of being happy and positive even if it is the hardest thing to do. Turn yourself over to God and allow his spirit to heal you. Get active in church, take up hobbies, or immerse yourself in a project to build your happiness again. In addition, you should be working on controlling your negative emotions daily and praying often for God to send you help in the form of signs, people, scriptures, or books to help you keep moving forward. Then repeat this to yourself often: This is one person out of millions of people on this planet who I could meet or be in a relationship with. I am not going to let this one person ruin my life or steal my happiness anymore. I am a son or daughter of our Heavenly Father. That means I have standards and a birthright for something better than what I have put up with in the past.

When you forgive, you are taking away the power the narcissist had over you. Instead, you are using that power toward your growth. In essence, you are making the statement as a son or daughter of our Heavenly Father that you will not allow what this person did to continue to control your life. In addition, you will not allow your anger over their behavior to prevent you from your life mission and happiness. Let go of your pain and soften your heart, my friend. God wants to heal you!

This Thing Called Closure: Is It Keeping You Possessed?

You don't drown by falling in the water. You drown by staying there. This is true of my experience of hanging out on narcissistic abuse recovery forums and Facebook pages. I can tell you that almost all of the abuse victims I encountered felt stuck on those forums because they thought they needed validation, when in reality they were looking for closure. This much is true: When you loved someone and had to let him or her go, there will always be that small part of yourself that whispers, "What was it that you wanted and why didn't you fight for it?" Sadly, narcissists are notorious for not giving you those answers. They don't have the decency to give you that sincere talk that finalizes everything. This is because the relationship didn't matter to them— at least not in the way that it mattered to you. If they want to keep a foot in the door for narcissistic supply, then giving you those answers isn't wise. As I mentioned in the first section of this book, narcissists get into a "relationship" for some combination of money, sex, attention/ego strokes, food/clothing/shelter, social status, or public appearance. They may have played the part of the loving significant other, but it wasn't because they ever truly felt that way about you. Narcissists are incapable of forming real bonds with people. When they said they loved you, it wasn't a true Christlike version of love, the kind of love where if you were disfigured in a car accident they would take you home from the hospital and become your caregiver. They are not that loving. They would see it as a burden and an unfair responsibility they would want to get rid of. Heaven forbid if your attractiveness were altered in that car accident. Then they would be planning to discard you without looking like a scumbag to his or her family and friends.

Sometimes we get obsessed with this need for closure. It consumes us. Most victims want to believe that the narcissist entered the relationship with them for the same reason—love. However, it isn't normal healthy love that made the narcissist do it. Maybe they loved what you could do for them or how you made them look. "But what about being with someone for a long time?" you say. Remember, you can meet someone tomorrow who has better intentions for you than someone you've known for years. Time means nothing; *character does.* My narcissist hacker was with his wife for a few years before he decided to hack my computer and cell phone. Time spent together didn't make him loyal; if anything, it made him bored.

I understand that you want closure, and I agree that it is important. You should always have clarity about why a relationship began and why it ended. However, narcissists do a good job of robbing you of this. The reason for this is because it is their way of leaving their foot in the door of your life so they can later use you for narcissistic supply. Remember that they get off on controlling people; therefore, leaving you dangling with confusing statements like "If it was meant to be, it will be" is just their way of hooking you or hoovering. They are not stupid individuals who don't know how to communicate or don't know what they want. They know darn well they left you with unanswered questions, and they love every minute of your attention because of this need for answers. Sometimes you just have to turn around, give a little smile, throw the match, and burn that bridge. Who needs answers? Isn't their cruelty answer enough?

However, I fully understand what it feels like to be heartbroken. I had several questions left unanswered from both of my narcissists:

- Why did you treat me this way when all I was trying to do was give you my love?
- Why are you telling other people all these awful things about me that are exaggerated and untrue?
- What did I do that made you hate me so much?
- Why do you expect me not to be upset at the things you have done to me?
- What can I do now to fix the situation? Maybe something was misinterpreted or left unsaid between us that could heal this mess.
- Why are you sending me mixed signals? Why did you have your friend contact me and your sibling send me clues that you cared, but now you are denying it?
- Why did you say I was beautiful and it was about timing between us, then turn around, steal my privacy, and act cruelly?

I had the above questions burning in my heart for a long time. However, I never got those answers, and it ate away at my happiness for quite a while. Things left unsaid unsettle me. Maybe you can relate. Anger and the need for closure are the two things that keep narcissistic victims from moving forward with their lives.

If you get to the point that you need to see your narcissist and ask for closure, then you should know what it is you are wanting from them. Makes sense, right? The need for closure can take many forms. This is what I have noticed on the narcissist abuse boards online. Sometimes the victim wanted their narcissist to admit that they hurt them and apologize. Others said they wanted to know why they were treated so badly after all the wonderful things they did for them. Still others said they approached their narcissist for closure but after deep reflection they realized what they really wanted was another chance at trying to fix the situation, or they wanted to know why the narcissist was still sending them mixed signals. So let's find out what your reasons are. Answer the following questions:

To-Do List

1. What are your reasons for wanting closure?
2. How would you have felt differently if you had gotten this closure? If the narcissist were standing right in front of you, what would they need to say specifically for you to move on?

3. Is it realistic that they will say this to you? I am not telling you not to march over to their house or apartment and ask them what is burning in your mind. If that is what you need, then do it. However, I am saying that you may not get it. In fact, they might just send more mixed signals (hoovering) to keep you in a state of wanting more answers.

4. Is your need for closure simply a deep-seated need for revenge so you can say everything you want to the narcissist? If so, do you really believe they will stand there, listen, and not retaliate? Do you really believe they feel sorry? If they did, wouldn't they have stopped their toxic behavior toward you?

Whatever your reason, I can guarantee you this much: You won't get what you are looking for. Closure happens after you accept that letting go and moving on are more important than projecting a fantasy of how the relationship could have been. It is stepping out of that fairy tale I have spoken so much about. It is realizing it was just a dream. There are moments that mark your life, moments when you realize that nothing will ever be the same and time becomes divided into two parts: *before* this and *after* this.

If your partner refuses to give you closure after you have repeatedly asked for it, then ask yourself whether the type of person you imagined him or her to be would have treated you better. Chances are the answer is yes. Therefore, you can begin to realize that you projected qualities onto the narcissist that are part of this dream you had, when in reality they are not true characteristics they possess. After you start to see the faulty patterns in your thinking, forgive yourself for seeing what wasn't there. The only closure you need is terminating communication with the toxic individual. That is the best closure you can have, because it increases your dignity! You have to accept that some chapters in our lives have to close without closure. There's no point in losing yourself by trying to fix what's meant to be broken.

Many victims are stuck on getting closure because it is a way of finalizing or putting an end to things. We can act like perfectionists. We want everything neat, tidy, and put away. There is a beginning and an end. Most definitely not a question mark! People who need control have the hardest time coping without it. If you are one of those people, don't rack your brain wanting to have closure, like a missing piece to a puzzle. If you wish to have a healthy version of closure, then make it about saying goodbye, not to your narcissist but to the "old version" of you. Your closure doesn't have to come from this person. It can come from yourself. Knowing deep in your heart that you did everything you could will help you get there. You went above and beyond for your narcissist. You more than compromised to the point that you became a whole other person to accommodate their needs, and it still wasn't enough. Maybe you can find peace in these words: Sometimes you have to realize that everyone isn't for everyone, and you and they were not meant for each other. You were meant to be a son or daughter of our Heavenly Father and have great dignity and respect for yourself. You have a life purpose to carry out, and God is going to open doors for you. He is going to bring someone who is worthy, and your narcissist wasn't that person.

Sometimes, the answer to why is as simple as accepting that some people are terrible human beings, and terrible people do terrible things. If you are racking your brain trying to understand it, it just means you're not one of those terrible people. Have you considered that God's blessings are not in what he gives but what he takes away? Trust him! Narcissists are notorious for not making a lot of sense. They do illogical things. Stop trying to figure out their craziness. Accept that they are crazy and their behavior is a by-product of that imbalance within them.

Not getting closure can be especially hard if you attach religious reasons to why the two of you met. The narcissist I was in a relationship with met me at church. I felt that God had brought us together. In the beginning, the relationship felt ordained. After the breakup, I was left scratching my head in bewilderment, wondering, "Why did I feel God had brought that thing into my life?" In my case, I wanted to believe in the idea that there were such things as soul mates. Yet there is nothing scriptural to support that claim, as I mentioned before. So many people could work as a potential mate. It seems rather silly to think that God only created one person, and I have to be somewhere at the right time and place to find them. What if I was sick on the day I was supposed to meet them and I had to stay home? You get the point.

Don't let your need for closure keep you tethered to a toxic person. Seeking closure has a way of changing a person into someone they are not. This was the case with my narcissist hacker's ex. Long before my narcissist started hacking my house, he told me that I was part of the reason why his relationship ended with his ex. She didn't trust his loyalty. Her hacking of my computer systems was her way of taking revenge because he was attracted to me. This made her bitter and jealous. Sadly, she still had feelings for him even after she ended the relationship. Unfortunately, it was too late. He moved on and found himself someone else. She posted her pain online in quotes. It was obvious to anyone who read her social media that she couldn't let him go. Her narcissistic ex knew that, so he threw her breadcrumbs to keep his foot in the door. Closure never came because it was never being offered. This is the one thing that you have to keep in mind with narcissists. They don't want to offer closure. They enjoy you not moving on. Why would they want to end the attention they are getting? I am sure she had a bunch of unanswered questions because of his mixed signals. However, here is the thing to remember: You will never find the real truth among people who are insecure or have egos to protect. Truth over time becomes either guarded or twisted as their perspective changes; it changes with the seasons of their shame, love, hope, or pride.

Unlike a movie or book, where there is a clear beginning, middle, and end, there usually isn't with life. While it can be difficult to live with not knowing why and not quite understanding, love can be like the weather. Meteorologically, we understand hurricanes. Emotionally, we don't. We will never get an answer to "Why did this hurricane destroy my house?" other than "You were in its path." So where do you go from here if your ex won't give you closure? The answer is this: closure is something you give yourself. However, if that is not enough for you, let's look at what your ex would give you as a reason for why the relationship ended or why they changed their feelings for you. However, remember this when you seek closure from a narcissist: *What they say is not what they mean.* They say and do things for their gain only. That means they will tell you what you need to hear, and the truth is something you rarely get to experience. Also, don't let their mixed signals fool you; indecision is a decision. **If someone wants to be a part of your life, they will make an effort that goes beyond throwing you crumbs.**

In the table below, you will see what narcissists have told their victims. This list was derived from what I observed on narcissistic abuse recovery boards. Victims shared online what they knew the real truth was behind what the narcissist was telling them.

What They Tell You	What They Mean but Won't Say
"We grew apart."	"I was bored and wanted someone else."
"You changed and expected so much."	"You wouldn't let me cross your boundaries anymore and do what I want in the relationship."
"We fought all the time."	"You didn't let me get away with anything, and I am the one in control."
"You need to find someone who makes you happy."	"I am pulling the victim card, so you feel guilty."
"If it was meant to be, none of this would have happened."	"I am going to blame it on fate because then I don't have to take responsibility."
"We just couldn't communicate. We are different people."	"You didn't let me control you, and therefore you're of no use to me if I don't get what I want."
"I didn't cheat on you. Your paranoia drove us apart."	"I don't consider flirtation, emails, or using family members to get another person to be interested in me cheating. I only consider sex cheating. Therefore, I am going to blame you for feeling insecure about my actions."
"We fought all the time. I just couldn't make you happy."	"It is your fault because all I ever tried to do was make you happy and it wasn't good enough, so you started all these fights with me."

As you can see, you might get an answer as to why from your narcissist, but even then you will need to do the detective work to decipher what they really mean. Narcissists don't want to give us the rules to succeed with them. They constantly change the rules, so we fail and they have someone to blame. They are not into brutal honesty, unless you tick them off, and then the truth might come out in rage. The best thing you can do is not to seek the answer to why, because the answer won't satiate you. You will go back for more and more clarification. Don't put the course of your life in the hands of someone else—waiting for answers, looking for a response, coveting an apology, or desiring an outcome solely dependent on them. By doing that, it's as if you handed them a pen and said, "Here, write the story of our lives, because you get to determine how it ends." That is not how it is supposed to work! No one can write our story better than God, but we have to wake up to being a son or daughter of our Heavenly Father and have enough dignity to say, "I am better than what you put me through, and I don't need anything else from you, so goodbye!"

You have everything you need to move on and create your own closure. You have courage, worth, wisdom, and God's helping hand. Angels are already preparing a way for your future. They are lining up new opportunities, new people to meet, and happier times. You have to let go. "Blessed are all they that put their trust in him" (Psalm 2:12).

Every man or woman who has finally figured out their worth has picked up their suitcase of pride and boarded a flight to freedom, which landed in the valley of change. And it's true! Realize that if you spend too long holding on to the one who treats you like an *option*, you'll miss finding the one who treats you like a *priority*.

A book you might consider when planning the new version of you is *Plan B* by Pete Wilson. Pete is a pastor who uses the Bible and his own stories to help those who are struggling to make sense of why things didn't turn out the way they had planned. I stumbled across his book years ago. He inspired me so much that I wrote him a letter of gratitude because his words helped me realize that Plan B can be just as wonderful as Plan A. You might consider getting that book to help you escape your need for closure.

Below is a list of things that will help you bring an end to a bad chapter of your life. Do your homework!

To-Do List

1. To get over a relationship and feel a sense of closure, it's essential that you give yourself the physical and emotional distance to move

on. This would obviously mean moving out, if you haven't done so already, and removing sentimental objects that remind you of the past relationship. Sometimes, ridding your space of reminders of the relationship can make it that much easier to work toward a sense of closure.

2. Cut off contact with your ex. This could be difficult if you share a child. However, anything is possible if other people help you. For example, if you moved back in with your parents, have one of them open the door if the ex comes by to pick up the kids. If that is not possible, have him or her pick the kids up from school, rather than your house. There is no reason to talk to them. You can handle things through third parties or stop the phone calls and resort to emails only.

3. Write a letter of closure to your ex. Maybe you just need to get it out of your system. Say what you need to in a letter. However, don't send it! It never goes over well when a narcissist receives such a message. It becomes an invitation for drama. You don't need them being mean to you because of something you said. Depending on their vindictiveness, they could submit it to the police and say that you are harassing them.

4. Do a letting-go ritual. I spoke about this in the last section. You need something that signifies the end of that relationship and the beginning of the new you. This could be a simple act, like lighting a candle and letting it burn to symbolize the closure of the relationship. On the other hand, you could do a more drastic ritual and burn personal possessions or objects that remind you of the relationship. Get creative!

5. Do self-care. After a breakup, it is important that you focus on your needs. This will help you deal with the emotions you are experiencing and allow you to put your attentions toward yourself rather than the breakup. As mentioned before, get those lab tests to see where your health has gone during your stressful relationship. Make an appointment with a weight-loss center if you have gained weight from stress. Start a workout routine. Get a massage or your hair styled. Sometimes seeing the changes on the outside makes it more real that you are becoming a new version of you, thus adding to your closure of the past.

6. Build a new social group. Maybe you and your narcissist had the same friends, and associating with these people brings back sentimental

feelings. It is okay to distance yourself from these people. You might consider building a new social group to rejuvenate you after your breakup. Not sure how to meet someone? You can go to Meetup.com, which is a website with clubs you can join in your community, or you could join a group at your church. This may be a good move if you and your ex had the same friends, as this will allow you to put further distance between the two of you.

7. Explore new areas alone or with friends. Changing your everyday scenery can also shake you out of your emotions and help you gain closure on your past relationship. Rather than going to the hangouts that you used to go to with your narcissist, you might consider saying goodbye to them and establishing new places in your life. You also might consider changing churches or times that you go to church, just in case your ex was attending with you.

8. Change the music. Music has a way of taking you down a backroad of bad memories. Turn off the radio and instead put on motivational CDs. Fill your house with music that doesn't remind you of your relationship. This is the time to explore other types of music. If your narcissist was into alternative rock, switch to something mellower. You get the idea. Take yourself out of situations that cause triggers of emotional pain.

9. Go on a retreat or a solo vacation. This was a definite must-do on my list for healing from narcissistic abuse. Instead of sitting around the house feeling miserable for myself because of the breakup, I took a trip to Disneyland. How can you be miserable at Disneyland? Even though the trip lasted three days, it gave me three days to not think about the breakup in great detail. It also shifted my mood to one I had when I was a young kid—carefree and excited.

10. Get inspired. I can't praise motivational coach and author Tony Robbins enough for helping me through my recovery. I bought almost all of his motivational CDs to help me figure out what I wanted in the future. The CDs are a little pricey, but I was able to get mine off eBay for a fraction of the cost. Every morning on the way to work, I would listen to one of his CDs, and his motivation set the tone for the day. I started with his Ultimate Edge collection. I purchased the *Inner Strength* audio program first, then *Get the Edge*. He offers many programs, but those two were the best to start with. Every day on the long commute to work, I popped them in the CD player and recharged my motivation to change my life.

Is No Contact Right for Me?

If you have spent any time on narcissistic abuse recovery boards or searching the internet on the topic of narcissism, then you have probably stumbled upon the recommendation to go "no contact" with your narcissist. This is the only way to send a clear signal to the narcissist that they are not welcome to play their games in your life anymore. While some narcissist websites will call no contact the ultimate revenge, I prefer to think of it as common sense. No contact is a part of your closure. It is you getting the last word, and it sends a clear message to your narcissist that you respect yourself enough not to associate with them. They have finally come to understand you know who and what they are and you're not interested in their manipulative games.

Not talking to someone sounds easy. You just don't answer text messages or respond to emails or phone calls. However, many survivors I have spoken to on narcissistic abuse recovery boards have told me it is difficult. The main reason most of them cited was that their narcissists were so convincing that this time would be different that they wanted it to be true. It is hard to walk away from someone whom you spent months or years with. It is difficult to disconnect from the dream you had about growing old together. It is also difficult to accept that you made a mistake and that the dream is going to be postponed until someone else comes along.

By the time we wake up and decide to put them behind us, the habit, obsession, and addiction to the idolization phase takes over and drives us to think, feel, and behave in ways that don't make any sense to us. Christian women in particular romanticize their relationships. They want to believe that the idolization phase is their narcissist being softened by God because of their prayers. It's as if Jesus performed a miracle transformation because their narcissist stopped putting them down for three weeks because of a church sermon they heard on kindness. The reality is that "Jesus" didn't do that much. Real change is lasting. The idolization phase is not a renewal of the repentant prodigal son; it is a cycle of a mental disorder. The romantic notion that this is a genuine change of heart is not to be relied on, unless they have admitted they are a narcissist and are in therapy. All cards should be on the table in your therapy sessions, and it should be made known to the narcissist by your therapist that he has taken you back through the idolization phase because of his change in behavior. The therapist should be working on them to break through manipulative barriers that might use this phase as a way to control.

As much as it might be a breath of heaven to be pursued again or get attention once more from your narcissist, I can guarantee you it is temporary. They have an established pattern, which is a part of their disorder that will put you back through the devaluation phase every time.

A nice side effect of going no contact with your narcissist is that after a few years you start to relax around people. You realize that not everyone wants to fight, not everyone is trying to manipulate you, not everyone is going to criticize or judge you, not everyone has ulterior motives and hidden agendas. For these reasons alone, it is strongly suggested that you go no contact. It is crucial in your recovery.

So let's write some rules that you will need to live by if you're going to go no contact. However, first let's be real about what can be done if your narcissist happens to be the father or mother of your children. In this situation, it is almost impossible to not have contact with your partner. Therefore, your communication should be short, monotonous, businesslike, and *boring*. Less is more when communicating with your ex. The goal of this approach is to give no invitation to elicit a fight through your tone. Once they see they can't get drama from you, they will look to their backup narcissistic supply for it. This minimizes their irritations with you and gives them other opportunities to seek it elsewhere.

Beside the typical suggestions I have already made in this book about sticking to strong boundaries, you will want to keep communication to email. Email is devoid of tone, unless you are using all capital letters, which you should avoid. Sift through the email communication between you and your narcissist, and only respond to the items that are relevant to co-parenting. They will try to push your buttons, so don't respond with anger. Save your frustration by sharing that with your therapist. Communicate only over important items such as medical care and education. Interact minimally, even if that means having separate birthday parties or holidays together with the kids.

The children will need to take all your focus, because they are trapped in a situation that might put them under the roof with the narcissist part-time. Whatever you experienced in your relationship, they will experience. Therefore, it will be important for you to be in tune not just with your narcissistic abuse recovery, but with their health as well.

If a narcissist or his enablers accuse you of running away from the problems in the relationship because you decided to protect yourself by going no contact, remember this: you can never solve a problem by letting another human being hurt and destroy your happiness. Detachment is letting another person experience the consequences instead of taking responsibility for them yourself. So let them learn. God has bigger plans for you than daily negative drama! The beauty of no contact is you don't have to say a word to get your point across. Your narcissist hears it loud and clear, as if you screamed at the top of your lungs, "Get thee to the depths of hell, you devil!" No contact is pure and sweet rejection. And no, it is not revenge. There is no revenge in wanting to be left alone to regain your health. Remember that Jesus didn't hang out with the Pharisees, because they were bad men. He surrounded himself with good men—his disciples. Cast the evil from your life. That is a reasonable request God desires of you so you can be spiritually healthy, don't you think?

To-Do List

1. Validate your kids' feelings. Your kids need acknowledgment that their feelings are real, that they matter, and that they are valid. Narcissists will try to use the same games on them that they used on you. Let the kids know that the treatment they are getting is not okay. If needed, you might consider therapy for the kids, depending on the abuse.

2. One thing narcissists like to do is blame. Helping your children understand that the narcissist's blame is unfounded, unfair, and not their fault is critical to their sense of an accurate reality, as opposed to a highly distorted one engineered by your narcissistic spouse. Seeing that they are not to blame or you are not to blame will help them.

3. Limit their contact. Narcissists need adoration and attention. They thrive on drama, so it makes sense that they will use the children to get what they need. Limiting the children's text messages with the narcissist is wise. Of course, there will be emergencies that arise, such as missing the bus and needing a parent to pick them up. However, less contact is best. This is a tricky thing to accomplish because the narcissist might see that you are manipulating the kids to break off

contact with them. This isn't the case if there is divided custody between you. You can most certainly allow conversations to continue once daily if the narcissist isn't hurting the child emotionally through manipulation or using them to gain information about you. However, once you see that is the case, you will need to talk to your child about the unhealthiness of the situation and get them to commit to a brief conversation less often with their narcissistic parent. Conversely, allowing your child to contact you about something your ex is doing invites triangulation. And don't let yourself fall into the trap of using the child for your gain.

4. Avoid demonizing your ex. You may want to avoid using the term *narcissist*, for example, until your child is older. Younger children might not understand what that means and will run back to the other parent and repeat what you said. I believe it is necessary at some point to tell your older kids that their parent has a mental disorder, but little kids don't need this knowledge. Simply stating that their mother or father is sensitive to criticism and overreacts is an approach you could take instead. As with many things, kids are usually your best guide to gauging what they are ready to hear. Waiting until your child asks about something is often the right way to introduce information. I recommend telling your older children that their parent has narcissistic personality disorder if you can trust that they are not going to run back to the ex and share this revelation. You don't want to start an unneeded fight. Tempering your own feelings about your spouse or ex, who may be highly abusive, can feel next to impossible. However, resisting your desire to cut loose with your own hurt, resentment, and anger is imperative in maintaining communication and trust with your kids, who are literally stuck in the middle.

5. Bringing up to older children that their parent has a mental disorder is an opportunity to help kids know it isn't something they said or did that caused their parent to be abusive. It is also an opportunity to teach about mental bias and stigma. They should learn that their parent could change if they wanted to, because narcissism can be managed if they seek medication, therapy, and spiritual recovery. However, if your ex is not doing these things, then it becomes an opportunity for your children to understand that God has given us all freedom of choice. They can pray for their parent, but they should not feel any blame because of the choices their parent makes that are not in accordance with Jesus's message of love for one another. Hearing it presented in this way takes the pressure off the child.

6. Don't take your child's anger personally. It can be just as frustrating for a child as it was for you in the narcissistic relationship. They might take their frustrations out on you because their narcissistic parent is too sensitive to hear their problems. You might be the only person they trust enough to act out with and show how they are really feeling. This can be hard on you if you are trying to recover from narcissistic abuse. The last thing you need is a child acting out by abusing you with their anger. This does not mean, however, that you should put up with abuse from your kids. That is when professional help is needed.

So let's recap the rules of no contact. Rip this list out of the book if you must and post it somewhere you can see it, like next to your computer or near the phone. You will want it to be a reminder of how you are to live now that you have accepted your partner is a narcissist and you don't ever plan to go back to that abuse again. This list is to be added to your boundaries. Here are the twenty things you should do if you go no contact:

No Contact Rules

1. I will not talk to the narcissist on the phone or text them. I will only respond if there is an emergency with our child. Communication will be through email or third parties only.
2. I will confine communication to email if I have children with the narcissist. If I have no children with the narcissist, I will have no contact with them.
3. My emails to the narcissist will be devoid of tone and boring. They will only address educational or medical topics that relate to the kids.
4. Custody and times will be arranged by the court system.
5. I will arrange for other people to drop the kids off at their house or have other people answer the door if the narcissistic ex has to pick them up. Or I will have them picked up at the school or the babysitter's house so there is no interaction.
6. I will not meet with them to discuss the relationship, because it is over with and they are simply hoovering.

7. I will not tolerate them dropping by unannounced. If they do this I will say, "I don't want contact with you. If you do this again, I will call the police because I see it as harassment."

8. I will box up their stuff and set it outside the house for them to retrieve. If this is not possible, I will have someone present with me when they pick up their belongings from the house.

9. I will not engage them in a fight or be in a room alone with them.

10. I will remove them from my Facebook page and all other social media. Plus, I will not change my Facebook cover or picture for a year. With nothing new to look at, they will stop stalking the page.

11. I will remove my status on Facebook if it states that I am "in a relationship."

12. I will remove all pictures of us together from my Facebook account or other social media, and I will make my account closed to the public so my narcissist can't read my page.

13. I will change my privacy settings on Facebook and other social media to only allow friends to view my page.

14. I will change internet passwords that my narcissistic ex might know.

15. I will remove my narcissist from all my checking accounts and credit cards if we shared these things. I won't be financially bound to them.

16. I will remove their name from all titles I have on cars or homes.

17. I will distance myself from people who are best friends with this individual, and they will not know the details of what is going on in my life, because I know they will be used to find out that information.

18. I will not attend church at the same time as my narcissist, even if it means changing where I go to church.

19. I will not discuss the details of my breakup with interested parties who know this individual or would tell him or her what I said.

20. I will not sit near this individual at any of my child's sporting events or school functions. In addition, I will not spend Christmas or other holidays with this individual for the sake of the kids. Holidays and birthdays will be separate.

How Can I Restore My Dignity?

What is dignity? We have talked about it throughout this book, and I hope by now the one major takeaway message in your recovery is to never lose it or give it away. If I had to define "dignity," it would look like this:

Dignity

/ˈdignitē/ noun

- The moment you realize that the person you cared for has nothing intellectually or spiritually to offer but a headache.
- The moment you realize God had greater plans for you that don't involve crying at night or sad Pinterest quotes.
- The moment you stop comparing yourself to others because it undermines your worth, education, and your parents' wisdom.
- The moment you live your dreams, not because of what it will prove or get you, but because that is all you want to do. People's opinions don't matter.
- The moment you realize that no one is your enemy, except yourself.
- The moment you realize that you can have everything you want in life. However, it takes timing, the right heart, the right actions, the right passion, and a willingness to risk it all. If it is not yours, it is because you really didn't want it, you didn't need it, or God prevented it.
- The moment you realize the ghost of your ancestors stood between you and the person you loved. They really don't want you mucking up the family line with someone who acts anything less than honorable.
- The moment you realize that happiness was never about getting a person. They are only a helpmate in achieving your life mission.
- The moment you believe that love is not about losing or winning. It is just a few moments in time, followed by an eternity of situations to grow from.
- The moment you realize that you were always the right person. Only ignorant people walk away from greatness.

I believe my gender has the hardest time maintaining their self-respect in relationships. So many books have been written on the topic of empowering women that I have concluded that too many women want a man to save them. However, they forget that two thousand years ago a man did save them, on the cross. If you are female, then I want you to pay careful attention to what I am going to tell you. Ladies, don't chase a man! When a man is truly interested in you, there will be no need for you to do the pursuing. Men are born to pursue women. Yes, you can pursue a man, but in most cases that's just an obvious sign that he's not into you. It's not natural for a man to sit back and make the woman do all the work. However, you will find it is natural to someone who is toxic. The toxic narcissist thrives off you doing all the work for his attention. For a man who claims to like or love you, it doesn't make sense for him to expect you to do all the texting, calling, date-night arrangements, or talks about the future. You have to understand the difference between someone who speaks to you on their free time and someone who frees their time to speak to you. He will make himself available to you if he is interested. There is a difference between someone who desires you and someone who would do anything to keep you.

The wife who hacked my cell phone is still in this evil man's life. She would tell you that she has worth and dignity. However, what she did to me proves otherwise. She still leaves her social media site open to the public. Her posts read like an open diary of someone who is being abused. She doesn't have the decency to keep her pain private, nor does she know where the delete button is on her computer keyboard. Yet she calls it love. Don't be like her! Don't lower yourself to win the affection of a cruel man and then naively call yourself a blessed daughter of God because he hasn't left you for another woman. God is not trying to keep you in a relationship where you will be abused. A daughter of God is not a doormat or an enabler. Remember that! Plus, don't post your pain in quotes on Pinterest or Facebook like she did. People can look that stuff up and instantly know the details of what is going on in your life. Have some self respect!

Author Steve Maraboli said, "Sometimes your knight in shining armor turns out to be an idiot wrapped in tin foil." Maybe this is true in your life, but I definitely know it was in mine. Ladies, trust God. He knows who belongs in your life and who doesn't. Whoever is meant to be there will fight for you. They won't be repeatedly taking you through the cycle of idolization and devaluation. They won't be giving you a bunch of excuses and lies to keep you appeased. They are not going to flirt with other women. Most definitely, he isn't going to be listening in to a beautiful woman's cell-phone conversations and lying to you by saying they weren't interested in dating that person. They won't be sending you mixed signals. They are actually going to be making changes in themselves to prove they respect and love you enough to keep you around. And if they don't, remember that sometimes God's blessings are not in what he gives but in what he takes away. Trust God!

To have dignity, you should have relationship rules you live by, don't you think? Here are my top ten things strong men and women never do in a relationship:

1. They don't allow disrespect.
2. They don't act needy or insecure.
3. They don't expect their partner to meet all their needs.
4. They don't give up their standards or identity as a child of God to please someone.
5. They don't give up their financial dependence.
6. They don't stoop to the narcissistic games in this book to get their way.
7. They keep their personal life private.
8. They don't ignore their family, friends, hobby, or careers and become addicted to their emotions about one person.
9. They don't let people cross their boundaries.
10. They don't let their partner make all the decisions.

What else would you add to the above list? The type of man you want is someone who loves God before he even knows you exist. He would fall to his knees and praise God without caring who was watching him. You want a man who knows that God is the best foundation to build a relationship on. Because he knows that is going to bring you and him closer. A man who loves Jesus will respect you. He will pursue you and treasure you. He will appreciate you as a gift and the beauty you are. He will worship with you. He will pray with you and for you.

The heart that is meant to love you will fight for you when you want to give up and pick you up when you're feeling down. He will never get strength from seeing you weak, power from seeing you hurt, or joy from seeing you cry. The heart that is meant to love you wants to see the best in you. Never forget that! All the men reading this need to be thinking along the same lines. There are many good Christian women out there worth pursuing.

Some of you see yourself as being broken. You look at the scars from the heartbreaks in your past and you believe you are not worthy of a good man or woman's love. You look down instead of up, as if you have something to be ashamed of. My dear brothers and sisters in the gospel, I am not going to ask you to wipe your tears. I know through my own narcissistic abuse that I had to cry it all out because my spirit couldn't hold the pain in. Get it all out of your system so not another person can ever hurt you like you were hurt before. However, when you are finished, I need you to stand up and hold your head high. Realize that you needed a little more time and inspiration to move forward. Take strength in remembering Ruth. Ruth didn't go back to what was familiar. She stepped out in faith and walked into the unknown. Her courage brought her to her divine destiny. Don't look back because the past is behind you for a reason.

The women whom I love and admire for their strength and grace did not get that way because stuff worked out. They got that way because stuff went wrong and they handled it. They handled it in a thousand different ways on a thousand different days, but they handled it. Those women are my superheroes. One of them was Queen Elizabeth. She once loved a man who kept his marriage to another woman secret from her. He continued to string along Queen Elizabeth's feelings for him, until she found out about his wife. She was heartbroken. However, she was a strong woman. She had boundaries. She didn't chase after him and beg him to leave his wife or convince him of her worth. She danced with the devil and won! She moved on. She wasn't afraid to be without a mate. She was a queen and knew her role in her kingdom and ushered in the golden era of English history. Take her example. There is nothing ordinary about you. You are a son or daughter of the King, and your story is significant!

We have covered a lot in this book. I hope that you will do the things I written in the preceding sections. They are there as a guideline to help you in your spiritual recovery from narcissistic abuse. Remember that God sometimes stirs us out of comfortable situations to stretch us and cause us to use our faith. We may not like it, and it might not always be comfortable, but God loves us too much to leave us the way we are.

I strongly believe that if you live by a code, then your decisions in life will be easier. So what is your code? What do you stand for and what will you not tolerate in your life as you try to be an example of Christ? "For we wrestle not against flesh and blood, but against principalities, against powers, against the rulers of the darkness of this world, against spiritual wickedness in high places" (Ephesians 6:12). You have spent too much time in darkness. God is asking you to take his hand and follow him to the light. Refuse to lower your standards to accommodate those who refuse to raise theirs. It is time you take back your control and happiness by standing for all that is true and right! It takes courage and bravery to recover as much as it does to walk away from the abuse. The giant in front of you is never bigger than the God inside you. Remember that bravery doesn't come with the absence of fear or hurt. Bravery is the ability to look those things in the eye and say, "Move aside, you are in my way!"

If you have done the work in this book, then I am proud of you! You are taking the steps needed to re-create yourself stronger and more faithful than you ever were before. God wants you to know he loves you. He wants you to trust in him and build a lasting relationship based on proclaiming his greatness through your happy life. Don't disappoint yourself by not stepping into the vision he has for you.

Following is a list of rules to live by. Post it somewhere so you can see it daily—it is who you are and how you are to be treated. It is second to your Bible; it is now your *code.*

My Pledge as a Son or Daughter of Our Heavenly Father

I pledge to have boundaries that safeguard my values and belief system. I know that Satan will test those boundaries, but I will hold strong because I know that I am a child of God deserving of respect.

I pledge to stand up for all that is true and right. I will not remain silent to evil done to others or to myself.

I pledge to not let fear of the unknown guide my choices in any of my relationships.

I pledge to put my God first over any relationship and will humbly do his will.

I pledge to not devote my entire life to changing another person, while letting it destroy my health and spiritual growth.

I pledge to live in reality and not a fairy tale that I have projected onto someone. I will always accept the truth of what the person is before me, not the person I want them to be.

I pledge to never let my children see their mother or father abused by their partner. I will show them my worth by leaving the situation if no other way presents itself.

I pledge to have faith in my Heavenly Father, and I will show this in prayer, in attendance at a church, and through bringing Christ's message into my family's life.

I pledge to find and fulfill my life mission by using the talents and blessings my Father in Heaven has bestowed on me.

I pledge to raise up a righteous family that will spread the message of Jesus Christ and live by his example.

I pledge to not be worldly, but to live as if God's Kingdom is all I need.

I pledge to be honest, fair, and kind to all I meet.

I pledge to forgive others because God has forgiven me.

I pledge to live by the laws of the land and the Ten Commandments.

I pledge to live authentically and not to be consumed with appearance or ego.

I pledge to spread Christ's message through sharing or example.

I pledge to be accountable for my sins and will go through the steps of repentance to be right with the Lord.

I pledge to love myself and treat myself with dignity in all situations.

I pledge to honor the diversity of men and women, respecting each other's faith choices, ethnicities, customs, beliefs, characteristics, and qualities—because what binds us is much stronger than what differentiates us.

I pledge to seek wisdom in all things, so I can be useful.

I pledge to be a person of integrity in character, in personal care, and in advice to others.

I pledge to be trustworthy. I don't engage in gossip but refrain from such evil.

I pledge to be accountable for myself, rather than rely on another to pull me through life.

I pledge to be sexually pure, meaning that I won't sleep with the people I date. I am worth a ring and the wait.

I pledge to not let pride dictate revenge and to live humbly God's law of forgiveness.

Do you see something missing off the list? Now is your turn to add a pledge. Write ten more pledges that pertain to your life.

1.

2.

3.

4.

5.

6.

7.

8.

9.

10.

I love to hear success stories from my readers. If my books have helped you and you want to share your story of recovery, you can reach me by emailing me at spulifecoach@gmail.com.

May God bless your life and help you leave the title of victim behind. You're a son or daughter of our Heavenly Father with an amazing life to live! God has never left your side and will see you through to the other side, where he has a great life planned for you. You just need to have faith and take action!

"God will give me justice."

—Alexandre Dumas,
The Count of Monte Cristo

Bibliography

American Psychiatric Association. (2013). Personality disorders. *Diagnostic and Statistical Manual of Mental Disorders* (5th ed.). Washington, DC: American Psychiatric Publishing Inc.

Barr, C. T., Kerig, P. K., Stellwagen, K. K., & Barry, T. D. (eds.). (2011). *Narcissism and Machiavellianism in Youth: Implications for the Development of Adaptive and Maladaptive Behavior.* Washington, DC: American Psychological Association.

Barry, C. T., Frick, P. J., Adler, K. K., & Grafeman, S. J. (2007). The predictive utility of narcissism among children and adolescents: Evidence for a distinction between adaptive and maladaptive narcissism. *Journal of Child and Family Studies, 16,* 508–521. doi:10.1007/s10826-006-9102-5.

Barry, C. T., Frick, P. J., & Killian, A. L. (2003). The relation of narcissism and self-esteem to conduct problems in children: A preliminary investigation. *Journal of Clinical Child and Adolescent Psychology, 32,* 139–152. doi:10.1207/15374420360533130.

Barry, C. T., & Lee-Rowland, L. M. (2015). Has there been a recent increase in adolescent narcissism? Evidence from a sample of at-risk adolescents (2005–2014). Personality and Individual Differences, 87153-157. doi:10.1016/j.paid.2015.07.038.

Bolles, Richard N. (2005) *How to Find Your Mission in Life,* Ten Speed Press, p. 6.

Brunell, A. B., & Campbell, W. K. (2011). Narcissism and romantic relationships: Understanding the paradox. In W. K. Campbell, J. D. Miller, W. K. Campbell, & J. D. Miller (eds.), *The Handbook of Narcissism and Narcissistic Personality Disorder: Theoretical Approaches, Empirical Findings, and Treatments* (344–350). Hoboken, NJ: John Wiley & Sons Inc.

Campbell, W. (1999). Narcissism and romantic attraction. *Journal of Personality and Social Psychology, 77*(6), 1254–1270. doi:10.1037/0022-3514.77.6.1254.

Campbell, W. K., Miller, J., & Widiger, T. (2010). Narcissistic Personality Disorder and the DSM–V. *Journal of Abnormal Psychology, 119*(4), 640–649. Retrieved March 7, 2014, from http://wkeithcampbell.com/wp-content/uploads/2013/08/MillerWidigerCampbell20101.pdf.

Crowell, S. E., Beauchaine, T. P., & Linehan, M. M. (2009). A Biosocial developmental model of borderline personality: Elaborating and extending Linehan's theory. *Psychological Bulletin 135.3*, 495–510. Web. 3 Apr. 2017.

Dhawan, N., Kunik, M. E., Oldham, J., & Coverdale, J. (2010). *Prevalence and treatment of narcissistic personality disorder in the community: A systematic review. Comprehensive Psychiatry, 51*(4), 333–339.

Edelstein, R. S., Newton, N. J., & Stewart, A. J. (2012). Narcissism in midlife: Longitudinal changes in and correlates of women's narcissistic personality traits. *Journal of Personality, 80*(5), 1179–1204. doi:10.1111/j.1467-6494.2011.00755.x.

Epictetus Quotes Goodreads (July 2019) http://www.goodreads.com/author/quotes/13852.Epictetus.

Franklin, Benjamin Quotes, Goodreads (July 2019) http://www.goodreads.com/author/quotes/289513.Benjamin_Franklin.

Furham, A., Richards, S. C., & Paulhus, D. L. (2013). The dark triad of personality: A 10 year review. *Social and Personality Psychology Compass, 7*(3), 199–216.

Hanh, Nhat Thich Quotes, Goodreads (July 2019) http://www.goodreads.com/author/quotes/9074.Thich_Nhat_Hanh.

Keller, Helen Quotes, Goodreads (July 2019) http://www.goodreads.com/author/show/7275.Helen_Keller

Loeber, R., Burke, J., & Pardini, D. A. (2009). Perspectives on oppositional defiant disorder, conduct disorder, and psychopathic features. *Journal of Child Psychology and Psychiatry, 50*(1–2), 133–142. doi:10.1111/j.1469-7610.2008.02011.x.

Maraboli, Steve (December 23, 2016 Post) http://www.facebook.com/authorstevemaraboli.

May, B., & Bos, J. (2000). Personality characteristics of ADHD adults assessed with the millon clinical multiaxial inventory-II: Evidence of four distinct subtypes. *J Pers Assess, 75*, 237–248. [PubMed].

Moses, Brittney, (July 2016), *"How To Set Healthy Boundaries With Toxic People"*, *Brittney Moses*, 21, Aug. 2016, http://www.brittney-moses.com/how-to-set-healthy-boundaries-with-toxic-people.

"My Life, My Love, My Legacy" Last Days & Legacy, The Martin Luther King Jr. Center for Nonviolent Social Change, Flip Schulke, 2018, http://www.thekingcenter.org.

Pappas, Stephanie, *"Narcissists Overconfidence May Hide Low Self-Esteem" LiveScience, 23 Oct. 2011,* Retrieved from http://www.livescience.com/16650-narcissists-esteem.html.

Presniak, M. D., Olson, T. R., & MacGregor, M. M. (2010). The role of defense mechanisms in borderline and antisocial personalities. *Journal of Personality Assessment, 92*(2), 137–145. doi:10.1080/00223890903510373.

Robbins, Tony (July 2019), http:/www.tonyrobbins.com.

Ronningstam, E., & Weinberg, I. (2013). Narcissistic personality disorder: Progress in recognition and treatment. *The Journal of Lifelong Learning in Psychiatry,11*(2), 167–177.

Simon, G. K. (2011). *In Sheep's Clothing: Understanding and Dealing with Manipulative People.* Tantor Media, Inc.

Smith, Ron Quotes, Goodreads (July 2019), http://www.goodreads.com/author/quotes/5009.Ron_Smith.

Stines, S. (2015). What is trauma bonding? *Psych Central.* Retrieved on July 31, 2018, from https://pro.psychcentral.com/recovery-expert/2015/10/what-is-trauma-bonding.

The Holy Bible, *King James Version*, Christian Art Publishers, Feb 2017

The Holy Bible, *New International Version*, Zondervan, Jan 2015.

Teresa, Mother Quotes (July 2019) http://www.goodreads.com/author/quotes/838305.Mother_Teresa.

Tucker, Max Quotes (July 2019), http://www.goodreads.com/author/quotes/5856.Tucker_Max.

Vernick, Leslie (July 2019), http://www.leslievernick.com.

Winfrey, Oprah. (July 2019), *Brene Brown: 3 Way to Set Boundaries*, Retrieved from http://www.oprah.com/spirit/how-to-set-boundaries-brene-browns-advice.

Zanarini, M. C., Frankenburg, F. R., Dubo, E.D., Sickel. A. E., Trikha, A., Levin, A., & Reynolds, V. (1998). *Axis II comorbidity of borderline personality disorder. Comprehensive Psychiatry, 39*(5):296–302.

About the Author

S hannon L. Alder is an inspirational author. She has been quoted in one hundred published books, by various relationship authors, and in several online magazine articles (*Psychology Today*, *Huffington Post*, etc.). When she is not cranking out another book for her bestselling 300 Questions series, you can find her off on some adrenaline-rush adventure trying to save the world.

Shannon is a volunteer search-and-rescue worker for her local police department and rescues missing hikers in the Sierra Wilderness. She also travels yearly around the world on humanity missions. Her last crusade was to Cambodia, where she was part of a team that rescued girls from human trafficking. Prior to that, she was a member of the ocean conservation society Sea Shepherd. She served on the Operation Jairo team, which rescued sea turtles off the Florida Coast.

In addition to her published books, Shannon wrote and produced the song "One Life" on iTunes to raise money for a terminally ill boy she met on her medical mission in Nicaragua.

Currently, Shannon is a rehabilitation therapist at an inpatient trauma hospital. She maintains a positive community on Facebook, called Staying Positive University. She loves to get email from fans and readers on her website, ShannonAlder.com.

Scan to visit

www.shannonalder.com